T0317168

A Strategic Myth

'Underdevelopment' in Jammu and Kashmir

SEHAR IQBAL

Tulika Books

Published by
Tulika Books
44 (first floor), Shahpur Jat, New Delhi 110 049, India
www.tulikabooks.in

First published in India in 2021

ISBN: 978-81-947175-6-0 (hardback)

Printed at Chaman Enterprises, New Delhi 110 002

To my grandmother who always knew I would write a book,
and to my father who didn't get to read it

'All truths are easy to understand when they are discovered,
the point is to discover them.'
– Galileo

Contents

Tables

CHAPTER SIX
From Tenants to Leaders: The Human Experience of Land Reforms in Jammu

Foreword

The two things the world knows – or thinks it knows – about Kashmir is that it was once a paradise, and that it has been blighted by conflict for about as long as anyone can remember. As with most enduring narratives, there is some truth in this. The Kashmir valley has a bewitching landscape and climate that has delighted and fascinated visitors since long before the Mughals declared it to be a paradise. And more than thirty years of conflict has brought grief to just about every Kashmiri home and made many Kashmiris feel disempowered and despairing as well as crimping the lives and ambitions of successive generations.

Yet, there is much more to Jammu and Kashmir, including a measure of rural well-being and of urban education that stands comparison to just about anywhere in the region. Dr Sehar Iqbal is a Kashmiri who has a deep pride in and concern for her homeland, combined with a commitment to scholarship and evidence-based research. In this exceptionally valuable book, Sehar Iqbal explores the landmark importance of the land reforms introduced across Jammu and Kashmir – in the face of Delhi's disapproval – from the late 1940s, which, while perhaps flawed, transformed the social and political landscape of the former princely state.

The impact of Sheikh Abdullah's radical 'land to the tiller' policy has often been mentioned by historians and commentators. Dr Iqbal goes beyond the simple phrases and generalizations to explore with rigour and detail the impact of the break-up of the large landed estates and redistribution of cultivable land. And that includes the really essential tasks of providing a village-level assessment of what land reform has meant, and exploring the impact of these changes on rural women and their status within the household and more widely.

She also demonstrates that in terms of human development, Jammu and Kashmir – in spite of insurgency, an overwhelming military presence and a deeply flawed democracy – has performed rather better than most of India. The economic problems facing the Kashmir valley in particular – the lack of industrialization and acute shortage of jobs for graduates – are inescapable, but the bald statements made by Delhi-based politicians about the underdevelopment of Jammu and Kashmir are deeply misleading.

This is of vital importance, because it challenges one of the most widely stated reasons for the abrogation in 2019 of Jammu and Kashmir's special status in India's Constitution. It is perhaps surprising, given the miseries that Kashmir has faced, that the measures of development there compare so well with other regions of India, but Sehar Iqbal's research both establishes that and explores the reasons and implications.

On a more sombre note, she also demonstrates the malign impact of the measures accompanying that constitutional change on access to health and education. The restricting of internet access and limits on movement, far from promoting the local economy or attracting private investment, have imperilled one of the more positive aspects of Kashmir's story: the gains achieved in economic and social development.

My own association with Jammu and Kashmir, first as a journalist and more recently as a historian, stretches back over almost thirty years. In fundamentals, depressingly little has changed over that period. One of the few bright spots has been the emergence of a new generation of Kashmiri scholars, writers and social activists committed to studying, chronicling and championing their homeland. Sehar Iqbal is among the most impressive of that group. Her research deserves and demands attention.

London   ANDREW WHITEHEAD
December 2020   Former BBC India Correspondent

Preface

I grew up listening to my great-grandmother's stories of feudal Kashmir. Her eloquence made the world of echoing *diwan khana*s (drawing rooms), endless hospitality, bountiful harvests and rural idyll come alive in my imagination. It was much later that I learnt about the deep inequities that prevailed in the feudal system. This made me uneasy about my family's identity as *jagirdar*s (landlords) in the old system and I began to dig deeper into my family's history. I found generations who had benefited from this system without questioning it. Simultaneously, I also discovered radical figures like my great-great-grandmother Khonam Ded, who defied the maharaja's officials and organized a huge community kitchen in the yard of her house during the famine of 1877. This was at a time when anyone who was seen cooking rice after the harvest could be arrested, beaten or sent for *begar* (forced labour) by cruel state inspectors called *shakdar*s, for not paying the state's share of grain first. Khonam Ded and my two great-grandmothers – Zainab Begum, who lost her husband at a very young age but took on the challenge of farming the land that fell to her young sons, and Hajra Begum, who gave away all of her personal property to orphans whom she had adopted and raised as her own – became sources of inspiration for me.

My university education gave me the tools to examine the feudal system critically and to appreciate the benefits of land reforms and debt conciliation for millions of people in Jammu and Kashmir. I came to the themes of this book from a personal understanding of how these two measures had changed my own family's fortunes. My father's family, who were both landlords and moneylenders, would have been reduced to near-penury but for the determined efforts of my paternal grandmother Ameena Begum, who went back to school after having two children, educated herself and got a job as a government teacher. The loss of landed estates also pushed my maternal grandfather M. Shamsuddin Ganaie on to a path of education, employment and public service. My maternal grandmother, Padishah Begum, made sure that her five daughters sought education and employment. She imparted to them a powerful work ethic that helped them through their journeys in life. For my family, land reforms were a lesson in pragmatism and self-reliance. For the strong women who anchored the new generation in the values of hard work, discipline and the primacy of education, they were stepping stones to a new life and new opportunities. But for the land reforms, I would not be the educated working woman I am today.

Accordingly, this book sees the radical developments in asset and debt distribution that took place in Jammu and Kashmir through the lens of empowerment and dignity that they brought to millions. It advocates my belief that real gains in development can only come when we put the interests of the vulnerable before our own.

> Who see self as other
> Other as self
> Day as night
> Night as day –
> They alone have seen the Teacher
> The first among the gods.
>
> – Lal Ded[1]

NOTE

[1] Lal Ded is a fourteenth-century Kashmiri female mystic and poet; translation by the author.

Acknowledgements

This book has been a four-year journey: juggling research and writing, walking through villages with a four-year-old in tow, packing school lunches and dressing scraped knees, and full-time work. It is a labour of love and a testament to the belief my family had in me. My husband has been a rock throughout, helping me in endless little tasks and taking on my social obligations. Without his support, this book would not have seen the light of day.

My mother has been my anchor. Without her shouldering the responsibility of my father's care in his final years, completing my research would not have been possible. My late father, M. Iqbal Khandey, who pushed me to focus on my research from his hospital bed, deserves special mention. To my parents and my husband, who put my quest for knowledge before their needs, I owe an endless debt.

I would like to thank my grandfather, M. Shamsuddin Ganaie, who painstakingly proofread the manuscript and helped me refocus at critical times.

Special thanks are due to my soul-sister, Dr Farah Qayoom, who helped me navigate through the complex world of academic research. She babysat my children between giving lectures at Kashmir University's Department of Sociology, while I spent hours in the library. She truly embodies the maxim, 'Women rise by lifting each other up.'

To Professor Jean Dreze, without whose patient guidance this book would have been a lot shallower, I owe special thanks. His work on turning rights into legal entitlements in India has benefited millions and is inspirational to activist-researchers like me.

To Indu and Basanta, who believed in this book and were patient with all my queries throughout – thank you.

Finally, to my children, Sajid and Sahir, who went to university before they went to school – thank you for understanding your mother's equally strong love for learning. May you grow up to be seekers of truth and knowledge, and be strong enough to act on both.

Introduction

Jammu and Kashmir has been, throughout the twentieth century and well into the twenty-first, different things to different people. To military analysts, it represents a strategically important territory; to political scientists, a complex political problem; and to social scientists, an important democratic experiment (being the only Muslim-majority state in the country, it has become a testing ground for the secular identity of India). Much has been written about the political upheavals in the state from these points of view – its transition from a princely state to a democratic one, the wars fought over it by India and Pakistan, and, more recently, the armed insurgency that the state went through from 1989 onwards. Recent academic debate in India around Jammu and Kashmir centres almost exclusively on the physical, social and psychosocial effects of violence on the people, and on whether the state has made the transition from a conflict to a post-conflict society.

There exists a sizeable gap in the available literature about the developmental journey and experience of the state, the relationship between its political and social development. This book is a small step in the direction of bridging this gap. It aims to study the social impact of the state development policy in Jammu and Kashmir from 1948 (when princely rule ended) to 1988 (the year armed insurgency emerged). It is the Indian state of Jammu and Kashmir that I focus on here specifically, and therefore Pakistan-administered Kashmir will not be considered for the purpose of this study considering that the administration and development experience of the area since 1948 has been noticeably different. With the abrogation of Article 370 on 5 August 2019, the special constitutional powers of Jammu and Kashmir have been taken away and the erstwhile state has been divided into two separate union territories (UTs), i.e. Ladakh (a UT with no legislature), and Jammu and Kashmir (a UT with a legislature). Since this book deals with how the princely state of Jammu and Kashmir which later came to be a state within the Union of India (October 1947–August 2019) created its own model of development, Chapters One through Seven refer to the state of Jammu and Kashmir in its past iteration. The last chapter deals with Jammu and Kashmir as a union territory.

The book first establishes the context of development in Jammu and Kashmir, i.e. the systematic deprivation faced by the people under feudal rule. Thereafter, it outlines the development of the state's economy and polity after 1948, when a government with non-monarchical representatives was formed for the first time. It illustrates this development through the progress of human development index (HDI) indicators till the start of militancy, which affected this progress, and the resulting impact on society.

The process of development in Jammu and Kashmir began with the end of princely rule.[1] After India and Pakistan achieved independence from British rule in August 1947, the rulers of princely states were given the option to sign up with one or the other. Because of its predominantly Muslim population, cultural affinity and geographical contiguity with Pakistan, the princely state of Jammu and Kashmir was expected to accede to Pakistan.[2] The maharaja hoped to stay independent and signed a standstill agreement with Pakistan, enabling Jammu and Kashmir to be an independent political entity from August to October 1947. In October 1947, armed tribesmen from Pakistan's North-West Frontier Province (now known as Khyber Pakhtunwa) entered Kashmir with a view to claim the territory for Pakistan. The maharaja was already facing an armed rebellion in Poonch and Mirpur, and a mass movement against his rule in the Kashmir valley; the initial gains made by the tribesmen in Uri and Baramulla forced him to flee to Jammu. There, he signed the Instrument of Accession on 27 October 1947, and Jammu and Kashmir acceded to the Indian Union: this was the pre-condition for India extending military support to the beleaguered maharaja against the tribal invasion.

The Instrument of Accession itself is a point of contention between India and Pakistan. India maintains that the maharaja signed it on 26 October 1947 while he was still sovereign, and that armed forces were sent into the Kashmir valley only after the signing. Pakistan contends that the Instrument of Accession was signed much later, after the maharaja was driven out by invaders from the Kashmir valley and thus was no longer sovereign. This, they say, invalidates the legality of the Accession itself. An interim government, headed by Sheikh Mohammad Abdullah,[3] was set up and continued to function till 1951 when the first elections were held.

With 'a meagre per-capita income of Rs 208 (at 1960–61 prices)' and a literacy rate of 'just about 5 per cent' (while the all-India literacy rate was 18.3 per cent), Jammu and Kashmir was one of the most backward states in India in 1950.[4] This was a direct result of the feudal administration under the Dogra rule, which viewed the people as little more than sources of revenue. Under this regime, taxation (in cash and kind) was high and the cultivators, who were primarily Muslims, 'had to pay much more than half the share of their crop to the state in the form of multifarious taxes'.[5] Famines and outbreaks of communicable diseases were cyclical, and indebtedness due to disease and over-taxation was high. In his report to the maharaja in 1932, English civil servant Bertrand James Glancy put the proportion of the rural population that were in debt in the princely state at 70 per cent.[6]

State-led Development

By the 1980s, the quality of life of the people of Jammu and Kashmir had improved to a remarkable degree, with 23.8 per cent living below the poverty line in the state as against a national figure of 38.9 per cent.[7] The literacy rate increased to 30.64 per cent,[8] against the all-India figure of 43.7 per cent.[9] These developments were primarily due to multifarious state policies that empowered the people economically and politically through redistribution of land, conciliation of debt, universalization of free education and other such measures.

This book argues that the common deprivations faced under the feudal system brought the masses together in resentment against princely rule. Political activism in the state had increased in the 1930s with the formation of new political parties and other groups/associations formed by educated young men of the state. Parties like the National Conference (earlier named Muslim Conference) used the politically charged atmosphere of the 1940s to develop an aspirational agenda for change – 'Naya Kashmir' (New Kashmir). This was the first attempt at a public expression of common aspirations – social, political and developmental. This document declared that human development (as we understand it now) should be the foundation of state policy. Its pro-people language helped the National Conference gain massive popularity in the years preceding the tribal invasion from Pakistan in 1947. In the period of war and political upheaval that followed, the National Conference, with support from the Indian government, was made part of an emergency administration set up in 1948. The maharaja was later compelled to leave the state by Jawaharlal Nehru, and this resulted in confusion amongst the beneficiaries of the old feudal system. The emergency administration, now firmly led by Sheikh Abdullah, thus received a historic opportunity to introduce radical redistributive measures such as the abolition of all private debt and the redistribution of agricultural land to the tillers (without compensation to landowners). This was in complete contrast to other princely states like Andhra Pradesh, Rajasthan and Madhya Pradesh, where land reforms initiated by the state were sabotaged by the collective efforts of the landed aristocracy and local politicians.

Firm legislative roots, deep ideological commitment, and the sweeping nature and rapid implementation of state-led reforms make the development experience of Jammu and Kashmir unique in India. This book aims at studying the development experience of Jammu and Kashmir as developed by state development policy, and contextualizing the same. In particular, it traces the influence of the 'Naya Kashmir' document as a developmental roadmap.

Further, it looks at the social impact of state-led modernization in Jammu and Kashmir to examine it in terms of the progress of human development indicators, and to see if some of the indicators, like per capita income and life expectancy, grew more rapidly than others like literacy (especially female literacy) and why. Particular emphasis is placed on looking at the equity of reforms and the distribution of the fruits of development across all sections of society, including disadvantaged sections like Scheduled Castes, Scheduled Tribes, women and manual labourers.

Research Hypotheses

Through macro and village-level data I aim to test the following hypotheses:

1. The development experience of Jammu and Kashmir is unique and distinctive. Amongst Indian states, it led the way in implementing far-reaching land reforms, debt conciliation and guaranteeing the economic and social rights of its people (including the marginalized) under the state constitution.
2. State development policy aimed at disassembling traditional structures of resource management, employment and ownership, and replacing them with modern alternatives.
3. The state used the major part of central assistance and domestic resources for the development of the social sector (and not the private sector).
4. This process had a positive impact on human development indicators like household income, access to education, life expectancy and access to food till 1988.
5. From the late 1980s, armed conflict adversely affected the enabling of a social environment for development through human, social and infrastructural damage.

Book Outline

The book is divided into eight chapters. Chapter One contextualizes the development process in Jammu and Kashmir. It argues that a solid legislative foundation for state development policy was provided by one document in particular – the 'Naya Kashmir' manifesto of the National Conference. When the National Conference came to power in 1948, this document became a roadmap for government policy and inspired many pioneering legislations relating to agrarian reform and debt reduction. The chapter further argues that the main emphasis of 'Naya Kashmir' on rights-based policy came from its preoccupation with many of the normative constructs and policy goals that are central to the human development approach in development economics today. To fully explore this point, the chapter compares 'Naya Kashmir' with Martha Nussbaum's ten principles of human development.

Chapter Two traces the progress of Jammu and Kashmir's development policies. It examines the aim of the state government's policies to bring about a transition from 'traditional' to 'modern' in Kashmir's economy, society and polity. It argues that from 1948, successive state governments aimed at building a new social, economic and political order on the pattern of 'modern' societies in the west, and continued to subscribe to 'Naya Kashmir' and formulate and execute policy based on its recommendations well into the 1970s.

Land reforms in Jammu and Kashmir were a defining feature of its development policy. In fact, their effectiveness in reducing rural poverty and impact on the lives of the people made them unique in India. Chapter Three deals with the land reforms, comparing them with similar reforms in other Indian states. It argues that no other state in India implemented land reforms as quickly and as comprehensively as Jammu and Kashmir. It firmly establishes the link between land reforms and increases in per capita income.

Chapter Four discusses the impact of state-led modernization on the society and environment of Jammu and Kashmir. Here, I analyse the changes in the state's society and environment, arguing, *inter alia*, that the redistributive initiatives of the state government brought about mutually reinforcing positive changes in the lives of the people. This is substantiated by tracing the changes in human development indicators from 1948 to 1988. The chapter also discusses the failings of the state development policy and its implementation, particularly with reference to obstacles to democratic action, education, environment and gender inequality. The increase in bureaucratic control over community resources which led to corruption and damage to the environment is also examined. The chapter argues that the greatest failing of state policy was its complete belief in modernization theory's structuralist logic, which assumed that Jammu and Kashmir had to develop *only* in a particular direction – along the western trajectory. This led to its rejection of the traditional in its entirety and thus elements were lost that are recognized as vital to development today: the emphasis on sustainability, participation, social cohesion, and responsibility towards the environment and every member in the community. It also led the state into decreasing the space for genuine democratic action and focus instead on unfettered implementation of government policy, often stifling dissent and hijacking democratic institutions.

Chapters Five and Six present the findings from studies of three villages – one in the Jammu region (Nangali in Poonch district) and two in the Kashmir valley (Peth Kanihama and Sehpora in Budgam district) – to add depth to the macro-observations of Chapter Four.

Chapter Seven looks at how events, people and legal provisions came together in the evolution of the unique developmental journey of Jammu and Kashmir. It concludes by reiterating the relationship between the political and social development of the state, and describing the wider significance of the development experience of Jammu and Kashmir.

Chapter Eight looks at the de-operationalization of Article 370, the division of the state into two union territories, and the impact this has had on Jammu and Kashmir's development.

NOTES AND REFERENCES

[1] Jammu and Kashmir was ruled by the Mughals, the Afghans, the Sikhs and finally by Hindu kings from Jammu – the Dogra dynasty who, in 1846, bought the territory with all its inhabitants for Rs 75 lakh from the British East India Company, which had defeated the Sikhs.

[2] Frank Messervy, 'Kashmir', *Asiatic Review*, vol. 45, no. 161, 1949; Christopher Snedden, *Understanding Kashmir and Kashmiris*, London: C. Hurst and Co., 2015.

[3] Sheikh Abdullah was one of the main architects of the anti-monarchical movement.

[4] M.L. Misri and M.S. Bhat, *Poverty, Planning and Economic Change in Jammu and Kashmir*, New Delhi: Vikas Publishing House, 1994: 38.

[5] Chitralekha Zutshi, *Languages of Belonging: Islam, Regional Identity and the Making of Kashmir*, Delhi: Permanent Black, 2003: 64.

[6] Bertrand J. Glancy, 'Enquiry Commission Report submitted to His Highness the Maharaja', Jammu and Kashmir State Archives, Jammu, 1932.

[7] 'Jammu and Kashmir Digest of Statistics, 1960–1990', Department of Planning and Statistics, Government of Jammu and Kashmir, 1991.

[8] Ibid.

[9] Census of India 1981, Planning Commission, Government of India.

CHAPTER ONE

Change as Key

'Naya Kashmir' and Human Development

Half a century before the concept of human development broadened the horizon of economics from a preoccupation with GDP (gross domestic product) growth to a rights-based approach, the 'Naya Kashmir' document of the National Conference made these rights the central concern of government policy. Viewed from this perspective, it is a historical document of outstanding value not just in the context of India but globally. This chapter explores the development of 'Naya Kashmir', its central concerns and its impact on the development policy of Jammu and Kashmir – in particular, how it provided a firm foundation for state policy and defined a unique developmental journey for the state. To understand this, one needs to understand the extremely stark social realities of the colonial period from which it evolved.

Development Context in Jammu and Kashmir: The Monarchical Period

Till 1948, extreme levels of poverty and deprivation were deeply rooted in Jammu and Kashmir.[1] Taxation was high, and extracted in both cash and kind.

> Maharaja Gulab Singh, determined to recover the 75 lakh he had paid to the British to purchase Kashmir (after the Treaty of Amritsar), and continued by his successors, had set the trend for exorbitant tax collection. Not only were

tax levels very high, but virtually nothing was exempt from taxation: crops, fruit, grazing animals, handicrafts (shawls, carpets, etc), marriage ceremonials, and labour services – including grave-digging and even prostitution.[2]

The predominantly Muslim peasantry 'had to pay much more than half the share of their crop in the form of multifarious taxes to the state'.[3] As the state and its feudal intermediaries appropriated three-fourths of all rice yields, the people had no stores of grain to fall back on. Famines were widespread, affecting the state three times between 1890 and 1910 alone. During the Great Famine of 1877–79, which was followed by a cholera epidemic, the death rate was so massive that local folklore grew around the notion that only eleven families had survived in the Kashmir valley. The actual figures showed that the population of Srinagar was decimated from '1,27,400 to 60,000 and the total number of survivors in the Kashmir valley to only two-fifths'.[4] Even worse, the famine could have been prevented if the people had been allowed to 'cut their crops and carry them',[5] but this was not allowed by the feudal functionaries and they were made to wait till revenue assessment was over, by which time the harvest had been washed away by incessant heavy rain.

Industrial development 'was almost negligible and the lack of infrastructure had crippled the economy and accentuated the poverty syndrome'.[6] Education levels were dismal with the first school being set up by the maharaja only in 1886.[7] Teachers were sent for training to Lahore till the first training facility for teachers was opened in Srinagar, in 1910. The low priority given by the maharaja's government to education is evident from the state council's 1893 statement that, 'mere literary education without a technical component only serves to create a class of discontented candidates for clerical duties whose aspirations the state could not afford to meet'.[8]

Access to education was the preserve of the feudal elite with only 5 per cent literacy in the state till as late as 1941. These figures were even worse for females: the first school for girls set up in Srinagar in the 1890s was closed within a year due to local hostility against female education.[9] The government then established a girls' school in 1911, but education remained the preserve mostly of upper-caste Hindus.[10] Even in 1947 schools across the whole state were very few in number, and fewer still in the villages. Free education was available only in girls' schools, where enrolment rates were very low. Only those who could pay school fees and pay for books, etc., could afford to send their male children to school. This ruled out most of the tenant farmers, subsistence agriculturists with no cash incomes, those who were indebted (which made up most of the Muslim population of the state), and those belonging to the Scheduled Castes and Scheduled Tribes.

Public health was another extremely neglected sector, apart from education, under the maharaja's rule, a fact illustrated by the maharaja's last budget in 1948 that classified both health and education as 'minor departments'. From 1892 to 1920, seven outbreaks of smallpox devastated all parts of the state, and the maharaja's health department was far too inadequate to control it. In 1920 alone, smallpox caused 237 deaths.[11] From 1950 onwards, mass vaccinations were carried out by the interim government. These proved to be successful and the disease was eradicated by 1975. From 1892 to 1934, cholera visited the state fifteen times, and the plague became endemic, particularly in Jammu, Samba and Akhnoor, causing 2,722 deaths in 1918 alone.[12] The maharaja's lack of concern for health is shown by the fact that there was no government facility/ department for dealing with epidemics in the state till 1925. Whenever an epidemic broke out, 'the engagement of temporary Assistant Surgeons and Compounders from Punjab [was necessitated] at the eleventh hour'.[13] An Epidemic Establishment was set up in the regions of Jammu and Kashmir in 1925, and rules for containing epidemics were drawn up and enforced as late as 1934.[14] Access to health facilities too was dismal – there was no medical department in the state till 1890, when two *sadar* (central) hospitals were set up in Jammu and Srinagar cities, and twelve dispensaries (functioning under hospital assistants) in the populous towns. Villages had no health-care facilities beyond visits by medical officers during epidemic outbreaks. The situation was not much better by 1947, with life expectancy in the state being as low as 27 years[15] as compared to 32 years for all of India.[16]

The condition of the Scheduled Castes and Tribes was wretched, with the state being oblivious towards them at best and exploitative at worst. Scheduled Castes that lived in the Jammu region were not allowed to own land or construct houses, and were routinely compelled to perform *begar* (forced labour). Even when they were employed, those employed in government departments were not entitled to pensions.[17] The Scheduled

Tribes were completely neglected by the state, and lacked even basic opportunities of accessing health and education.

The standard of living of the people, across regions, was very poor. William Moorcroft and George Trebeck, officials of the British East India Company recorded the condition of mass hunger in Kashmir in 1837. They observed that '*singhara* [water chestnut] constituted almost the only food of at least 30,000 people for five months in a year and *nadru* [lotus-stem] of about five thousand people in Srinagar city for nearly eight months'.[18] Bamzai wrote that the diet of the majority of people consisted of boiled rice and vegetables, although 'a great number' lived on water chestnuts, maize and barley.[19] Both these accounts show the acute scarcity of foodgrains for the common people of the state, explaining why a single failed harvest could lead to a famine. In his administrative report of November 1944 to the maharaja, Ganga Nath, a senior minister at the Dogra court, painted a dismal picture of housing facilities: 'Even the best house . . . could afford no better shelter in the rain than a chinar tree. These huts were made like log cabins and were covered with mud plaster.'[20] Add to this the difficulty in accessing basic health and education, and it is clear that the overall development scenario of Jammu and Kashmir was bleak indeed till 1948.

This was by no means true of all princely states in India at the time. The princely state of Travancore, in what is now central and south Kerala, had built an effective education system (including mid-day meals for children as early as the 1940s) and a modest health system. The king, Balarama Varma, had also issued the famous temple proclamation of 1936 which allowed members of all Hindu castes to visit temples, a freedom denied to the lower castes till then. The princely state of Cochin (Kochi), similarly, was forward-looking and had taken steps to encourage genuine local self-government, with the establishment of town councils in Mattanchery and Ernakulam in 1896, as well as a thriving state legislature that included the first female legislator of India, Thottakattu Madhaviamma, in 1925. Significantly, only ten of the forty-five members of the Kochi Legislative Assembly were officially nominated, the rest being elected.

In both cases, the development process initiated by the government was spurred by the threat of annexation by British authorities on charges of misrule.[21] But it was the growing sense of a common identity in the 1900s that inspired the Malayali people to unite and demand better public services and a share in employment.[22] In Jammu and Kashmir, the threat of annexation by the British was always imminent, particularly after the Great Famine of 1878, when the Officer on Special Duty F. Henvey wrote a series of letters to the Secretary to Government of India. In these reports, he mentioned that after the famine three-fourths of all peasants had either died or left the state for Punjab, and in Srinagar city, out of 40,000 shawl weavers only 4,000 remained.[23] This and other correspondence from Henvey specified how the maharaja failed to provide food and relief works (food-for-work programmes) to the stricken population despite repeated directions from Simla.

These reports, and the discovery of letters written by the maharaja to the rulers of Russia and Afghanistan seeking help against the British,[24] prompted the colonial administration to intervene unambigiously. A Permanent Resident to the maharaja's court was appointed in 1888. In 1889, the Resident divested Maharaja Pratap Singh of his administrative powers and set up a four-member Council of Regency, to be headed by the Resident. In a direct blow to the maharaja, his half-brother Amar Singh was appointed to this council. The publication of Robert Thorp's *Kashmir Misgovernment*, followed by his mysterious death in Srinagar (allegedly through poisoning on the maharaja's orders), also influenced these decisions. But the increased British presence and interference in the maharaja's administration did not have the same effect in Jammu and Kashmir as in Travancore and Cochin. The reason for this was that the British understanding of Jammu and Kashmir's importance as a buffer state between British India on the one hand, and Afghanistan and Russia on the other, overshadowed their other priorities.

> The British Resident concerned himself more with the reorganization of the army, construction of roads to border areas like Gilgit and Ladakh and the supply of a huge contingent of 50,000 soldiers for the imperial war effort in the First World War. The British ignored Settlement Commissioner A.A. Wingate's recommendation that proprietary rights be granted to the tenants instead of the tenants-at-will status that they had.[25]

This demonstrates quite clearly that their focus was on defence and not development. Token measures were initiated in education and health, including the setting up of two schools by the government and two hospitals by Christian missionaries in Jammu and Srinagar, but these were not the government's priority.

Till 1905, when power was handed to the new maharaja, the Regency Council 'recruited educated Punjabis from outside the state to serve in high positions in the state administration prompting Dogras and Kashmiri Pandits (till then the administrative elite) to launch a campaign against the appointment of these *ghairmulki*s (foreigners)'.[26] The lack of educational opportunities for the Muslim majority meant that it was not till the 1920s (till there was a critical mass of educated Muslims) that they 'joined the chorus against *ghairmulki*s, prompting Pratap Singh's successor Hari Singh to pass a law providing state's preference for hiring educated *mulki*s (natives) in 1927'.[27] The Mulki agitation was not a mass movement but it accelerated political activity in the state. Till 1920, 'the only public activism allowed by the Dogra state was under the auspices of societies for socio-religious reform'.[28] In the 1920s and 1930s, people from all communities began to form associations like the Sanatan Dharm Yuvak Sabha (in Kashmir), Reading Room Party (in Srinagar) and the Young Men's Muslim Association (in Jammu). Political parties like the Kisan Mazdoor Party, the Muslim Conference (later renamed the National Conference), the Hindu Maha Sabha and many others were also formed during this period. The people of the state began demanding better services in health and education, culminating in the presentation of the 'Naya Kashmir' agenda to the maharaja by Sheikh Abdullah in 1944.[29] As a result, the maharaja's government took measures to increase expenditure on health and education after 1944, but this process was interrupted by the tribal invasion of 1947. The development trajectory of the princely state of Jammu and Kashmir was thus late in starting, and was interrupted by external geopolitical factors, more so than in Travancore and Cochin.[30]

A Common Identity?

According to Prerna Singh, a sense of common identity or 'we-ness' can generate a 'more progressive social policy and a greater popular involvement with the public goods provided, which combine to give rise to higher levels of social development'.[31] She uses the development experience of Kerala in the twentieth century to argue that, from the 1890s to 1950, the emergence of Malayali 'subnationalism' led the people of Kerala to demand better services in health and education. This process was initiated by elite, well-educated sections of the Nair, Christian and

Ezhava communities against the domination of non-Malayali Brahmins at the court (and in government service), but by the 1920s crystallized into the 'Aikya Keralam' (United Kerala or Malayali homeland) movement in the two princely states of Travancore, and Cochin and Malabar, then a part of the British-ruled Madras Presidency.

> A powerful sense of Malayali subnationalism fostered the understanding that the well-being of all sections of the population was the collective responsibility of all Malayalis. This appears to have enhanced the willingness of upper castes and classes to move beyond narrowly defined self-interest and work for the good of other members and of the subnational community as a whole.[32]

The people began to demand better services in health and education, and equal rights for all Malayalis including the Scheduled Castes. This led the rulers of Travancore and Cochin to ensure better representation of Malayalis in government services, set up a large number of schools and implement mid-day meals, establish an effective health system and municipal system, and allow Scheduled Castes access to temples. This subnationalism was facilitated by a common language (Malayalam) and a common history.

The princely state of Jammu and Kashmir was – to borrow an expression – a very different animal. It had a variety of native languages: Kashmiri, Dogri, Ladakhi, Shina, Gojri and Pahari, to name but a few. It had distinct ethnic groups and different religions. Even at the regional level, Jammu, Kashmir and Ladakh had no common ethno-religious or linguistic identity. Other than a shared history imposed on them by the Dogra rule, the princely state's constituent regions had been historically distinct, with Kashmir more in line with Central Asian influences through the Silk Route, Ladakh having close historical and religious links to Tibet, and Jammu tied to political developments in Punjab. So the process of developing a common identity remained very much a project of the educated elite, particularly the Muslim Conference – renamed the All Jammu and Kashmir National Conference in 1939[33] – which aimed at ending monarchical rule in the state through popular agitation.

The strong socialist ideals of the National Conference gave it support from the impoverished masses in all regions of the state, particularly in the valley. The emergence of the National Conference as a secular political platform followed the culmination of the Mulki movement. Hence, it was very conscious of the need for consolidating the prevailing sense of a common identity and building on it politically. It tried to do this systematically for the first time during the anti-monarchical uprising of 1931, but was unable to find adequate support amongst the Hindu elite who were invested in the feudal state.

This lack of support from the Hindu elite might have continued but for unwitting facilitation by the Dogra state itself. The introduction of Urdu as the state language by the maharaja in 1889 meant that the elite had to study Urdu in order to get into government service or gain more favours at the Dogra court. The proportion of those literate in Urdu increased by 99.2 per cent from 1921 to 1931.[34] Urdu was subsequently used by the National Conference for dissemination of pamphlets advocating a common identity and common responsibility to rise up against imperial rule, especially after 1944. Because of the common language, these messages were understood, in some measure, in all regions of the state; if not for the introduction of Urdu, such transregional understanding would not have been possible. After the killing of unarmed protestors by Dogra soldiers in 1931, counter-protests by the people and excessive use of force by the Dogra state became a cyclical process in the Kashmir valley. This converted the anti-monarchical push by the educated elite (essentially a top–down process) into a mass movement (bottom–up). As Gul Wani observes, 'The history of [monarchical] oppression was bound to create in the minds of the people of the state an intense desire for self-government and independence.'[35]

However, the Dogra state actively worked against this movement, supporting religious leaders from all communities against the National Conference and lending a sympathetic ear to the breakaway faction of the National Conference (that retained the old name, Muslim Conference) under Ghulam Abbas. Amongst the Sunni Muslims, Mirwaiz Yusuf Shah, arguably the most important religious leader in the valley, stood in public opposition to Sheikh Abdullah with the support of the Dogra state.[36] The confrontation between the supporters of Mirwaiz and Sheikh Abdullah was divisive and violent but was limited to only Srinagar city.

This opposition did not reach the National Conference's main support base – the rural hinterland. The peasantry supported the National Conference because of the party's ideological commitment to end feudal hegemony over resources and society. The end of the *jagirdari* system gave the exploited peasantry a common goal to rally behind. Though this agenda was not unique to state-based political parties of pre-independence India, the National Conference was unique in incorporating these concerns into a composite socialist agenda – 'Naya Kashmir'. This document was used thereafter as the main tool of the anti-monarchical struggle, and as a future constitution for a democratic state.

After 1947, the National Conference devoted itself with singular focus to the articulation of a common identity, to try and redefine the anti-monarchical movement into something higher. Accordingly,

> . . . selected cultural fragments from an imagined past were collected to construct a *Kashmiriyat* (sense of common Kashmiri identity) that would draw in both Pandits and Muslims. This was evident, for instance, in the periodization adopted by Sheikh Abdullah and his associates in their recounting of the history of the valley. Their reconstruction of the 'biography' of Kashmir moved not from periods of Hindu to Muslim to Sikh rulers but from an age of Kashmir rule, through a long interregnum of 'foreign' dominance beginning with the Mughals in 1586 before the end of Dogra hegemony marked a triumphant return to rule by Kashmiris.[37]

Looking at these facts, it cannot be claimed that a sense of subnationalism, however diffuse, was the precursor or the catalyst for social development in Jammu and Kashmir, as in Kerala. The state was too ethnically and linguistically diverse for the development of a common identity or 'we-ness'. Though there was a Mulki movement to petition the maharaja to employ state subjects in government service, similar to the movement against non-Malayali Brahmins in Kerala, its proponents were mainly Kashmiri Pandits, Dogra Hindus and a handful of the Muslim elite. Since a sufficient number of Muslims were not educated, this was a non-issue for the majority of people in the state. The spread and benefits of the Mulki movement remained confined to the elites. Similarly, though Maharaja Hari Singh issued a proclamation allowing the Scheduled Castes access to temples, government schools and other public places in 1932, this was not the result of any agitation by the Scheduled Castes or any other social group but in line with his idea of what a 'benevolent ruler' should do.

What drove the people together across religious, ethnic and linguistic lines was widespread poverty, unemployment and a desire for self-government, not a common identity. Kuldip Singh Bajwa describes it thus:

'By the 1930s, the general poverty and lack of employment opportunities had bred some discontent against the autocratic Dogra rule.'[38] In the Kashmir valley, this discontent was accelerated by the escalation of violence by the Dogra state. Even the common language of the resistance movement, Urdu, was an imposed and not a native language (like Malayalam). Members of the elite from both Jammu and Kashmir regions came together with Muslims under the banner of the National Conference to demand better services from the maharaja, in the form of 'National Demands' and then 'Naya Kashmir', but this *preceded* the *final* construction of 'we-ness' (*Kashmiriyat*), a process that began later in the 1940s.

Thus, Singh's concept of subnationalism, as it stands, cannot be applied to pre-1948 Jammu and Kashmir as an explanation of what prompted people to come together. However, there was a firmly rooted interdependence, mutual aid and sense of social solidarity at the community level that facilitated this process (see Chapter Five).

Drafting 'Naya Kashmir': Clashing Versions

According to Rasheed Taseer, the idea of drafting a constitution based on socialist principles came from Dr Kanwar Ashraf who arrived in Kashmir after a visit to the Soviet Union in 1940: 'The idea became popular within the Muslim Conference[39] the largest political party in Jammu and Kashmir at the time.'[40] In his autobiography, *Aatish-e-Chinar* (Flames of the Chinar), Sheikh Abdullah records that he asked his friend Baba Pyare Lal Singh Bedi to draft the document. Bedi and his wife Freda were committed socialists and edited a political quarterly in Lahore.

The official version put out by the National Conference was that intellectuals, artists and politicians, including Dr Kanwar Ashraf, Danyal Lateefi (advocate), Pandit Jia Lal Kilam (landlord), Mohammed Din Taseer and the poet Ihsan Danish[41] came to Delhi Hotel, Lahore to meet the Bedis and contribute their ideas for the document. It was through discussion and debate with this group that Bedi came up with the actual text of 'Naya Kashmir'. Many believe that Freda Bedi typed up the document and was responsible for including the section on rights of women. But a closer inspection reveals major holes in the official account. For instance, it is not clear which sections were specifically authored by Bedi and which by others. Also, as Andrew Whitehead points out, the drafting of 'Naya Kashmir' was less a product of pure intellectual debate and more a loose act of plagiarism on Bedi's part:

> In fact, the document was largely lifted from the constitution Stalin had introduced in the Soviet Union and which Bedi knew well, having republished it in full in 1937 in a political quarterly he edited in Lahore, *Contemporary India*. There were some concessions to Kashmir's particular circumstances – notably an acceptance of a constitutional monarchy – but it was a thoroughly radical prescription for the state: freedom of conscience, worship, speech, press and assembly was to be enshrined in law; there was to be free and universal elementary education conducted in the mother tongue; women were assured of equal rights, including equal wages; there would be a planned economy; and a National Assembly was to be elected by secret ballot, with everyone aged over eighteen able to vote.[42]

Even though only eight of the 50 clauses in the text were original, 'Naya Kashmir' was a powerful document, designed to fire up the imagination of the most marginalized. The language and imagery used (the cover of the English version had a gun-toting Kashmiri woman) were evocative.

Sheikh Abdullah regarded 'Naya Kashmir' as 'a revolutionary document'.[43] He lost no time in employing it to galvanize public opinion and increase support for his party's agenda. Accordingly, the document was translated into Urdu by Maulvi Mohammed Sayeed Masoodi and publicly distributed to garner support for the party. In 1944, Sheikh Abdullah presented the document to Maharaja Hari Singh, the ruler of Jammu and Kashmir, on his return from the Imperial War Cabinet in England. The objective of this public act was to showcase the National Conference as the true representative of the common aspirations of the people of the state, and to present Sheikh Abdullah as their undisputed advocate.

On 3 August 1945, the National Conference formally adopted 'Naya Kashmir' in its annual session at Sopore, Baramulla and set about propagating the central ideas of the new constitution. A Working Committee of twenty-one members, which included Pandit Kashyap Bandhu, Sardar Budh Singh, Pandit Jia Lal Kilam, Lala Girdharilal Dogra and Pandit Prem Nath Bazaz, was nominated for the dissemination programme. Within a short time, 'Naya Kashmir' became a unifying force for the anti-monarchical movement in the state. Though 'Naya Kashmir' drew support from the intelligentsia and the peasantry, particularly the

Kashmiri Muslim peasants who were the worst off under the feudal system, it antagonized the Dogra upper castes and Kashmiri Pandits who were the main beneficiaries of the feudal dispensation comprising the largest number of landlords, government officials and soldiers. A few right-leaning elements including the Muslim Conference, Mirwaiz Yousuf Shah and some members of the Kashmiri Pandit-dominated Yuvak Sabha opposed it. But since the opponents did not have a significant grassroots presence across most of the state, their reaction did not pose that formidable a challenge.

The Contents of 'Naya Kashmir'

The stated aims of 'Naya Kashmir' were: 'To raise the standard of living of our people, enhance the wealth of the community, and to eradicate all invidious social divisions.'[44] The document was divided into two parts: the Constitution and the National Economic Plan. The Constitution laid out the basic rights and obligations of citizenship and the structure of the legislative, executive and judicial organs of government, as well as the process of amendments to the Constitution. The National Economic Plan included the aims of planning and the outline of a planned economy model. Notably, it included charters for the rights of peasants, labourers and women, and contained clear provisions for the economic and social upliftment of Scheduled Castes and Tribes.

As Kashmir was primarily a feudal agrarian economy, agriculture was viewed as the starting point for change. The backwardness of the state was attributed mainly to the 'common peasant suffering in the clutches of landlordism'. 'Naya Kashmir' sought to change the social relations of production in the agrarian sector by giving ownership rights to tenant farmers through state-wide land reforms. This was to be supplemented by 'economic remedies like improvements in the production technique and agricultural equipment of all kinds, better marketing facilities and consolidation of holdings'.[45] Accordingly, mechanizing agriculture and introducing high-yielding varieties of seeds, which in turn required the import and use of pesticides, insecticides, etc., were defined as a developmental priority.

Regarding manufacturing, 'Naya Kashmir' advocated rapid industrialization, and diversification from traditional small-scale industries like handicrafts to medium and heavy industries like cement. Industrialization was envisaged as developing from a 'take off' in agriculture, brought about by changing the traditional agrarian structure (primarily through land reform). 'From the land must come more food to feed the people as well as the goods by the exchange of which machines can be bought to industrialize the country and mechanize agriculture itself.'[46]

On the political front, it initially demanded 'responsible government' by the maharaja (a constitutional monarchy with the maharaja as head of state and of the armed forces), but later its demands became more radical: complete overthrow of the monarchical system, and the establishment of 'Awami Raj' (popular rule) and democratic institutions. On this basis, it can safely be said that 'Naya Kashmir' made change the key aim, indeed the *basis*, of state development policy.

Perhaps the most radical part of the document was its unequivocal advocacy of women's rights. The charter for women not only gave them the right to education, right to work with equal pay as men, right to consent to marriage, but also paid maternity leave, right to medical assistance at childbirth and right to inheritance.

Influence on State Development Policy

In 1947, against the backdrop of a tribal invasion from Pakistan, an interim government under Sheikh Abdullah was established in Jammu and Kashmir. To give legal sanctity to 'Naya Kashmir', the government tasked the existing Praja Sabha (State Assembly convened by the maharaja) with adopting the 'Naya Kashmir' Constitution. 'The Jammu and Kashmir Constitution Act of 1939 was then subjected to a process of repeated modifications through the passing of a number of amendment acts' that did away with the powers of the monarch and delegated them to the Constituent Assembly.[47] The Dogra dynasty was formally abolished by The Jammu and Kashmir Constitution Amendment Act of 1952.

From 1947 to 1956, when the Constitution of Jammu and Kashmir was ratified by the Constituent Assembly, the Jammu and Kashmir Constitution Act of 1939 was in force as an 'interim' Constitution. But it may be argued that 'Naya Kashmir' functioned as the *de facto* Constitution, as the government was guided chiefly by its social, political and developmental objectives. It lost no time in implementing the redistributive provisions, including land reforms and the dissolution of debt. The centrality of 'Naya Kashmir' to public opinion and political legitimacy can be gauged from the fact that even the governments that followed the interim government, including the undemocratic regime of Bakshi Ghulam Mohammad, made repeated public declarations that their policies were in line with 'Naya Kashmir'.

In 1956, 'Naya Kashmir' became part of the Directive Principles of State Policy in the new Constitution of Jammu and Kashmir, thus remaining continually relevant to the development context in the state. The Directive Principles of State Policy are an important illustration of the developmental priorities of the state – a public, legal representation of the aims of governance. Though they are not enforceable – for instance, by a court of law – it is the legal duty of the government to keep them in mind when making government policies. The primary objective of the Directive Principles of State Policy in Jammu and Kashmir comes straight out of 'Naya Kashmir', emphasizing 'the promotion of the welfare of the mass of the people by establishing and preserving a socialist order of society wherein all exploitation of man has been abolished, and society wherein justice – social, economic and political – shall inform all the institutions of national life'. Article 38 Section 1 of the Constitution of India which contains the Directive Principles of State Policy declares: 'The State shall strive to promote the welfare of the people by securing and protecting as effectively as it may a social order in which justice, social, economic and political, shall inform all institutions of the national life.' Only in 1978 did the 44th Amendment to the Constitution of India add: 'The State shall, in particular, strive to minimize the inequalities in income, and endeavour to eliminate inequalities in status, facilities and opportunities, not only amongst individuals, but also amongst groups of people residing in different areas or engaged in different vocations.'

It is noteworthy that the emphasis on ending exploitation in 'Naya Kashmir' legally became a central concern of government policy in Jammu and Kashmir by being a part of the Directive Principles. This is not to say that all state policy in Jammu and Kashmir was enacted to end exploitation, or that it was not so in the rest of India. But this legal conception of the state as a force to defeat exploitation showcases Jammu and Kashmir's greater legal commitment to the principles of human development. The Constitution of India is much more modest in its Directive Principles which vow to secure and protect '*as effectively as it may,* a social order based on justice' (emphasis added).

Comparison with the Indian Constitution

To understand how far ahead of its time 'Naya Kashmir' was as a document, a comparison with the Constitution of India (arguably the oldest and most liberal one in the subcontinent) is most useful. This is not a comparison between the Constitution of Jammu and Kashmir and that of India, but it does help to establish the legal context of the development experience of Jammu and Kashmir, particularly from 1948 to 1956, when 'Naya Kashmir' was the *de facto* Constitution. It explains how Jammu and Kashmir was able to legally implement radical land reforms and debt conciliation in 1948 and 1950, and why this did not happen in the rest of India – simply because 'Naya Kashmir' was a more radically redistributive Constitution. Though not all the provisions of 'Naya Kashmir' were implemented during this time, land reforms, debt conciliation and universal free education were.

Right from its first draft, 'Naya Kashmir' guaranteed fundamental rights to all citizens including the right to employment, right to leisure time, right to provision of basic living requirements, right to education, etc. It also detailed the fundamental duties of citizens including universal military service. In comparison, fundamental rights were included in the working draft of the Constitution of India in December 1948, eight months after the submission of the Kripalani subcommittee's Report on Fundamental Rights. Fundamental duties of citizens were added even later – by the 42nd Amendment in 1976, upon the recommendation of the Swaran Singh Committee constituted by the government earlier that year. Further, while the right to education had been guaranteed under 'Naya Kashmir' more than fifty years earlier, it was only in 2002, with the 86th Amendment, that the right to education was converted into a fundamental right in the Indian Constitution. Unlike the Constitution of India, 'Naya Kashmir' guaranteed citizens the right to property but with reservations, notably that a person who did not contribute to the economy of the state by doing productive work would forfeit this right. This made redistribution of feudal properties a main aim of government policy in Jammu and Kashmir.

Article 12 of 'Naya Kashmir' guaranteed equal wages for women and men. It declared:

In all spheres of national activities whether economic, cultural, political or any other aspects of national service there would be equality between men and women. To guarantee this right, women would have the same conditions of service and get the same wages as men in every job. Women would have equal rights with men, regarding right to leisure, right of association and right to education.[48]

Importantly, the Women's Charter of 'Naya Kashmir' advocated universally paid parental leave, an unprecedented provision at the time. It was not till the enactment of the Equal Remuneration Act in 1976 that equal remuneration to men and women workers and prevention of discrimination on grounds of sex were granted to women by the Constitution of India.

'Naya Kashmir' declared that 'All citizens will have the right to work, that is, the right to receive guaranteed work with payment for their labour in accordance with its quantity and quality, subject to a minimum and maximum wage as prescribed by law.'[49] The Constitution of India still does not guarantee this right, though it has taken a step in this direction through the enactment of the Mahatma Gandhi National Rural Employment Guarantee Act (MGNREGA) in 2005. This Act provides a hundred days of labour at minimum wage for rural workers and helps engage them to create much-needed local infrastructure. Sadly, the employment scheme under MGNREGA has recently suffered from an appalling lack of financial support from the central government.

'Naya Kashmir' was far ahead of the Constitution of India in terms of providing a separate charter for the rights of peasants, labourers and women, and providing special legal safeguards against the exploitation of children and the elderly. Through its emphasis on broadening human freedoms and reducing social divisions, it can be said to be a precursor to the human capabilities approach in development economics that was developed half a century later.

'Naya Kashmir' and Human Capabilities

The human capabilities approach was developed within development economics in the last decade of the twentieth century, primarily through the work of noted economist Amartya Sen and philosopher Martha Nussbaum. It uses basic human freedoms and opportunities available to the citizens of a country, in addition to economic measurements, in the assessment of a country's well-being. It has emerged as a valuable alternative to indices that use GDP growth alone as a measure of a country's economic development, giving as it does a comprehensive picture of a people's standard of living and access to means of improving the same.

Sen received the Nobel Prize in economics in 2000 for his work on human capabilities. Nussbaum's work is equally notable as it provides the philosophical foundation of the human development index (HDI) approach. She has defined ten basic human capabilities that should be supported by all democracies – namely, life, bodily health, bodily integrity, senses, imagination and thought, emotions, practical reason, affiliation, concern for other species and control over one's environment – as central to any conception of development.[50] A close study of 'Naya Kashmir' reveals how the document outlines almost all these capabilities, and makes the state responsible for supporting and implementing them.

1. *Life.* Nussbaum defines this right as a person 'being able to live to the end of a human life of normal length'[51] and 'not dying prematurely'. 'Naya Kashmir' dedicates itself to eliminating all barriers to this including death by disease, death during childbirth, death due to starvation and death due to lack of medical facilities.

2. *Bodily health.* To Nussbaum, being 'able to have good health, including reproductive health; to be adequately nourished; to have adequate shelter' is essential.[52] 'Naya Kashmir' pledges that 'safeguarding of the health of citizens of the State is the primary duty of the State'. It includes a National Health Charter that makes extensive provisions for providing healthcare and health education to all citizens. Especially noteworthy is the guarantee that

> all women, whether in town or village, in Frontier areas, among nomad tribes or living in boats shall be afforded the greatest help and protection in fulfilling their labour of motherhood including: ante-natal treatment, medical arrangements for childbirth, adequate nursing arrangements for the lie-in period, and extension of the district nursing system.[53]

It also places 'special emphasis . . . on recruitment and training of woman doctors'.[54]

The National Economic Plan further promises 'a reasonable standard of living' including:

a. *Better nutrition*: a balanced diet, necessary vitamins and protective foods; a total of 2,400 units of calorific value for a full-grown worker;

b. *More clothing per head annually*: an increase to at least thirty yards per head, with guaranteed provision of woollen garments for the winter;

c. *Adequate housing*: weatherproof accommodation of at least 100 square feet per person in town and country;

d. *Water supply*: adequate and accessible, allowing the use of twenty-five gallons per person daily;

e. *Lighting arrangements*: according to local needs;

f. *Education for all*: according to the basic 'National Plan';

g. *Provision of food stores and cooked-food shops under hygienic conditions*: at least one for every thousand inhabitants;

h. *A postal service*: well-regulated and supplemented by a network of telephone exchanges all over the State, aiming at the closer linking up of remote areas, frontier districts, and isolated populations, with the capitals;

i. *Insurance*: a universal system against all disabilities and calamities;

j. *Banking facilities*: the recognition of banking as a necessary concomitant of national life; one bank office for 25,000 people;

k. *Medical arrangements* and nursing facilities free for all.[55]

3. *Bodily integrity*. Nussbaum conceptualizes this as 'being able to move freely from place to place; . . . to be secure against violent assault, including sexual assault and domestic violence; having opportunities for sexual satisfaction and for choice in matters of reproduction'.[56] Not only does 'Naya Kashmir' include this but its Women's Charter assures women 'freedom from assault and molestation' and also protection from 'trafficking' and 'unduly heavy work during pregnancy'.[57]

4. *Senses, imagination and thought*. Being able to use one's mind (where that mind has been developed 'by an adequate education, including, but by no means limited to, literacy and basic mathematical and scientific training') freely and to express one's thoughts freely is to Nussbaum an essential human capability.[58] This is embodied in the commitment of 'Naya Kashmir' to provide education not 'limited to the three Rs',[59] and its promotion of 'freedom of speech, freedom of the Press, freedom of assembly and meetings and freedom of street processions and demonstrations'.[60]

5. *Emotions*. To Nussbaum, supporting this capability means that the state should support 'forms of human association that can be shown to be

crucial in the [emotional] development [of its citizens]'.[61] 'Naya Kashmir' pays special attention to the family as it supports the emotional and social development of its citizens and recognizes it as 'the basic social unit'.[62]

6. *Practical reason.* According to Nussbaum, this means being able to 'form a conception of the good and to engage in critical reflection about the planning of one's life'.[63] The state's duty is to ensure protection of the liberty of conscience and religious observance. 'Naya Kashmir' deals with this quite directly in Article 2 where it says, 'Freedom of conscience and of worship shall be guaranteed for all citizens.'[64]

7. *Affiliation.* Nussbaum sees affiliation as a duality:

a. Being able to live with and toward others, to recognize and show concern for other humans, to engage in various forms of social interaction; to be able to imagine the situation of another. . . . (Protecting this capability means protecting institutions that constitute and nourish such forms of affiliation, and also protecting the freedom of assembly and political speech.)

b. Having the social bases of self-respect and non-humiliation; being able to be treated as a dignified being whose worth is equal to that of others. This entails protections against discrimination on the basis of race, sex, sexual orientation, caste, religion, ethnicity, or national origin.[65]

'Naya Kashmir' recognizes affiliation in both these forms. Article 4 provides a legal foundation for promotion of public institutions based on affiliation. 'In conformity with the interests of the people and for the purpose of developing self-expression . . . all citizens shall be ensured the right of combining in public organizations . . . women's and youth organizations, . . . political parties, and cultural, scientific and technical societies.'[66] Article 1 establishes equality before the law and non-discrimination 'on account of nationality, religion, race or birth'.[67] Here, birth is intended to cover sex, class, caste and disability. The propagation of religious, racial or national exceptionalism or hatred is declared punishable by law.

8. *Other species.* 'Being able to live with concern for and in relation to animals, plants, and the world of nature'[68] is the only human capability that does not find an equivalent in the 'Naya Kashmir' document.

9. *Play.* 'Being able to laugh, to play, to enjoy recreational activities' is an essential part of human capabilities.[69] Article 1 of 'Naya Kashmir' guarantees every citizen the right to rest and the National Economic Plan

envisages the 'establishment of centres of recreation for the organized use of leisure'.[70]

10. *Control over one's environment.* Again, Nussbaum expresses this as a duality:

> a. *Political*: Being able to participate effectively in political choices that govern one's life; having the right of political participation, protection of free speech and association.
> b. *Material*: Being able to hold property (both land and movable goods) . . . and having property rights on an equal basis with others; having the right to seek employment on an equal basis with others; having the freedom from unwarranted search and seizure. In work, being able to work as a human, exercising practical reason and entering into meaningful relationships of mutual recognition with other workers.[71]

Articles 3 and 4 of 'Naya Kashmir' guarantee the right to association and Article 15 the right to property as basic rights of citizens, and, crucially, make the state responsible for the protection of these rights. The spirit of all ten capabilities defined by Nussbaum is succinctly expressed in the commitment of 'Naya Kashmir' that 'All children born in the State shall be ensured equality of opportunity irrespective of accidents of birth and parentage.'[72]

Conclusion

'Naya Kashmir' as a policy document is unique in India. No other contemporary document, including the Fundamental Rights Resolution of the Karachi Session of the Indian National Congress comes close to being as comprehensive. It derived some of its ideas from dominant ideologies popular at the time, like socialism (particularly the emphasis on redistributive measures in agriculture and ending private debt) and modernization theory (the stress on changing the traditional society of Jammu and Kashmir on the pattern of 'modern' societies in the west by bringing about industrialization, urbanization and economic growth through technology transfer). However, it went over and beyond these ideologies to guarantee the masses fulfilment of basic needs like food and education as rights backed by law. Some rights like the right to work that it pledged to citizens more than half a century ago have yet to find equivalents in the Constitution of India. 'Naya Kashmir' made these rights the underlying concern of government policy. It made the extension of human capabilities, as we understand it today, the basis of state legislation.

'Naya Kashmir' enabled the rapid and total dismantling of the feudal system and put in place redistributive measures like land reforms and abolition of private debt. This was in stark contrast to other princely states like Rajasthan, Gujarat and Andhra Pradesh, where the landed aristocracy lobbied successfully to keep their land, thus defeating state government-initiated land reforms. The success of 'Naya Kashmir' in enforcing these changes may be attributed to many factors. Perhaps the most influential were its ideological commitment to socialist reforms, the popular widespread support it was able to garner in large numbers from the Kashmiri intelligentsia and largely landless working classes combined with the united political leadership which, due to the declaration of an emergency, enabled them to act in ways unhindered by electoral concerns between 1948 and 1950.

In the absence of a constitution during 1948–52, 'Naya Kashmir' gained quasi-constitutional status and became the document that determined the policy-thinking of the emergency-era administration and those that followed. Viewed from this perspective, 'Naya Kashmir' firmly set Jammu and Kashmir on to a distinctive developmental path by providing a strong constitutional basis for recognizing the human being as the main subject of development and redistribution as a major policy objective. After 1953, the real influence of 'Naya Kashmir' declined as various unrepresentative governments, propped up by the centre, worked to demolish the legal and financial independence of Jammu and Kashmir, and enacted several misguided development measures. But it laid a unique foundation for development policy in the state.

NOTES AND REFERENCES

[1] This despite the fact that Hari Singh, the last maharaja of Kashmir, had a reformist outlook on the exclusionary system of governance put in place by his predecessors. He abolished forced labour (*begar*); passed legislation to allow the lower castes to enter temples and public places, to allow remarriage of Hindu widows, to prevent child marriage, to outlaw moneylending, to establish panchayats; set up cooperative societies for disbursing (though rather limited) agricultural credit; and doubled state expenditure on education.

[2] Iffat Malik, *Kashmir: Ethnic Conflict, International Dispute*, Karachi: Oxford University Press, 2005: 26.

[3] Chitralekha Zutshi, *Languages of Belonging: Islam, Regional Identity and the Making of Kashmir*, Delhi: Permanent Black, 2003: 64.

[4] Walter Lawrence, *The Valley of Kashmir*, Delhi: Kashmir Kitab Ghar, 1996: 213.

[5] Ibid.: 214.

[6] M.L. Misri and M.S. Bhat, *Poverty, Planning and Economic Change in Jammu and Kashmir*, New Delhi: Vikas Publishing House, 1994: 28.

[7] Amar Singh Chohan, *Development of Education in the Jammu and Kashmir State, 1846–1947*, New Delhi: Atlantic Publishers, 1998: 11.

[8] Administration Report of Jammu and Kashmir State, 1893–94: 46.

[9] Ibid., p. 30.

[10] Census of India 1921, vol. 22, part 2, Lahore: Mufid-i-Aam Press: 50.

[11] Annual Administration Report (General) of His Highness's Government, Medical Department, 1936–37: 86–89.

[12] Annual Administration Report (General) of His Highness's Government, Medical Department, 1934: 88.

[13] Amar Singh Chohan, *Health Services in Jammu and Kashmir 1858–1947*, New Delhi: Atlantic Publishers, 1994: 33.

[14] Ibid.: 34.

[15] R.C. Bhargava, 'Economic Background', in Baghwan Sahay, ed., *Jammu and Kashmir*, Srinagar: Universal Publications, 1969: 119.

[16] Preetika Rana and Joanna Sugden, 'India's Record since Independence', *The Wall Street Journal*, 15 August 2013.

[17] Address of Mahasha Nahar Singh, Budget Session, Jammu and Kashmir Legislative Assembly Debates, 6 May 1952: 25.

[18] William Moorcroft and George Trebeck, *Travels in the Himalayan Provinces of Hindustan and the Punjab in Ladakh and Kashmir in Peshawar, Kabul, Kunduz and Bokhara: From 1819 to 1825,* vol. 1, New Delhi: Asian Educational Press, 1837: 132.

[19] Prithvi Nath Kaul Bamzai, *History of Kashmir*, vol. 1, Delhi: Metropolitan Book Co., 1962.

[20] Ibid.: 132.

[21] P.K. Michael Tharakan, 'Socio-economic Factors in Educational Development: Case of Nineteenth Century Travancore', *Economic and Political Weekly*, vol. 19, no. 45, 1984: 196.

[22] Prerna Singh, 'We-ness and Welfare: A Longitudinal Analysis of Social Development in Kerala, India', *World Development*, vol. 39, no. 2, 2010: 285.

[23] F. Henvey, 'Condition and Prospects of Kashmir on the 1st of June, 1880', letter to Secretary to Government of India, Jammu and Kashmir State Archives, Jammu.

24 A. Lamb, *A Disputed Legacy: 1846 to 1990*, Karachi: Oxford University Press, 1991: 29.

25 Ashiq Hussain Bhat, 'Pratap Singh's British Rule', *Kashmir Life,* 3 March 2014.

26 Ibid.

27 Ibid.

28 Zutshi, *Languages of Belonging*: 219.

29 The document was presented in the form of a memorandum in English titled 'New Kashmir'; it was reprinted in 1945. It was later translated into Urdu as 'Naya Kashmir: Siyasi Ayeen aur Iqtisadi Mansuba' (Naya Kashmir: Political Constitution and Economic Plan) for mass distribution by the National Conference, and was further adopted as its manifesto. This book refers to the document as 'Naya Kashmir', as it is widely and popularly known, and all references to it here are from the 1945 reprinted version.

30 For a detailed discussion on the development of a Kashmiri identity, see Karan Arakotaram, 'The Rise of Kashmiriyat: People-Building in 20th Century Kashmir', *The Columbia Undergraduate Journal of South Asian Studies,* Fall 2009.

31 Singh, 'We-ness and Welfare': 282.

32 Ibid.: 284–85.

33 My grandfather, as an idealistic, curly-haired eleven-year-old, was one of the many people who had gathered to witness this special session. In an interview, he described the atmosphere as 'electric'.

34 Rai Bahadur Pt. Anant Ram and Pt. Hira Nand Raina, 'The Census of India 1931', vol. XXIV, part 1, Jammu and Kashmir State, 1933: 257.

35 Gul M. Wani, 'Political Assertion of Kashmiri Identity', in N.A. Khan, ed., *The Parchment of Kashmir: History, Society, and Polity*, New York: Palgrave Macmillan, 2012: 127.

36 Ibid.: 143.

37 Mridu Rai, *Hindu Rulers, Muslim Subjects: Islam, Rights and the History of Kashmir*, Princeton: Princeton University Press and New Delhi: Permanent Black, 2004: 282.

38 Kuldip Singh Bajwa, *Jammu and Kashmir War 1947–1948: A Political and Military Perspective*, New Delhi: Har Anand Publications, 2003: 71.

39 On 11 June 1939, the Muslim Conference was renamed the National Conference in a special session held at Patthar Masjid, Srinagar: a commendable display of secular commitment in a religious place.

40 Rasheed Taseer, *Tehreek-i-Hurriyat-i-Kashmir: 1931 to 1939,* vol. 1, Srinagar: Muha'afiz Publications, 1968: 29.

41 Rasheed Taseer acknowledges the contribution of Kilam in his book, even though it is unacknowledged by Sheikh Abdullah in his memoir, *Aatish- e- Chinar.*

42 Andrew Whitehead, 'The Rise and Fall of New Kashmir', in Chitralekha Zutshi, ed., *Kashmir: History, Politics, Representation*, New York: Cambridge University Press, 2018: 75–76.

43 Ibid.: 76.

44 'Naya Kashmir', published by All Jammu and Kashmir National Conference, Lahore, 1945: 2, Jammu and Kashmir State Archives, Jammu.

45 Speech by Mirza Afzal Beg in the State Legislative Assembly, 1951, Jammu and Kashmir State Archives, Jammu.

46 J.K. Banerji, 'Agrarian Revolution and Industrialization in Jammu and Kashmir', in S.R. Bakshi, ed., *History of Economic Development in Jammu and Kashmir*. Srinagar: Gulshan Publishers, 2002: 227.

47 A.S. Anand, *The Constitution of Jammu and Kashmir: Its Development and Comments*, seventh edition, Delhi: Universal Publications, 2017: 116.

48 'Naya Kashmir': 43.

49 Ibid.: 14.

50 For a full discussion, see Martha C. Nussbaum, *Beyond the Social Contract: Capabilities and Global Justice,* Oxford Development Studies, vol. 32, no. 1, Taylor and Francis, 2004; Martha C. Nussbaum, *Women and Human Development: The Capabilities Approach,* New York: Cambridge University Press, 1999.

51 Nussbaum, *Women and Human Development*: 78.

52 Ibid.

53 'Naya Kashmir': 43.

54 Ibid.: 38

55 Ibid.: 24.

56 Nussbaum, *Women and Human Development*: 78.

57 'Naya Kashmir': 43.

58 Nussbaum, *Women and Human Development*: 78–79.

59 'Naya Kashmir': 34.

60 Ibid.: 13.

61 Nussbaum, *Women and Human Development*: 79.

62 'Naya Kashmir': 13.

63 Nussbaum, *Women and Human Development*: 79.

64 'Naya Kashmir': 13.

65 Nussbaum, *Women and Human Development*: 79.

66 'Naya Kashmir': 13.

67 Ibid.

68 Nussbaum, *Women and Human Development*: 80.

69 Ibid.

70 'Naya Kashmir': 40.

71 Ibid.: 80.

72 Ibid.: 15.

CHAPTER TWO

Restoration, Reformation and Redistribution

Post-1948 State Development Policy

Introduction

Maharaja Hari Singh had signed the Instrument of Accession to India in October 1947, when the tribal invasion from Pakistan was ongoing. Soon after the accession, under pressure from Jawaharlal Nehru, an emergency administration was set up in Kashmir by the maharaja who invited Sheikh Abdullah to take over as head. Abdullah moved swiftly to put in place the policy measures envisioned in 'Naya Kashmir'. The reason was two-fold: the National Conference wanted to enact concrete redistributive measures before the remnants of the old feudal administration could regroup during peacetime, and to garner maximum popular support before the forthcoming election.

Accordingly, they issued a number of decrees post-1947 that stopped both *muafis* (exemptions of land revenue to feudal subsidiaries) amounting to Rs 7 lakh and *mukarrarees* (grants in kind to families considered loyal by the maharaja) amounting to Rs 31.2 lakh paid by the state treasury to feudal subsidiaries; granted wasteland to tillers who wished to cultivate it; and stopped forcible ejectment of peasants.[1] A 'land to the tiller' committee was established to recommend the direction that agrarian reforms should take. At the same time, serious thought was also given to the eradication of rural debt that stood at Rs 3.66 crore (or a per capita debt of Rs 482).[2]

Land Redistribution

'Naya Kashmir' declared, 'The development of agriculture shall be the foremost task of the government.'[3] This preoccupation with the reformation of agriculture led to direct intervention in the traditional system of production through land reforms. The Grow More Food scheme was launched in 1948, whereby nearly 3 lakh kanals (1 kanal = 0.125 acre) of cultivable wasteland were allotted to landless peasants. The Big Landed Estates Abolition Act of 1950 transferred land to the tiller without any compensation to the landlords. Approximately '2.3 lakh acres of land were distributed to 2 lakh tillers by the end of 1953'.[4] This was followed by the Agrarian Reforms Act that continued to operate till 1979. In total, the ownership rights of some 49.5 lakh kanals (3,31,964.23 acres) of land were transferred to tiller families.[5] It was hoped that thereby rural inequalities, deemed the basic cause of underdevelopment, would be reduced and agricultural output increased. Despite the socialist emphasis, giving land to individuals without a serious attempt to cooperatize ownership actually led to the strengthening of individual property rights – a capitalist outcome.

Besides redistribution, the state also invested heavily in providing better facilities and modern technologies to farmers. To reduce farmers' dependency on rainfed agriculture, an irrigation department was set up. It immediately started construction and repair work on ten irrigation canals. The Awantipora Canal, completed at a cost of about Rs 8,22,000, was the largest of these canals and irrigated an area of 4,000 acres of land.[6] In the 1960s, the government started the Intensive Agricultural District Programme and the High Yielding Varieties Programme by which new hybrid varieties of seeds as well as subsidized fertilizers and pesticides were provided. This yielded positive results in the form of 'high yields of food and non-food crops especially paddy, wheat, maize and apples'.[7]

Debt Conciliation

According to government estimates, the total debt in Jammu and Kashmir in 1948 stood at Rs 3.66 crore. Of this, rural debt amounted to Rs 3.10 crore and urban debt to Rs 56 lakh, which meant a per capita debt of Rs 48 on average.[8] As mentioned earlier, the emergency administration declared a moratorium of six months on the realization of all debts in

February 1950. Three months later, it introduced The Distressed Debtors' Relief Act. This Act enabled the setting up of Debt Conciliation Boards all over the state which had jurisdiction over debts up to Rs 5,000 in cases where the total assets of the debtor were not greater than Rs 5,000. The Act, by later amendment, excluded commercial loans, arrears of wages or rent, land revenue and debts to the government or banks/corporations.

The Debt Conciliation Boards were given sweeping powers – 'the decision of the Board would supersede any previous rulings of any civil court and all civil courts were directed to transfer cases relating to debt (up to the amount described previously) to the local Debt Conciliation Board'.[9] It was made mandatory for all creditors and debtors in the state (in cases where the amount borrowed was up to Rs 5,000) to appear before their local Board with evidence of the amount borrowed, rate of interest, amount repaid and terms of the loan if any. If the debtor proved that he/she had paid the principal amount and 50 per cent of the interest, the Board would designate the debt as discharged and the debtor had to pay no more. Any amount in excess of 150 per cent of the principal would be refunded to the debtor. In cases where the amount repaid or any other terms of the loan were not established, the Board was authorized to decide on the basis of available evidence how much of the loan had been repaid and how much was still due. After this, the debtor was allowed to repay the loan in small instalments over twenty or thirty years.[10]

The effectiveness of the Act cannot be overstated. By 1953, it had scaled down debts of more than Rs 1 crore (Rs 1,11,22,054) by 80 per cent (Rs 88,97,643)[11] and liquidated mortgage debts of more than Rs 14 lakh (Rs 14,38,000).[12] It also allowed debtors easier terms and from two or three decades to repay outstanding amounts, thus ensuring that the economic gains from land redistribution would not be lost to servicing debt. The Restitution of Mortgaged Properties Act came into force in 1949. Under its provisions, 'mortgaged properties worth 37 lakh rupees were restituted to 34,000 debtors who had mortgaged it'.[13] These were mostly illiterate peasants who had lost properties to unscrupulous moneylenders.

Such legislation was unparalleled in the subcontinent where informal systems of lending had crushed the illiterate masses under debt over generations. The effects of the Act are still visible in the state with 25 per cent of its total households in debt, of which only 11 per cent have debts of more than Rs 1 lakh.[14]

State Education Policy

When Jammu and Kashmir became independent in 1947, only 5 per cent of its population was literate, and there were very few educational institutions in the state, mainly concentrated in the cities and larger towns.[15] The interim administration created a Ministry for Education for the first time.[16] It also took immediate measures to restore education services that had been suspended in the wake of the tribal invasion, such as 're-opening schools, repairing damaged buildings and giving jobs to refugee teachers'.[17]

In line with the objective of 'Naya Kashmir' of having an 'active and progressive policy of education which may carry the light of knowledge to the farthest and most backward areas of the state',[18] a committee was instituted to reorganize education in order to increase enrolment and literacy levels, and open new institutions. In its 1950 report, the committee proposed a systematic plan for school education beginning with enrolling children at three years of age at the kindergarten level and continuing till the secondary level at sixteen years. By May 1953, as many as '200 kindergartens were set up and training facilities for teachers extended. A Textbook Advisory Board was established to formulate textbooks in local languages and adult education centres set up.'[19] For training teachers in rural areas, mobile training centres were established. Significantly, even during the severe cash scarcity in the wake of the tribal invasion, funds for education were allotted promptly; as Sheikh Abdullah declared publicly, 'Land to the tiller and education for everyone were the two basic needs which brooked no delay for fulfilment.'[20] Expenditure on education was raised from 7 per cent of state revenue in 1946 to 11 per cent in 1950.[21]

School education was subsidized but students still had to pay for books and stationery. Higher education received official attention too – the two existing colleges were reorganized into full-fledged institutions offering four-year degree courses. Two new colleges were set up at Anantnag and Sopore so students from the villages could access higher education more easily. The first university in the state was established in November 1948, expanding to separate universities in Jammu and Kashmir by 1969. The Board for Secondary Education (later named the Jammu and Kashmir State Board of School Education) was established in 1975. Most significantly, in 1954, the state government made education free from primary to postgraduate levels.

In the five-year plans (FYPs) too, there was an increase in the expenditure on education. These efforts paid off as the literacy rate began to rise: from 5 per cent in 1950, it rose to 11.03 per cent by 1961 and to 32.68 per cent by 1981.[22] However, the primary emphasis of these policies remained on the short-term social goal of increasing the literacy rate; in the initial period, the government failed to prepare long-term employment plans for its population. Despite the emphasis on education in 'Naya Kashmir' and the initial investment in building educational infrastructure, the government underestimated the resistance to modern education (as against the *madrasa* and *pathshala* systems). This was particularly relevant in the sphere of female education, where the lack of a sufficient number of female teachers and girls-only schools was a big hurdle in overcoming resistance within families to send girls to school. Drop-out rates were also a big concern, reaching 55 per cent in 1989.[23] But the government did not tackle this proactively.

State Employment Strategy

The state created an employment policy that attempted to provide the required number of jobs to educated youth in the civil administration sector. Over the years, this led to the creation of the largest bureaucracy in the country. As political pressure built up to provide more white-collar jobs, the government kept repeating the same strategy.

Educated youth who did not find employment in civil administration or industry could not be absorbed into the largest economic sector – agriculture – due to the changes brought about by the land reforms of 1950. Shrinkage in the size of average landholdings and increased labour-replacing technology meant that the agrarian sector 'could not provide jobs in spite of its growth in output'.[24] The government's emphasis on providing jobs win the civil administration sector therefore provided a solution.

Thus, following the recommendations of 'Naya Kashmir', the state government not only introduced reforms that would over time move the traditional concentration of employment away from the agricultural sector, but also, to overcome this problem, tried to provide the required jobs in the public sector, particularly in civil administration.

State Health Policy

In 1947, there were just two hospitals in the state, one in Jammu and the other in Srinagar, and 87 dispensaries concentrated mainly in the larger towns. After 1948, all these institutions were consolidated under a Directorate of Health Services. The emphasis of 'Naya Kashmir' on public health delivery led the state to invest heavily in building new hospitals, particularly a hospital for women and an adjacent one for children at Lal Mandi. By 1964, the state's health network had been expanded remarkably to include 32 hospitals and 429 dispensaries.[25] Care was taken to provide public health institutions at district and village levels. The Sher-i-Kashmir Institute of Medical Sciences (SKIMS) was set up at Soura in 1982 as a tertiary health care institute focused on medical research into diseases endemic to the valley.

Expenditure on health kept increasing with successive budgets, from an abysmally low 0.04 per cent (18 lakh) in 1948[26] to 16 per cent of the revenue by 1952.[27] Import duties on life-saving drugs were reduced from 30 per cent to 12.5 per cent.[28] Mass vaccination was introduced from the 1950s onwards with mobile teams of doctors and assistants touring villages to vaccinate children. This culminated in a full-fledged immunization programme with its own budget head in 1978, where the thrust was on universal coverage. These efforts paid off as smallpox was eradicated in the state by 1975, and there was no outbreak of cholera in the period from 1948 to 1988.[29]

From the 1950s, the state government started granting student loans for up to 50 students a year to study in other medical institutions across India. The first medical college in the state was started at Hazuri Bagh in 1959. Thereafter, separate government medical colleges were set up in Jammu and in Srinagar. Significantly, Jammu and Kashmir reserved 50 per cent of the seats in medical education across all specialities for women in 1983, in order to improve women's access to health care which had been restricted by a lack of female doctors and due to conservative attitudes coming in the way of approaching male doctors, particularly in the villages. It reserved half of all seats in engineering colleges for women as well. It is the only state in India to have implemented such affirmative action for women.

State Industrialization Policy

Industrialization was viewed by the state as an essential component of development as it would 'absorb rural surplus labour in non-agricultural occupations and raise incomes and standards of living of wage workers'.[30] The growth of indigenous industries, like cement, plywood and the manufacture of silk, was based on locally available raw materials. The government organized and subsidized cottage industries making carpets, shawls, wooden furniture, papier-mâché, metalwork and other handicraft items. Depots for handicraft items were set up in New Delhi, Amritsar, Bombay, Simla, Lucknow, Madras and Calcutta, managed by the Kashmir People's Cooperative Society. The tourism industry was given special attention. Despite the major role of industrialization in the period of the first two five-year plans,[31] there was growing concern within the government that industrialization in the state was trailing behind the rest of the country. The state government declared in its Third Five-Year Plan that it would 'establish basic industries based on our natural wealth'.[32] Accordingly, it increased public sector investment in the industrial sector and established a number of corporations over the years, such as J&K Industries, J&K Minerals and J&K Cement. 'By 1975 the total output from the various units operated by these corporations stood at Rs 8.19 crore.'[33]

The government also set up organizations like the State Industrial Development Corporation and State Financial Corporation to provide infrastructure and raw material to these industries where 'private investment was not available'.[34] In addition, the Development Committee's Report in 1975 laid renewed stress on the need for the government to increase the rate of development and emphasized that, to further this aim, 'steps must be taken to welcome the maximum possible investment of private capital and entrepreneurship in the state'.[35]

Rural Development Programme

A number of development programmes were introduced from the 1950s onwards, mostly conceived of and funded by the Indian central government, aimed at the socio-economic transformation of rural areas. These included the Intensive Agricultural Development Programme and Intensive Area Programme of 1964, both a part of the Green Revolution programme to make the country self-sufficient in food. The central government also introduced programmes to develop rural infrastructure and bring about social development in villages.[36] Public works like the provision of piped water to villages were attempts to better the lives of the rural population by providing them with modern facilities. The various programmes introduced by the state led to a total of '4,200 villages, covering a population of 25.86 lakh [being] provided with piped water supply by 1985–86'.[37] The state's road network was also expanded considerably, tripling in length in twenty years from 1965, with special emphasis on connecting rural and border areas to the rest of the state. Efforts to develop rural areas within the state continue even today.

The Five-Year Plans

'Naya Kashmir' borrowed quite generously from the Soviet model of development in that it aimed to bring about the 'development, in a planned manner [of] the productive forces of the country with a view of enriching the material and cultural life of the people'.[38] Consequently, development in Kashmir followed, like in the rest of India, the planned economy model.[39] Drawn up in 1950 under Sheikh Abdullah, the First Five-Year Plan for Jammu and Kashmir was ideologically oriented towards socialist principles and designed to make the state economically independent. The primary aim of the plan was development of infrastructure and agrarian reform.

At the same time, the plan had to balance these aspirations with meeting economic challenges that stemmed from the conflict from 1948 onwards, particularly with regard to depletion of the state treasury and food shortages, especially in the cities. Customs barriers between Jammu and Kashmir and the rest of India were kept intact, and tuition fees were imposed on boys from class 8 onwards and on girls from college level.[40] The imposition of fees, in addition to the cost of stationery and books, certainly would have acted as a deterrent to higher education. It must also have had some effect on new enrolments as well, in what was still an economy where the majority of parents had little cash to spare. Many considered the fee imposition a betrayal of 'Naya Kashmir', with some socialist commentators like Bazaz calling it 'a new taxation'.[41] It also prompted student protests, particularly in colleges in Srinagar. The government saw it as a necessary evil – a short-term strategy to maintain the financial independence of the state and still cater to rebuilding efforts after the invasion. Its focus was directed mostly towards increasing primary school enrolment. This continued till the mid-1950s, when all education was made free. But overall, the government continued to persist with this short-term approach towards education. It gave the highest priority to physical infrastructure, investing heavily in public works, primarily road-building and supply of water and electricity, in an effort to rebuild and modernize the infrastructure of the state. It promoted urbanization and the expansion of existing cities like Srinagar and Jammu. The continuation of the much-maligned Dogra tax of *mujawaza* – an imperial levy collected from farmers as a portion of the rice harvest and stored in government granaries in the cities to feed the urban population – even after 1948 is evidence of this. Siddhartha Prakash has observed that 'the government [post-1948] introduced the "*khush-kharid*" [surplus foodgrain procurement at the will of the tiller] and "*mujjwaza*" [sic]. . . . Peasants had little capital to sustain their own livelihoods, therefore surpluses for sale to the government have been limited.'[42] But he has his facts wrong. *Mujawaza* was a Dogra practice that was developed to support shawl-weavers in Srinagar, to ensure the continuation of the heavily taxed shawl trade. After 1948, though the interim government renamed it *khush kharid* (voluntary purchase) in an attempt to remove old negative associations, peasants trying to feed their families in the aftermath of the tribal invasion were still resentful. The Bakshi government abolished *mujawaza* following the Wazir Committee's recommendation of 1953. However, power subsidies to urban centres continued, as Table 2.1 shows.

Development of the industrial sector was given priority and allocated Rs 83.12 lakh. The building of industrial infrastructure was stressed, with proposals even to export natural products like silk, skins and hides to Czechoslovakia in exchange for machines. As part of the First Five-Year Plan, a large chunk of expenditure was also allocated to irrigation and administration. This pattern continued for the next three five-year plans, but because some sectors like industry, irrigation and administration did not generate sufficient returns on the amounts invested in them, the state was faced with recurring budget deficits – for example, Rs 58.55 lakh in 1956–57.[43] The First Five-Year Plan was not without problems, with some experts pointing to a 'lack of study

TABLE 2.1 *Detailed Expenditure under the First Five-Year Plan (1951–56), Jammu and Kashmir* (in Rs lakh)

Head of work	Plan provision (1951–56)
Power	295.08
Irrigation	268.68
Road development	254.97
Rural and urban water supply	99.76
Cottage and small-scale industries	83.12
Education	66.06
Tourism	50.46
Health services	44.83
Miscellaneous	27.50
Animal husbandry	24.38
Agriculture	20.43
Housing	13.32
Soil conservation	9.92
Drug farming	8.48
Forest works	6.85
Total	1,274.15

Source: 'First Five-Year Plan Document', Department of Planning and Development, Government of Jammu and Kashmir, 1951.

of resources and proper investigation into the technical feasibility of . . . projects',[44] and others saying that it was too modest to cover the state's needs. Again, this was because Sheikh Abdullah's government wanted the state to be economically self-reliant. It was concerned about recurrent budget deficits after the tribal invasion and wanted to keep these to a minimum. After Sheikh Abdullah's arrest and the coup in 1953, Bakshi Ghulam Mohammad took over. To give his government some degree of legitimacy he needed to impress the public, who still supported Abdullah, with grandiose displays of money and power. Thus began eleven years of development – a spectacle – with the emphasis being on huge infrastructure projects that could symbolize development. As B. Puri notes: 'Big buildings like the Secretariat, the Tourism Reception Centre, stadium, the legislature complex in Jammu, roads, bridges, etc. became

Bakshi's public ideograms. He presided over public *durbar*s every Friday, abolished *mujawaza* and subsidized rations up to 75 per cent.'[45]

All this needed huge inflows of cash. Bakshi appealed to the centre for more funds for the First Five-Year Plan. The plan was revised in 1954 and 'the plan provisions went up from Rupees 700 lakh to Rupees 973.21 lakh in the central sector and from Rupees 300 lakh to Rupees 300.94 lakh in case of the state sector'.[46] The Second Five-Year Plan was even more ambitious, aiming for an expenditure of Rs 26 crore. The outlay of the plan was around Rs 34 crore. It brought Jammu and Kashmir under the Indian tax regime and removed customs barriers. Overall, it was designed to achieve financial integration of the state of Jammu and Kashmir, till then an autonomous unit, into the Indian Union. By ratifying the Instrument of Accession, Bakshi had already integrated the state politically into the Union of India.

With the Third Five-Year Plan, Bakshi began to look at how planning could affect people's lives and not just state infrastructure. Accordingly, a key objective was included into the plan: 'To increase employment opportunities and spread the benefits of increase in the state income as evenly as possible.'[47] But the focus of the plan continued to be to bring about a substantial increase in the state income; to develop the state's power resources and establish industries based on the state's natural wealth; and to achieve self–sufficiency in foodgrains and increase agricultural production.[48]

During the second and third plan periods, the state domestic product (SDP) grew by 8 per cent, fuelled in part by generous central assistance, and in part by the rise in agricultural productivity after land reforms and the introduction of modern agricultural techniques. However, despite being placed in the 'special' category of states by the Fifth Finance Commission in 1969, Jammu and Kashmir received plan assistance at the rate of 70 per cent as loan and 30 per cent grant till 1990 – and not 90 per cent as grant-in-aid and 10 per cent in the form of loan, which other special category states like Assam and Nagaland received. This tied up the bulk of the state's financial resources in debt repayments to the centre.

The Fourth Five-Year Plan prioritized development of agriculture, power, communications and expansion of irrigation. Jammu and Kashmir received financial assistance of Rs 140 crore from the centre in addition to Rs 17 crore which was the state's own contribution. It was not till the Fifth

Five-Year Plan (1974–78)[49] that the government adopted a more human-centred approach towards planning and development. An increase in per capita income, creation of employment opportunities, and reducing poverty and inequality across groups and regions were the aims of this plan. The plan coincided with Sheikh Abdullah's release in 1972 and return to power in 1975 after the Indira–Sheikh Accord or the Kashmir Accord, which meant that Abdullah too was thenceforth committed to a loan-heavy, dependent economic relationship with New Delhi.

It is clear that the five-year plans were based on the modernization theory, as they aimed to eradicate the 'characteristics of a backward economic region, the predominance of the agricultural sector, low degree of urbanization, inadequately developed infrastructure, low industrial development and low levels of investment'.[50] The Sixth and Seventh Five-Year Plans were on similar lines as the Fifth Five-Year Plan. Per capita expenditure in the five-year plans increased from Rs 34 in the First Plan to Rs 556 in the Seventh Plan. The grant pattern continued as before, however, and the state grew more and more indebted to the centre, although plan assistance from the centre did not cover the growing resource gap in the non-plan budget up to the Seventh Plan.[51]

Two points are worth highlighting here. First, the focus on infrastructure development started by the Bakshi government in 1954 perpetuated itself though the top–down system of planning that characterized the five-year plans.[52] This domination of infrastructure development within budget allocations continued till the 1980s, with lower amounts being allocated for social services, particularly education.[53] Though Sheikh Abdullah created District Development Boards in 1976 to facilitate 'planning from below', the strain on the state's financial resources due to debt repayments rendered such experiments much less effective than they would have been if the state had more money of its own to spend.

Second, in India today, there exists a common misperception that Jammu and Kashmir's 'weak' economy was shored up by heavy financial grants from the centre right from Independence. While such analysis gets the numbers right, it gets the pattern wrong. As stated earlier, its special category status entitled the state of Jammu and Kashmir to 90 per cent grants from the centre, which were not allotted till 1990. The loans that were given instead of grants slowed economic growth in the state, as the bulk of its resources was tied up in debt servicing. As Prakash points out,

'In 1978–79, fifty per cent of the state's expenditure comprised of debt and interest repayments and the debt servicing liability on one rupee loaned by the centre to Jammu and Kashmir had reached over 5 rupees.'[54]

Conclusion

The observations and data vis-à-vis the state development policy of Jammu and Kashmir from 1948 to 1988 presented here supports the following three hypotheses.

1. The development experience of Jammu and Kashmir is distinctive. Amongst the Indian states, it led the way in far-reaching land reforms, debt conciliation, universalization of free education from primary school to university level, and in guaranteeing the social and economic rights of people, including the marginalized, under the state's constitution.
2. State development policy was aimed at disassembling traditional structures of resource management, employment and ownership, and supplanting them with 'modernized alternatives'.
3. The state used the major part of central assistance and domestic resources for development of the social sector (and not the private sector).

The tense circumstances surrounding the beginnings of the development process in Jammu and Kashmir were reflected in the state development process. From 31 October 1948 to 5 March 1948, a dual governance system operated in Kashmir, with Sheikh Abdullah operating as head of the emergency administration of the National Conference and the maharaja's prime minister, Mehr Chand Mahajan, heading the maharaja's cabinet. This caused the privileged feudal classes and their adherents to vehemently oppose any reforms proposed by the National Conference, particularly those aimed at democratization, asset redistribution, and the extension of social, economic and political rights to the common people, inspired by 'Naya Kashmir'. The maharaja's cabinet publicly criticized Abdullah's plans for the abolition of *jagir*s, redistribution of land and dissolution of debt, even appealing to the Congress government in New Delhi against these. To end this confrontation, the maharaja, under pressure from Nehru, issued a proclamation on 1 March 1948 establishing an interim government with Sheikh Abdullah as prime minister and calling for the convening of a Constituent Assembly as soon as conditions allowed. In 1949, Maharaja Hari Singh, again at Nehru's insistence, left permanently for Bombay after declaring his young son Prince Regent. Even after the monarchy was formally abolished on 24 July 1952 by the India–Kashmir agreement, traces of the feudal system remained in the administration and in society. Feudal adherents, particularly the Rajput Sabha and the Jammu Chamber of Commerce, opposed various legislations enacted by the interim government, especially those related to the abolition of *jagirdari*, redistribution of land and debt reconciliation. They tried to rally support against these legislations, calling upon their members to boycott the same, but could not gather much public support.[55] The people of the state, across lines of religion, caste and region, were overwhelmingly supportive of the National Conference's 'Naya Kashmir' project.

But there were other problems. On the ground, the various government departments, from revenue to industry, were staffed by monarchical appointees. The tribal invasion from Pakistan's North-West Frontier Province had caused devastation, rendering more than 600 people dead and 43,000 people homeless, and causing economic losses of more than Rs 1.83 lakh.[56] The expenditure on relief and rehabilitation caused recurrent deficits in the state budget between 1950 and 1953. But despite these challenges, the interim government plowed through with major reforms to ameliorate anomalies in agriculture, massively scale down private debt, develop industry, expand secondary and tertiary employment, and develop modern infrastructure to increase economic growth. It came up with a highly centralized model of development inspired by 'Naya Kashmir' that aimed for structural changes in the traditional social, economic and political structures. At the same time, the focus of state development policy remained on improving the lives of the people of the state, as can be seen in the spending priorities of successive state governments. Legislation was the main weapon with which feudal systems were attacked. From the Big Landed Estates Abolition Act to the Distressed Debtors' Relief Act, major blows were delivered to asset inequality, indebtedness and poverty. Through the five-year plans, expenditure on health, education, irrigation, communications and rural development was maximized, the bulk of central assistance going to public spending rather than any other sector. No other state in India, including Kerala and West Bengal under communist governments, have implemented such a systematic and comprehensive dismantling of the feudal system, and provided assets (in the form of agricultural land) and freedom from debt to the masses. The redistribution of land was particularly effective in raising the economic position of the masses, with some commentators calling it 'the most sweeping agrarian reform undertaken in the Indo-Pakistan sub-continent since Partition'.[57]

NOTES AND REFERENCES

[1] 'In Ninety Days: A Brief Account of Agrarian Reform Launched by Sheikh Abdullah's Government in Kashmir', Ministry of Information and Broadcasting, Government of Jammu and Kashmir, Srinagar, (n.d.): 14.

[2] *The Times of India*, New Delhi, 21 April 1950.

[3] *The Constitution of Jammu and Kashmir*, Government of Jammu and Kashmir, Srinagar: Government Press, 1956: 2.

[4] Up to 8 lakh acres were transferred till 1961. Thereafter, the Agrarian Reforms Act was promulgated to make the land reforms more effective. See M.L Misri and M.S. Bhat, *Poverty, Planning and Economic Change in Jammu and Kashmir*, New Delhi: Vikas Publishing House, 1994: 71.

[5] Department of Revenue, Government of Jammu and Kashmir; government figures tabled in the Jammu and Kashmir State Assembly in June 2016.

[6] Joseph Korbel, *Danger in Kashmir*, Princeton: Princeton University Press, 1954: 212.

[7] Siddhartha Prakash, 'Political Economy of Kashmir Since 1947', *Economic and Political Weekly*, vol. 35, no. 24, 2000: 2051–60.

[8] *The Times of India*, New Delhi, 21 April 1950.

[9] M. Brecher, *The Struggle for Kashmir*, Toronto: Ryerson Press, 1953: 159.

[10] Ibid.

[11] Ibid.

[12] Prakash, 'Political Economy of Kashmir Since 1947'.

[13] P.N. Bazaz, *The History of Struggle for Freedom in Kashmir*, New Delhi: Kashmir Publishing Company, 1954: 298.

[14] United Nations Development Programme (UNDP), *Jammu and Kashmir Human Development Report*, UNDP, 2010: 205.

[15] Misri and Bhat, *Poverty, Planning and Economic Change*: 28.

[16] Brecher, *The Struggle for Kashmir*: 153.

[17] *Kashmir Information Series: Education*, Government of Jammu and Kashmir Srinagar: Government Press, 1951: 3.

[18] 'Naya Kashmir', published by All Jammu and Kashmir National Conference, Lahore, 1945: 38, Jammu and Kashmir State Archives, Jammu.

[19] Brecher, *The Struggle for Kashmir*: 154.

[20] Sheikh Abdullah's address to the Educational Reorganization Committee, Jammu and Kashmir Legislative Assembly Debates, Jammu, December 1950.

[21] Budget Address by Mr G.L. Dogra, Jammu and Kashmir Legislative Assembly Debates, Budget Session, 1952: 41.

[22] Misri and Bhat, *Poverty, Planning and Economic Change*: 38.

[23] T. Kawoosa, 'Over 60 per cent Leaving Midway', *Epilogue,* issue 10, November 2008: 10.

[24] 'Jammu and Kashmir State Development Report', Planning Commission, Government of India, 2003: 67.

[25] Directorate of Health Services in Jammu and Kashmir, 'History of Modern Healthcare in Kashmir', *Kashmir Health Line*, vol. 2, 2010: 3.

[26] 'Budget 1948', His Highness's Government, Jammu and Kashmir, Srinagar: Sri Ranbir Government Press: 62.

[27] Jammu and Kashmir Legislative Assembly Debates, Budget Session, 1952: 41.

[28] Ibid.

[29] Directorate of Health Services in Jammu and Kashmir, 'History of Modern Healthcare in Kashmir': 2.

[30] Misri and Bhat, *Poverty, Planning and Economic Change*: 4.

[31] In the Second Plan (1956–60), 8.4 per cent of planned expenditure was allocated to industry. See 'Report of the Development Review Committee on Jammu and Kashmir, Part V: Agriculture and Irrigation', Government of Jammu and Kashmir, 1975: 11.

[32] Draft of Third Five-Year Plan, Planning Department, Government of Jammu and Kashmir, 1966: 13.

[33] Prakash, 'Political Economy of Kashmir Since 1947': 2056.

[34] 'Jammu and Kashmir State Development Report', Planning Commission, Government of India, 2003: 96.

[35] 'Report of the Development Review Committee on Jammu and Kashmir, Part V: Agriculture and Irrigation', 1975: 33.

[36] For example, employment schemes like Training of Rural Youth for Self Employment (TRYSEM) and Jawahar Rozgar Yojna, and rural housing schemes like Indira Awaas Yojna.

[37] Misri and Bhat, *Poverty, Planning and Economic Change*: 41.

[38] 'The Constitution of Jammu and Kashmir and Plan Documents of the Jammu and Kashmir Government', 1956, Jammu and Kashmir State Archives, Jammu: 1.

[39] The planned economy model was first developed by the Soviet Union. In India, this model ran from 1947 to 2017. The Planning Commission (and, since 2015, its successor the NITI Aayog [National Institution for Transforming India]) would draw up detailed economic plans for central economic assistance to the states every five years. These were known as the five-year plans.

[40] Budget address by G.L. Dogra, Jammu and Kashmir Legislative Assembly Debates, Budget Session, 6 May 1952: 25.

[41] Bazaz, *The History of Struggle for Freedom in Kashmir*. 493.

[42] Prakash, 'Political Economy of Kashmir Since 1947': 2054.

[43] 'J&K Review of Progress', Department of Planning and Statistics, Government of Jammu and Kashmir, 1961: 3.

[44] I. Bhatnagar, 'Planning in Kashmir', *Kashmir Today*, vol. 4, no. 3, Srinagar: Department of Information, Government of Jammu and Kashmir, November 1959: 3.

[45] B. Puri, *Triumph and Tragedy of Indian Federation*, Delhi: Sterling, 1981: 129.

[46] S. Gupta, *Kashmir: A Study in India-Pakistan Relations*, Bombay: Asia Publishing House, 1967: 397.

[47] 'Jammu and Kashmir: A Review of Progress', Department of Information, Government of Jammu and Kashmir, 1969: 1–2.

[48] Ibid.

[49] The plan only covered four years and was succeeded by the rolling plan initiated by the Janata Party government from 1978 to 1980.

[50] 'Jammu and Kashmir State Development Report', Planning Commission, Government of India, 2003: 25.

[51] *Jammu and Kashmir: Fifty Years*, Srinagar: Department of Information, Government of Jammu and Kashmir, 1998: 286.

[52] His obsession with infrastructure did not help Bakshi win popular support. The public still saw him as a backstabber. Public processions were frequent during Bakshi's regime, with people chanting insulting slogans against Bakshi. One of these was '*Warnyi hyind nechwyo, bokwach phachiyo*' ('You son of a midwife, may you die the most painful death!'), which is as personal an attack as any.

[53] This was true for most Indian states at the time and not limited to the state of Jammu and Kashmir.

[54] Prakash, 'Political Economy of Kashmir Since 1947': 2053.

[55] For example, the Jammu Chamber of Commerce, dominated by upper-class Hindus, asked its members to suspend all loans till the Distressed Debtors' Relief Act was withdrawn.

[56] 'Relief and Rehabilitation in Kashmir', Kashmir Bureau of Information, 24 May 1949: 2.

[57] Brecher, *The Struggle for Kashmir*. 159.

CHAPTER THREE

Land to the Tiller

Agrarian Reforms in Jammu and Kashmir

Introduction

Poverty remains a deeply rooted problem in India. According to 2016 World Bank figures, one in every five Indians is poor, which means that a staggering 270 million Indians live in poverty![1] Poverty alleviation, therefore, is an important policy goal for the government. According to Chenery *et al.*, 'Throughout the postcolonial period, improvement in the asset base of the poor has been viewed as a central strategy to relieve endemic poverty.'[2] While it may seem that the link between land reforms and poverty alleviation is a direct one, economic studies over time have reflected mixed views on this. There have been conflicting views regarding the role of land reforms vis-à-vis poverty reduction. While some see land reforms as having a *direct* effect on reducing poverty through asset redistribution,[3] others see the effect as an *indirect* one – as land reforms reduce the size of landholdings the productivity of land increases, in turn affecting incomes.[4] While Alesina and Rodrick[5] are of the view that land reforms inhibit economic growth and hence have a negative impact on poverty reduction, Hoff and Lyon[6] show a positive relation between land reforms and economic growth, and, by extension, between land reforms and poverty alleviation. This conflict of theoretical views has not been put to rest conclusively by empirical studies. In India, particularly, there is a scarcity of empirical work at the village level on the link between land reforms, incomes, access to agricultural credit and rural poverty. However, this interplay can be understood to a great extent by studying the experience of different Indian states in the implementation of land reforms. Studies by Besley and Burgess, Banerjee, Gertler and Ghatak and others have established empirical links between land reforms and poverty reduction in India, though their findings are based mostly on reforms relating to security of tenancy rights.[7] Besley and Burgess, in particular, focus on data relating to land reform legislations in sixteen Indian states for the period 1958–92.[8] This leads them to miss the enactment of the Big Landed Estates Abolition Act, 1950 and the amendment to the Jammu and Kashmir State Tenancy Act of 1924, which granted the status of 'protected tenants' to tenant farmers across the state. And because they use land reform legislation (and not implementation) as a variable, their study does not shed much light on the extent and effect of land reform implementation on the ground.

The gap in theory could have been supplemented by empirical studies on land reforms and poverty alleviation, particularly in villages. But thus far, most such empirical studies carried out by researchers or government agencies in India have come up against a deplorable lack of data for the pre-Independence period, and so have failed to quantify the full extent of land reforms. In Jammu and Kashmir, empirical studies have been even rarer. With the exception of Tareak Rather,[9] who has done valuable work on the extent and effect of land reforms in Kulgam district in south Kashmir from a sociological perspective, not much micro-level study has been undertaken. Macro-level studies such as those by Mohamed Aslam, and M.L. Misri and M.S. Bhat, are useful, but because of incomplete data provided by official sources, are not comprehensive.[10] As a result, misconceptions abound. Most researchers and policy-makers at the national level are convinced that the most effective land reforms in India took place in West Bengal and Kerala.[11] Both nationally and internationally, not much is known about the agrarian reforms in Jammu and Kashmir which started in 1948 and continued till 1979.

Jammu and Kashmir is a land-scarce state. This may not appear to be an accurate statement at first glance, but consider the fact that of the total land area of 4.4 crore kanals that comprised the princely state of Jammu and Kashmir, only 2.7 crore kanals fall in the state of Jammu and Kashmir at present. And of this, the vast majority is dominated by rocky mountainous expanses typical of the Himalayas where the state is located. Only '30 per cent of the state's land area is suitable for cultivation'.[12] This amounts to just 1.3 crore kanals, out of which '31 lakh kanals is sown twice'.[13] Compare this with the population of the state that stood at over 1.25 crore in 2011,[14] and one gets an idea of the kind of land scarcity the state struggles with.

Agricultural land historically has been considered a valuable economic resource and, since it is an economy dominated by agriculture, a significant source of revenue for the state. Before 1931, all the land in Jammu and Kashmir was considered to be in the personal ownership of the maharaja and those who were in possession of agricultural land were considered his tenants-at-will.[15] This was because of the nature of the Treaty of Amritsar (1846) whereby Gulab Singh bought the valley of Kashmir, including all its land and all that it contained, including its 25 lakh people and natural resources, for Rs 75 lakh (*nanakshahi*) from the British (who had won it from the Sikhs after the Third Anglo-Sikh War, 1846). The maharaja retained ownership of some of the land directly and the rest was granted to '1.5 lakh absentee landlords classified into *Jagirdars* or major landlords and *Pattadars* or minor landlords. 8 lakh cultivating peasants were also the Maharaja's tenants. 3 lakh landless farmers cultivated the lands belonging to the landlords.'[16]

The Exploitative Feudal Administration

Maharaja Gulab Singh, who had paid the British an enormous sum of money for the state, was determined to make up the amount in the shortest time possible. Land revenue was identified as the quickest and easiest way of doing this. Accordingly, the Dogra administration fixed land revenue at three-quarters of all yields on rice, maize and millets (after 1860, this was fixed at one-half of all yields). Francis Younghusband describes how, 'after paying land revenue to the state and the multiple intermediaries or revenue farmers (like the *Patwari, Qanungo*, etc) the cultivator was left with just a quarter of his yield'.[17] This quarter-share was burdened with even more taxes, including '*Nazrana* [gift to the monarch] that was levied four times a year and *Tambol* [a tax levied whenever there was a wedding in the Maharaja's family]'.[18] To extract the maximum amount of tax from the economy, the Dogra state had devised a complex web of taxation that included not just 'crops but fruit, grazing animals, handicrafts (shawls, carpets, etc.), marriage ceremonials, and labour services including grave-digging and even prostitution'.[19] Adding insult to injury, the peasants had to pay even for the upkeep of the *shakdar*s or watchers of the land, who were appointed by the maharaja to prevent the peasants from keeping an excess amount of grain for themselves at harvest time.

As compared to the miserable lot of the peasant, the *jagirdar* had the following privileges:

1. Grazing fees for all cattle within his *jagir* (estate).
2. Rights to the forests within his *jagir*.
3. If any landowner died heirless within the *jagir*, his land devolved on the *jagirdar*.
4. Hunting rights to game without licence.
5. Right to state compensation if his land was acquired.
6. All village headmen were appointed by him.
7. Income from all watermills in his *jagir*.
8. Exemption from appearance in civil courts.

In addition, *jagirdar*s had proprietary rights over state lands (*khalsa sarkar*) and tenancy rights over wastelands (*banjar*). They also had powers to recover arrears of land revenue.[20]

The National Conference launched a popular campaign in 1930 to pressurize the maharaja into granting proprietary rights to farmers. The campaign was successful and proprietary rights were bestowed by the maharaja in 1931 on all those in possession of land; the 'beneficiaries included absentee landlords and cultivating peasants but significantly, the 3 lakh landless tillers were left out'.[21]

The National Context

In the pre-Independence period, the Indian National Congress was ideologically opposed to the feudal system and in favour of land reforms. In its Quit India resolution adopted on 8 August 1942, the All India Congress Committee clearly stated that 'the power when it comes would belong to *the toilers in the fields*, factories and elsewhere' (emphasis added). A far-reaching programme on agrarian reforms was included in the Congress election manifesto in 1937, with Jawaharlal Nehru, Mahatma Gandhi and Babu Jagjivan Ram as its vocal advocates.

The All India Kisan Sabha (AIKS) drafted the All India Kisan Manifesto at its first meeting in Lucknow in 1936. This included the abolition of zamindari ownership without compensation, the abolition of all debts, redistribution of government lands and wastelands to the landless, tax reductions for all farmers and tax exemption for all families earning less than Rs 500 annually, occupancy rights for tenants, agricultural credit at cheaper interest rates, and subsidized seeds and fertilizers. The *kisan* movement was not restricted to meetings and documents alone. Uttar Pradesh and Bihar saw powerful farmer agitations in the years leading up to Independence.[22] On 8 August 1947, the zamindari system in Uttar Pradesh was abolished by law. However, in practice, sharecropping and other exploitative forms of tenancy remained largely undisturbed.

Soon after Independence, in December 1947, the president of the Indian National Congress appointed an Agrarian Reforms Committee. In its report published in July 1949, the Committee recommended land ceiling and legal protection of tenants' rights whereby a tenant who had cultivated the same plot of land for six years could not be dispossessed even if the land in question fell within the ceiling limit. The First Five-Year Plan made redistribution of land and some degree of change from individual to a cooperative pattern of economic activity a part of the strategy to develop agriculture. It also endorsed the recommendation of the Agrarian Reforms Committee of the Congress to fix a ceiling of three times the family holding both for direct cultivation by owners and for land that could be resumed from tenants-at-will for personal cultivation.

From 1949 to 1952, states dominated by zamindars, such as Bihar, Assam, Orissa, Uttar Pradesh, Rajasthan, West Bengal and Hyderabad, enacted legislation to abolish intermediaries, as a result of which 20 million tenant farmers came into a direct tax relationship with their respective state governments. But 'the governments had to pay rupees 3340 million as compensation to the landlords'.[23] This put many other states off land reforms.

> Without consistency in tenancy reform laws the peasants' lot did not improve much. Rent varied from one-fifth of the gross produce in some states to one-fourth in others. In Bombay and Hyderabad, legislation provided for the category of protected tenant whereas in Andhra Pradesh and Tamil Nadu, it did not. Across the board, state legislations fell short of the recommendations of the Planning Commission.[24]

The exceptions were Kerala and West Bengal, where progress was made in tenancy reforms through legislations that made tenancy rights stronger, inheritable, and raised tenant incomes. In West Bengal, the legislation was in direct response to the Tebhaga agitation in the late 1940s that united impoverished sharecroppers (*bargadars*) to seek security of tenure.[25] In the late 1970s, the Left Front government in West Bengal consolidated the progress made by launching Operation Barga. Panchayats, local labour organizations and Left Front workers helped register sharecroppers, and legislations gave them access to subsidized agricultural credit, fertilizers and high-yielding seeds. Further, Operation Barga firmly placed the onus of disproving *bargadari* rights on the landowners.

Despite the recommendations on land ceiling given by the Planning Commission in 1953, land reforms fell under the state list. Most states did not pass legislation to this effect till 1960–61.

> The majority view in the Congress party was that land ceiling would decrease productivity (though later agrarian and economic studies disproved this assumption). The zamindars thus got seven to eight years to arrange transfer of holdings to different family members before the ceiling laws were passed. On the ground, little changed, in fact, the early fifties saw mass eviction of tenant farmers from land in the name of personal cultivation. Fake co-operative farms were created by landlords to defeat the purpose of the land ceiling legislation. Traditional share-cropping continued to exist on a large scale while new (and insidious) forms of disguised tenancies began to emerge.[26]

As far as land redistribution was concerned, even fewer states carried this out. Again, Kerala and West Bengal led the way, redistributing 66,984 acres[27] and 1.04 million acres[28] of land respectively. The fact that both state governments were dominated by Communist Parties may be considered as the main reason for this.

Jammu and Kashmir enacted laws for tenancy reform, abolition of intermediaries and land ceiling, and at the same time carried out major land redistribution. It started this process in 1948 and carried it on till 1979. The initial impetus for land reforms in Jammu and Kashmir came from a single political party – the National Conference.

Emergence of the National Conference

The National Conference had emerged as the most powerful political group within the anti-monarchical movement in Jammu and Kashmir. Its leaders were 'mostly young men who had come into contact with communists in Punjab while studying at Lahore'.[29] As such, their ideas on resource ownership and government were similar. They demanded reforms in agriculture, education, employment, health and public infrastructure. This helped their party gain popular support across social groups – from the educated youth who could not find employment easily within the maharaja's administration dominated by upper-class Hindus, to the peasantry that was suffering from high taxation and scarcity, to the people in towns and villages being subjected to recurring epidemics.

The National Conference was ideologically close to the Congress – particularly with regard to its anti-monarchical and pro-people stance. The dominance of zamindars, princes and religious feudatories in the Muslim League was one of the main reasons Sheikh Abdullah refrained from allying his movement with it. But it had a core of members committed to communism. In his introduction to 'Naya Kashmir', Sheikh Abdullah is quite direct about this: 'In our time, Soviet Russia has demonstrated, before our eyes . . . that real freedom takes birth only from economic emancipation. [This] . . . is an unanswerable argument for the building of our democracy on the cornerstone of economic equality.'[30]

The ideology and strategy of the National Conference leadership were heavily influenced by communism and global events. Andrew Whitehead describes in his book how 'Naya Kashmir' was 'a determinedly left-wing social and political programme', and that the 'trace of Socialist ideology was also prevalent in the National Conference's choice of flag, a white plough on a red background'.[31] The 1950s was the decade when land reforms were topical and debate on them was globally widespread. How important this debate had become at the time can be gleaned from the United Nations' resolution on the issue. In its fifth session on 20 November 1950, the United Nations passed a resolution recommending that the Secretary General prepare 'an analysis of the degree to which unsatisfactory forms of agrarian structure, and in particular, systems of land tenure, in the under-developed countries and territories impeded economic development'. It further requested the Economic and Social Council to 'consider the analysis referred to above and to prepare recommendations to the General Assembly'.[32] The Department of Economic Affairs of the United Nations published a report in 1951 which stated that '. . . agrarian conditions which persist in many underdeveloped countries and territories constitute a barrier to their economic development because such conditions are a major cause of low agricultural productivity and of low standards of living for the populations of those countries and territories'. The report identified the tenancy system as a powerful obstacle to economic development because it decreases the tenant's incentive to produce more, reduces the peasant's share of the produce to a bare minimum and obstructs investment in agriculture.

Many countries experimented with land reforms (particularly with regard to tenancy) before and after the 1950s, but the case of the USSR impacted Jammu and Kashmir significantly. In 1928, all land in the USSR was declared the property of the state and millions of individually owned farms were consolidated into state-run collective farms. Farmers protested this collectivization by destroying livestock or leaving them to starve.

> More than fifty percent of horses, forty four percent of cattle, sixty six percent of sheep and goats and forty three percent of the total population of pigs died. This led to an acute shortage of milk, meat and dairy products as well as livestock for ploughing the land. Ten years after, there was a reversion from strict collectivism to the more devolved *Kolkhoz system* whereby the farmers pooled their land & livestock and elected a management committee from amongst themselves to run these farms.[33]

This Soviet experience of collectivization was fresh in the minds of the National Conference leaders, which is why they made no serious attempt to cooperativize ownership after land redistribution, even ignoring the recommendations to this effect by the Land to the Tiller Committee. Ironically, this led to a strengthening of individual property rights – a capitalist outcome even by their standards.

'Naya Kashmir' and Peasants' Rights

'Naya Kashmir' drew heavily on the All India Kisan Manifesto with its emphasis on the abolition of landlordism, dissolution of debt and modernization of agriculture. However, it went much further than the Manifesto in its plan for agriculture – advocating cooperative association and distributing land to the tiller. The 'Peasant's Charter' as laid out in 'Naya Kashmir' included the following:

1. Every peasant has the right to work on the land unless he is provided with alternative and congenial work on equal conditions.
2. All land which at present belongs to the landlords will revert to the peasants, when social parasitism is abolished.
3. Every peasant family will be guaranteed a higher standard of living in accordance with the national norm.
4. The right of the peasant to maintenance from village produce will be recognized as the first claim on it.
5. All feudal dues, levies and forced labour to be completely abolished.
6. Rural indebtedness has been the millstone of the peasantry of the state. The peasant must be made completely debt-free. Wherever the borrower has paid off the original amount, there shall be no further payment of interest.
7. The peasant, in common with all other workers of the state, is entitled to all the benefits of social insurance.
8. The peasant, in a planned economy, will be protected against famine, flood, frost, crop pests, fire, and cattle and animal diseases.
9. The peasant will have the benefit of a modern scientific research.
10. Cheap and steady transport facilities to be provided for all peasants.
11. The peasant will be provided with cooperative marketing facilities to eliminate wastage of labour power.
12. The peasant shall be ensured the benefits of local forest produce and freedom from harassment by forest officials.
13. The peasant shall have the right to free medical and nursing facilities under the plan.
14. The peasant has a right to a clean, weatherproof and healthy home in a planned village with pure drinking water supply.
15. The peasant has the right to recreation based on a village hall as an expression of a common village life, provided with a radio and facilities for indoor and outdoor sport.
16. The peasant has the right to education, not only in the three Rs [Reading, Writing and Arithmetic] but with special application to land and its problems, up to the highest point to which he is capable, through the medium of national education.[34]

Jammu and Kashmir, Post-1947

In March 1948, the National Conference came to power as an emergency administration and Sheikh Abdullah made his first radio broadcast to the people of Jammu and Kashmir. Amongst other things, he pledged:

> Inevitably, the government will, as conditions permit, implement the economic programme of 'New Kashmir' which has inspired hope into the hearts of millions of our countrymen. The tiller of the soil and the labourer, the *kisan* and the *mazdoor*, the skilled and the unskilled worker, in the factory as well as the cottage industry, the endless agriculturist, the petty shopkeeper, the petty farmer and other neglected sections of our people will be given a fair deal.

Almost immediately, the changes envisaged in 'Naya Kashmir' were put into motion. To test the waters, the government first abolished *jagirs* as well as *muafis* (land revenue exemptions granted by the maharaja) and *mukarrarees* (cash grants amounting to Rs 5,6,313 awarded by the maharaja to those who had performed services to him). Other reforms put in place were the distribution of wastelands amongst the landless, a moratorium on all non-commercial debts and stopping ejectment proceedings against tenants for a period of one year. Significantly, the privileges of *chakdars,* a powerful group of nobles and state officials (mostly Dogras, Kashmiri Pandits and naturalized Punjabi officials) who had grabbed land greatly in excess of their original grants and become emblematic of the systemic injustice of princely rule, were withdrawn in totality.[35]

> In October, 1948 the State Tenancy Act of 1924 was amended to give tenant farmers the status of protected tenants who could not be ejected at will. The same amendment reduced the rent for all tenancies above 12 and a half acres – benefiting about 60 per cent of all cultivators in the state.[36]

The Grow More Food scheme was launched by the administration to give cultivable wastelands to the landless: 'As many as 1,85,583 kanals, mostly adjoining forests and lakes, were allotted to the landless during the year 1948–49 and in 1949–50, 49,547 kanals, a total of 2 lakh 35 thousand one hundred and thirty kanals.'[37]

Towards the end of 1949, the government appointed a Land to the Tiller Committee to submit a detailed plan for the reorganization of agriculture in the state. It comprised representatives of the government including the revenue minister Mirza Afzal Beg, landlords and peasants. The Committee deliberated over issues like the optimum amount of land a landowner would be permitted to own, compensation to the landowner for resumption of proprietary rights by the government, prevention of fragmentation of landholdings, etc. In its report, in 1949, it made the following recommendations:

1. Immediate legislation to transfer land to the tiller;
2. Appoint peasant committees in each district to oversee the transfer to land to the cultivators. The committee would also include the local functionaries of the National Conference;
3. Food production should be increased through the introduction of modern techniques of agriculture and by bringing more wastelands and forests land under cultivation.[38]

The recommendations of the committee were, for the most part, practical and locally sensitive, but the issue of compensation to landlords could not be adequately settled. The matter was therefore referred to the Constituent Assembly of the state, which appointed a ten-man committee to look into the matter. The Committee, in its report, had decided in favour of no compensation because:

1. The tillers are a poor and exploited class. There can, therefore, be no question of recovering the price of the land from them;
2. The State's resources are limited and it is too poor to pay compensation from its revenues;
3. Apart from these considerations there is no moral, economic or social basis for compensation.[39]

Opposition to Agrarian Reforms

'It is a well-known fact that in feudal times, Hindus constituted the majority of landlords and moneylenders.'[40] Despite the formation of the emergency administration in 1948, Sheikh Abdullah and the maharaja's prime minister, Mehr Chand Mahajan, were to share power under its auspices. The monarchy still existed legally (and would do so till 1952) and the maharaja strongly opposed the redistributive agenda of the

National Conference. He saw the resumption of *jagir*s as an anti-Hindu measure and refused his consent for its implementation.

> Sardar Patel, the home minister, supported the Maharaja and his private secretary wrote to Sheikh Abdullah on May 4, 1948 stressing that resuming *Jagirs* without compensation was contrary to government policy. He further stated that since the *Jagirdars* were mostly non-Muslim, this measure would create discontent and ill-feeling against the government among the minority community.[41]

Nehru too held similar views. Though a committed socialist, he shared the Congress party's elitist perception of land redistribution without compensation as destabilizing and disruptive. He wrote to Abdullah imploring him to reach a compromise with the maharaja to 'avoid conflict and new problems'.[42] However, the National Conference was publicly committed to land reforms. Abdullah and Beg, by then the revenue minister, went ahead with the enactment of the Big Landed Estates Abolition Act in 1950 without approval from the centre: 'Land to tillers became a reality and Nehru was enraged . . . on phone [sic] he told the Sheikh that Pandit community [sic] are the only sufferers.'[43] To this Abdullah replied, 'I lead the downtrodden and oppressed; India is too big to take care of oppressors.'[44] It is widely believed by political historians that this was the beginning of the Sheikh's falling out with Nehru, which eventually led to his long incarceration.

But this was not all. Soon after the promulgation of the Act, the leader of one of the two dominant sects of Shias in the valley, Aga Syed Yousuf Al Mosvi Al Safvi, issued a religious decree against the land reforms. Though a friend of Sheikh Abdullah, he saw the reforms as 'un-Islamic' because of the clause that denied compensation to landlords. Speaking to this author, Aga Yousuf's son Aga Mehmood explained that his late father was not against the reforms *per se*, but believed that under Islamic law, a person's property cannot be taken away without compensation.

Accordingly, in his capacity as a *mujtahid* (designated Shia religious thinker), he publicly gave a religious opinion (*fatwa*) that asked Muslim tillers to either pay a sum of money mutually agreed upon to the landowner as the price of the land or, if they were not able to, return the land to the original landowner. This opinion had the validity of law amongst his followers, a number of whom returned the lands allotted to

Aga Syed Yousuf Al Mosvi Al Safvi
(Reproduced with kind permission of Aga Yousuf's son, Aga Mehmood)

them.[45] There was some effect on the Sunni communities adjoining the
Shia communities as well, with there being recorded cases of Sunni tillers
getting the landowners (mostly Pandits) to declare publicly that they were
willingly foregoing their rights to the produce from, or in compensation
for, their land. This declaration, called *bakshaish* in Kashmiri, was elicited
by the Sunni tillers as a way of complying with the religious concerns raised
by the above-mentioned *fatwa* and still keeping the land apportioned to
them by the Act, particularly in the districts of Budgam and Baramulla,
where they lived in close proximity to the Shias.

Key Legislations

On the anniversary of the first popular protest against the maharaja's rule in 1950, the following measures were announced.[46]

1. Any individual institution or religious organization in the state which owned more than 1000 kanals of land was left with only 160 kanals of cultivable land for its maintenance and the remaining lands were transferred in proprietary ownership to the cultivators who were then cultivating them;

2. All those who allied themselves with the invaders were deprived of their land which henceforth was recognized as being owned by those who were cultivating them;

3. All the tenants-at-will in Poonch territory were declared owners of their holdings; and

4. The hunting preserves in Udhampur district which were carved out of previously cultivated lands were abolished and the peasants given freedom to cultivate these preserves.[47]

On the same day, the Big Landed Estates Abolition Act was passed. Under its provisions,

. . . all estates, private or religious in nature were abolished. A ceiling of 22.75 acres was imposed on all land ownership and land in excess of this was transferred to the actual tillers. No tiller could hold land in excess of 160 kanals (22.75 acres). In the initial phase implementation, approximately 9,000 proprietors, mostly *Jagirdars* and *Pattadars,* were expropriated from 4.5 lakh acres of land, 2.3 lakh acres of which was distributed to 2 lakh tillers by the end of 1953. The remaining land vested in the state.[48]

The tillers were expected to pay a 'land development cess' to the government which would be used to improve the land. A contemporary historian, D.N. Dhar, described the effect of the Act thus:

At the sunrise [sic] on the beautiful morning of 14 July 1950, when the peasant cultivator of Kashmir walked over his fields, he could not believe that the land belonged to him now and that he had overnight become its master . . . on this great day he was walking with his head held high in an atmosphere of complete freedom; freedom from feudal bondage.[49]

The Act had some interesting features, one of which was that the landowners were given one month to select which area of their estates they wished to retain under the ceiling, failing which 'a revenue officer not below the rank of *tehsildar*' would allot the area to them. Also, all orchards in excess of the ceiling were to be 'nationalized' – a measure that demonstrated the government's conception of orchards as important sources of cash income.[50] The most important feature of the Act was that no compensation was paid to the *jagirdar*s or other landowners, despite the recommendations of the Land to the Tiller Committee. This was unprecedented in India at the time. The success of the Big Landed Estates Abolition Act was evident in the total dismantling of the feudal system. The success of all the legislations that followed can be estimated from the fact that 'out of 9.5 lakh acres of land distributed throughout India till 1970, about half (i.e. 4.5 lakh acres) was distributed in Jammu and Kashmir alone'.[51]

To review the working and impact of the Act, the government appointed a committee in 1952 under Justice Wazir, a respected High Court judge. The committee recommended a lower ceiling on land, and that lands attached to Buddhist *gompa*s in Ladakh be exempted from implementation of the Act due to low yields and harsh climatic conditions that severely hampered agriculture. The government took note and passed further legislations: 'In 1965 all non-occupancy tenants admitted after 1955 were given the status of protected tenants provided their land did not exceed two acres of *aabi* (irrigated) and four acres of *khushki* (unirrigated) in Kashmir and four acres of *aabi* and six acres of *khushki* in Jammu region.'[52] The differential ceilings were because of the scarcity of arable land in the Kashmir valley. The rights of protected tenants were made inheritable, not transferable. All holdings subject to an annual land revenue of Rs 9 were exempted from payment from the kharif season of 1967 onwards.[53]

The Jammu and Kashmir Agrarian Reforms Act I was passed in 1972, declaring the proprietary rights of those not cultivating land personally as 'extinguished' and prescribing an even lower ceiling of 12.5 acres. 'Tillers who acquired the land expropriated would get ownership rights after twenty years during which period they were to pay rent to the former owners according to the existing rates. The payment of rent and the delay in acquiring ownership disappointed cultivators who put their concerns before the government.'[54] The government ordered an investigation into the implementation of the Act and passed a new legislation. A new version of the Act, The Jammu and Kashmir Agrarian Reforms Act 2, was passed on 1 May 1976 and given retrospective effect from May 1973. By its provisions, land in excess of the 12.5 acre ceiling was divided into two halves. One half was transferred directly to the tiller without any stipulation of rent. Five acres from the other half were retained by the landowner to

TABLE 3.1 *District-wise Allocation of Land, Jammu and Kashmir* (in kanals)

	Land allocated
Kashmir	
Srinagar	20,943*
Budgam	7,36,188**
Anantnag	2,14,660
Kulgam	40,833
Bandipora	70,988
Kupwara	1,31,844
Ganderbal	55,351
Baramulla	69,336
Shopian	55,903
Pulwama	1,08,152
Ladakh	
Leh	17,614
Kargil	12,608
Jammu	
Jammu	7,77,508^
Doda	1,58,271
Reasi	5,59,981
Kathua	4,47,825
Udhampur	4,76,543
Kishtwar	63,332
Samba	1,20,405
Ramban	1,66,955
Rajouri	6,58,939
Poonch	3,462^^
Total	49,67,641

Note: * Least in Kashmir; ** Most in Kashmir, second overall; ^ Most overall, ^^ Least overall

Source: Department of Revenue, Government of Jammu and Kashmir. Figures tabled in the Jammu and Kashmir Legislative Assembly, 2017.

cultivate in lieu of the rent payable to him by the cultivator, and the rest of the land was reverted to the state. This Act was received well by the farmers due to its consideration of the financial concerns of all parties.

In total, the government's legislation on land reforms enabled the ownership rights of more than 49,67,000 kanals of land to be transferred to tillers, without any compensation paid to the *jagirdars, pattadars* and other landowners. The largest amount of land was distributed in Jammu district and the least in Poonch district, as two-thirds of Poonch was subsumed under Pakistan-administered Kashmir after 1948. Srinagar, being mostly urban, had little agricultural land and so had the least amount of land redistributed in Kashmir province.

This achievement becomes even more significant when one recalls that the total land under zamindars was 55 lakh kanals;[55] and that according to the Census of India of 1941, agriculture supported 87.5 per cent of the total population. The district-wise allocation of land was as given in Table 3.1.

Critique

As we have seen, the land reforms in Jammu and Kashmir were radical and unique. They represent one of the most sweeping and effective legal poverty alleviation measures in the world. However, since comprehensive data on the subject are not available to researchers till date, misconceptions have been passed on as fact by many authors without providing figures to back their claims. We shall evaluate each of these critiques in turn.

The most cited critique of the land reforms is that they were implemented by officers of the revenue department who had been recruited previously by the maharaja's administration. Daniel Thorner, in particular, saw this as problematic because of the corruption endemic in the revenue department and the lack of accountability in their fieldwork.[56] These concerns are echoed by Riyaz Punjabi and Siddhartha Prakash.[57] But none of them offers empirical proof of systematic wrongdoing.

On the other hand, it can be argued that though the Land to the Tiller Committee had recommended peasants' committees to supervise land redistribution, Sheikh Abdullah realized that the formation of these would take considerable time if all the villages were to be covered, particularly as the aftermath of the 1948 tribal invasion and the conflict that followed had damaged large parts of rural areas. Both he and his revenue minister, Mirza Afzal Beg, wanted the land reforms to be effected before the zamindars had a chance to unite and resist. These facts seem to justify the haste in implementation of the reforms through the revenue department. Also, as my field study suggests (Chapter Five), the officials of the revenue department largely implemented their allotted task honestly in both Jammu and Kashmir regions. So branding them 'corrupt' by association could be simplistic and presumptuous.

Wolf Ladjensky, while commenting on the implementation of the land reforms in Jammu and Kashmir, wrote:

> . . . whereas virtually all land reforms in India lay stress on elimination of the Zamindari (large estates) system with compensation, or rent reduction and security of tenure (for tillers), the Kashmir reforms call for distribution of land among tenants without compensation to the erstwhile proprietors . . . [and] whereas land reforms enforcement in most of India is not so effective, in Kashmir enforcement it is *unmistakably rigorous*.[58] (Emphasis added.)

Thorner, an agrarian historian and economist, visited the valley in 1953 to study the land reforms. At the time, he observed that 'land reforms in Kashmir has clearly done away with the *Jagirs*, and has weakened the position of all the great landlords. . . . It has done the least for the petty tenants and landless labourers, these two categories being the largest in the countryside.'[59] However, in his second term as head of state (1975 onwards), the Agrarian Reforms Act 1976 was promulgated by Sheikh Abdullah specifically to overcome this deficiency. This prompted Thorner to change his assessment. In 1976 he wrote: '. . . many tillers have become land owners and some land has even gone to the landless. The peasantry of the valley was not long ago fearful and submissive. No one who has spent time with Kashmiri villagers will say the same today.'[60]

A second critique is that the Big Landed Estates Abolition Act, 1950 did not impose ceilings that were strict enough on some types of land – *kahikrisham* (grass cultivation) could be owned beyond limit and the ceilings for orchards were so generous as to make them ineffective.[61] Siddhartha Prakash goes as far as to say that 'some landowners converted their estates into orchards, thereby avoiding the ceilings'.[62] Again, no empirical data is offered to support this claim. Prakash does not take into account that irrigated paddy land is mostly low-lying and does not easily lend itself to being converted into orchards as fruit trees need more well-drained soil in the absence of easy access to heavy earth-moving machinery, which was the situation in Jammu and Kashmir till the 1990s.

To understand why these types of land did not attract smaller ceilings, it is necessary to understand that the government at the time viewed horticulture as an income-generating activity and agriculture as a means of subsistence. This seems to be a reasonable policy premise, keeping in mind the absence of mass industrialization. Also, there was the matter of costs. The high volume and price of inputs required for horticulture (price of saplings, pesticides, pruning, etc.) could not have been borne by individual farmers with little cash in hand. This was because the maharaja had introduced new European plant varieties which, though high-yielding, needed a large amount and repeated application of pesticides and fertilizers to thrive in their new environment. Also, the government did not completely absolve orchard owners from sharing their wealth – they had to pay a tax of Rs 800 per acre on such portions of their orchards that exceeded the land ceiling of 12.5 acres, according to the provisions of the Agrarian Reforms Act 2.[63] With regard to grasslands, the village grazing system in Jammu and Kashmir was collective, and pastures needed to be large and proximate to habitations. So *kahikrisham* and *shamilat* (village commons) lands were not partitioned.

A third common critique is that the land ceiling norms as enacted by the Big Landed Estates Abolition Act and the Agrarian Reforms Acts 1 and 2 were set in relation to an individual and not a family – some *jagirdars* were thus able to save land from redistribution by dividing it up in the names of their male heirs by registering them as cultivators (*kashtkar*). But considering that the *jagirdars* were not given any compensation by the government, this oversight could well have saved them from destitution. Land reforms also put tremendous pressure on the joint family system, particularly in the Kashmir valley,[64] and a large number of *jagirdar* families actually split up, with the sons setting up independent homes and farming their own land even during the father's lifetime.[65] In this way, they could be counted as independent farmers supporting their families. This is borne out by figures which show that the pattern of landholding moved decisively from large estates to small ones. As Siddhartha Prakash observes:

In 1953, 42 per cent of holdings were below one hectare, constituting only 14 per cent of the total land. By 1986, 73 per cent of total holdings constituted 0–1 hectare, and their share of total area doubled to 32 per cent. Conversely, over the same period, large holdings of more than 4 hectares, constituting 6 per cent of total holdings and 22 per cent of the total land, fell to 2 per cent of total holdings and 16 per cent of the total area.[66]

Currently, the proportion of households with land in the range of 40–100 kanals in Jammu and Kashmir is less than 3 per cent.[67]

Consequences

From 1948 to 1979, the National Conference government and other governments that followed redistributed nearly half of all the cultivated land amongst tillers and nearly 3 lakh kanals to the landless. This substantially decreased the systemic inequality in asset ownership between the *jagirdars* and big farmers on the one hand, and tenant farmers and the landless on the other. When we consider that according to the Census of 1941, this land supported 87.5 per cent of the population through agriculture, we can begin to appreciate the real difference agrarian reforms made to the lives of farmers and their families. These gains in asset ownership have endured over time with '68 per cent of households in the state still retaining some amount of agricultural land and the average amount of land possessed by a household being 13 kanals'.[68] Only '14 per cent of rural households in Jammu and Kashmir have no land', which is a policy triumph, considering the scarcity of land.[69]

However, it is the equity of agrarian reforms *across social groups* that is most interesting. For example, '2 lakh 50 thousand Hindu tillers belonging to the "untouchable" community in Jammu region gained proprietary rights through the Big Landed Estates Abolition Act of 1950'.[70] Since the census figures for Jammu and Kashmir for 1941 or 1951 are not available, the percentage of the Scheduled Caste population that received land out of the total population cannot be calculated. However, as a reference figure it may be noted that the population of Scheduled Castes in Jammu and Kashmir in 1961 was above 2.80 lakh (2,84,131),[71] which indicates that more than 87 per cent of them had received land. Most of the beneficiaries of the redistribution of land in Ladakh belonged to the Scheduled Tribe category.[72] Fifty thousand kanals of government-owned (*khalisa sarkar*) land were given free of cost to landless labourers across the state to build houses.[73] This measure has been particularly successful with '98 per cent of all households in the state owning their own houses, and these figures remain consistent across per capita income'.[74] Similarly, 'most of the land distributed under the Grow More Food scheme went to the Gujjar and Bakerwal communities who belonged to the Scheduled Tribe category of the population and had been eking out a meagre living tending animals in meadows adjoining forests'.[75] The scheme helped them acquire land so that they could live in settled communities and farm. As far as the impact of land reforms on women is concerned, exact figures on the number of female beneficiaries are not available. However, figures from the Registrar General of India (2011) show the number of female cultivators (main and marginal) in the state is nearly 5 lakh (4,79,789) and the number of male cultivators is over 7.5 lakh (7,65,527). Historically, families in the state, across religions or regions, would not give land to females. Muslim communities, despite religious guidelines to the contrary, would make the daughters or sisters of a deceased give away their rights to a share in the family's land.[76] Currently, the share of female cultivators is 38.52 per cent of the total number of cultivators. A part of this share certainly owes to land titles being transferred to women during land reforms,[77] the rest being a result of changing attitudes towards gender as a result of higher levels of education. Thus, it can safely be said that land reforms made a direct impact on the asset base, incomes and prospects of the most disadvantaged sections of society.

Though exact figures on poverty levels from the time immediately after the implementation of the Big Landed Estates Abolition Act in 1950 are not available, per capita income (at 1960–61 prices) in Jammu and Kashmir increased from a meagre Rs 208 in 1950 to Rs 1,536 within just a decade of land reforms,[78] despite the rehabilitation costs for refugees and infrastructure from the tribal invasion and floods in 1949 and 1951. Poverty in the state is much lower than in the rest of the country, which, in the absence of mass industrialization, points to a significant rise in agricultural incomes. According to Planning Commission figures, in 1973–74, when the first phase of land reforms had been carried out, the percentage of people living in poverty in Jammu and Kashmir was 40.83 per cent as against the all-India percentage of 54.88 per cent. In 2011–12, this further decreased to just over 10.3 per cent, against 21.9 per cent

TABLE 3.2 *Increase in Foodgrain Production*

Year	Foodgrains (in quintals per hectare [QH], in thousands)					Increase in foodgrain production (%)
	Rice	Maize	Wheat	Other cereals	Total	
1951–52	2,288	989	409	581	4,267	–
1961–62	3,563	2,833	930	630	7,976	+86.00
1971–72	3,701	3,633	1,676	280	9,290	+ 16.47
1981–82	5,507	4,613	2,037	252	12,409	+33.57

Source: 'Jammu and Kashmir Digest of Statistics, 2000–01', Department of Planning and Statistics, Government of Jammu and Kashmir, 2002.

nationally.[79] Even more interesting is the much lower incidence of rural poverty in the state, 11.5 per cent, as against the national figure of 25.7 per cent.[80] It is clear that this rise in rural incomes is due to the fact that 'more than 25% of the household earnings in J&K are from own cultivation'.[81] This percentage is much higher than in India's agricultural heartland, Punjab (18 per cent).

The third positive effect of land reforms was related to productivity. According to government figures, 'the increase in the produce of foodgrains was estimated at about 2,00,000 *maunds* by 1950'.[82] The increase in productivity continued till the 1980s. This is consistent with studies by Shaban, Besley and Burgess, Deininger, Jin and Yadav and others, which observe that all other things remaining the same, productivity from the same piece of land increases when the farmer either acquires security of tenancy or when he is farming his own piece of land.[83]

Land reforms also had a positive effect on labour supply and wage rates. As people got their own land to farm, the reserve of landless labourers was reduced. As Haseeb Drabu points out: 'The economic enfranchisement of the poorest in J&K is borne out by the near-absence of landless labour; less than 2% of the work force are agricultural labourers. The all-India average for the incidence of agricultural labourers is 23%.'[84]

Because there were fewer landless labourers in Jammu and Kashmir due to land reforms, the wage rates increased across sectors. This trend has continued, and even 'the average wages for skilled and unskilled labour in Jammu and Kashmir are higher than the rest of the country at Rs 750 a day and Rs 450 a day respectively'.[85]

Lastly, because of the land ceiling, the state government itself received land, which it used for building schools, hospitals, electricity grids, water supply schemes and other developmental infrastructure. While this might not seem significant at first glance, when considering the land scarcity in Jammu and Kashmir, this increase in the land held by the government did have a substantial positive effect on development.

Conclusion

The overall effect of land reforms on the lives of the people in Jammu and Kashmir was overwhelmingly positive. Administrative reports from the maharaja's time, including those by Wazir Ganga Nath and Bertrand J. Glancy, an English civil servant, describe the pitiful conditions of peasants in Jammu and Kashmir, and Robert Thorp's seminal work, *Kashmir Misgovernment*,[86] points to the much worse condition of the average Kashmiri Muslim peasant in comparison to his Indian counterpart. The monetary payment made by the maharaja after the Treaty of Amritsar meant that he effectively bought the land and the people of the state. As such, the 'ruthless feudal taxation regime was geared towards maximizing [the] return on his personal investment'.[87] Recurrent famines throughout the nineteenth and the early twentieth centuries meant that the cultivators had to live on very little indeed, after the state and intermediaries collected their share of *shali* (unhusked rice). They survived on water chestnuts and lotus roots from nearby lakes for about four months a year.[88] When the peasants were not dying of starvation or due to the epidemics that followed, forced labour or *begar* killed thousands more. *Begar* was not limited to just Kashmiri peasants; the Scheduled Caste community in Jammu was also a victim of the same.[89] To these cultivators, land reforms came as salvation – as a minimum means of subsistence for the whole year, at a maximum means to a cash income.

Jammu and Kashmir not only implemented laws regarding *all* of the Planning Commission's recommendations vis-à-vis tenancy reform, land ceiling and abolition of intermediaries, it followed these up by large-scale land redistribution *without compensation to landlords*. Large-scale debt reconciliation was also undertaken to prevent indebted farmers from having to sell their newly acquired land. Till date, Jammu and Kashmir is the only state in India to have done so.

This is not the state's only achievement in this regard; what is equally noteworthy is that the entire process was largely free of violence. If we compare this to the violence that accompanied proposed or actual land reforms in the rest of India, or that is still taking place in some places, it makes the land reforms carried out in Jammu and Kashmir even more remarkable. Take the case of Bihar, for example. In 2008, the Bihar Land Reforms Commission chaired by D. Bandyopadhyay (who had been in-charge of the land reforms in West Bengal decades earlier) submitted its report to the state government. This report saw the inequities of land distribution across caste as a direct cause of the regular incidents of caste violence in the state (in which hundreds of Dalits have lost their lives). It recommended that the Bihar government allot between 1 acre and 0.66 acre of land above the existing land ceiling limit to landless agricultural workers comprising 16.68 lakh households. It also recommended distribution of land to the homeless for the purpose of building houses, over and above the distribution of agricultural land.

The Bihar state government sat on these recommendations for years, fearing that implementing them would result in the loss of upper-caste support in the elections. In 2018, when the government finally started redistribution of excess agricultural land to lower-caste groups, the upper castes unleashed a campaign of open violence, including physical assaults and petrol bombs, on those about to receive land.[90] This led to the entire land reforms process being shelved by the beginning of 2019.

The lack of litigation in Jammu and Kashmir with regard to land redistribution is also a remarkable phenomenon. The fact that not even a single court case was filed by erstwhile landowners has an interesting explanation. In the princely state of Jammu and Kashmir, the ultimate power of deciding judicial appeals lay with the maharaja and his four councillors. With the Accession, the maharaja lost most of his real power and, crucially, the monopoly over violence in the state. This was exercised by the Indian army and the armed volunteer corps of the National Conference instead. With the establishment of the interim government and the dissolution of the monarchy, the maharaja lost his remaining powers, including the power to decide appeals. From 1950, when the land reforms started, to 1957, when the Constitution of Jammu and Kashmir came into force fully, there was no legal provision that the landlords could have used to appeal for restitution of property. Even more interestingly, the National Conference had ensured that the Constituent Assembly did not include fundamental rights in the state's Constitution, specifically because they wanted no legal challenge mounted against the land reforms. In 1954, the jurisdiction of the Supreme Court of India was extended to Jammu and Kashmir for the first time. Article 32(2-A) of the Constitution of India gave the state's High Court the power to issue writs for enforcing fundamental rights in the state, to the extent that they applied. These included the right to property, but by that time the land had changed hands and the landowners did not wish to fight costly legal battles with their constrained finances. This still leaves the question of why the land redistribution of 1975 was not challenged in court. Perhaps, by this time people had accepted that land reforms were the government's priority and that they were backed by the full force of the law.

Notes and References

[1] World Bank Group, 'India's Poverty Profile', 27 May 2016, available at https://www.worldbank.org/en/news/infographic/2016/05/27/india-s-poverty-profile, accessed 19 October 2020.

[2] Hollis Chenery, Montek Ahluwalia, Clive Bell, John Duloy and Richard Jolly, *Redistribution with Growth,* Oxford: Oxford University Press, 1970, p. 46.

[3] Ashutosh Varshney, 'Why Have Poor Democracies Not Eliminated Poverty? A Suggestion', *Asian Survey*, vol. 45, no. 5, 1999, pp. 718–36.

[4] Hans Binswanger, Klaus Deininger and Gershon Feder, 'Power, Distortions, Revolt, and Reform in Agricultural Land Relations', in Jere Behrman and T.N. Srinivasan, eds, *Handbook of Development Economics*, Amsterdam: Elsevier, 1995: 2659–772.

[5] Alberto Alesina and Dani Rodrik, 'Distributive Politics and Economic Growth', *The Quarterly Journal of Economics*, vol. 109, no. 2, May 1994, pp. 465–90.

[6] Karla Hoff and Andrew B. Lyon, 'Non-leaky Buckets: Optimal Redistributive Taxation and Its Costs', *Journal of Public Economics*, vol. 53, 1995, pp. 365–90.

[7] Timothy Besley and Robin Burgess, 'Land Reform, Poverty Reduction, and Growth: Evidence from India', *The Quarterly Journal of Economics*, vol. 115, no. 2, May 2000, pp. 389–430; Abhijit V. Banerjee, Paul J. Gertler and Maitreesh Ghatak, 'Empowerment and Efficiency: Tenancy Reform in West Bengal', *Journal of Political Economy*, vol. 110, no. 2, April 2002, pp. 239–80.

[8] Besley and Burgess, 'Land Reform, Poverty Reduction, and Growth'.

[9] T. Rather, 'Agrarian Transformation in Rural Kashmir: A Sociological Study of Kulgam Tehsil', PhD thesis submitted to the Centre of Central Asian Studies, University of Kashmir, 2002.

[10] Mohamed Aslam, 'Land Reforms in Jammu and Kashmir', *Social Scientist*, vol. 6, no. 4, November 1977: 59–64; M.L. Misri and M.S. Bhat, *Poverty, Planning, and Economic Change in Jammu and Kashmir,* Delhi: Vikas Publishing House, 1994.

[11] P.K. Agarwal, *Land Reforms in India: An Unfinished Agenda,* Delhi: Concept Publishing Co., 2010.

[12] Siddhartha Prakash, 'Political Economy of Kashmir Since 1947', *Economic and Political Weekly,* vol. 35, no. 24, 10 June 2000: 2051–60.

[13] N.S. Gupta and A. Singh, *Agricultural Development of States in India,* vol. 1, New Delhi: Seema Publications, 1979: 32.

[14] Census of India 2011.

[15] Aslam, 'Land Reforms in Jammu and Kashmir': 59.

[16] M.A. Beg, 'On the Way to Golden Harvests: Land Reforms in Jammu and Kashmir', Land Reforms Office, Government of Jammu and Kashmir, Jammu: Government Press, 1952: 5.

[17] F. Younghusband, *Kashmir,* London: Adam and Charles Black, 1909: 174.

[18] A.A. Wingate, 'Rules Regarding Grant of Waste Land for Cultivation as Sanctioned by His Highness the Maharaja Sahib Bahadur', Jammu and Kashmir State Archives, Jammu, 1917: 18–20.

[19] Iffat Malik, *Kashmir: Ethnic Conflict, International Dispute,* Karachi: Oxford University Press, 2005: 26.

[20] Beg, 'On the Way to Golden Harvests': 27.

[21] H.D. Malviya, *Land Reforms in India,* New Delhi: Sri Gauranga Press, 1954: 428.

[22] M. Dandavate, 'Land Reforms in Free India', *Mainstream,* vol. 11, nos. 1 and 2, 1972–73: 31–33.

[23] S. Ali and K.K. Singh, eds, *Role of Panchayati Raj Institutions for Rural Development,* New Delhi: Swarup and Sons Publishers, 2001: 79.

[24] G.S. Bhalla, 'Agrarian Transformation: Interaction between Tradition and Modernity', *Yojana,* vol. 37, nos. 14 and 15, August 1993: 36–44.

[25] United Nations Development Programme (UNDP), *West Bengal Human Development Report,* UNDP, 2004: 26.

[26] P.R. Dubhashi, 'Land Reforms: Intention, Implementation and Impact', *Kurukshetra,* vol. 35, no. 1, October 1986: 14.

[27] Anishia Jayadev and Huong Ha, 'Land Reforms in Kerala: An Aid to Ensure Sustainable Development', in Huong Ha, ed., *Land and Disaster Management Strategies in India,* New Delhi: Springer, 2015: 58.

[28] UNDP, *West Bengal Human Development Report*: 34.

[29] Rather, 'Agrarian Transformation in Rural Kashmir': 91.

[30] 'Naya Kashmir', published by All Jammu and Kashmir National Conference, Lahore, 1945: 1, Jammu and Kashmir State Archives, Jammu.

[31] A. Whitehead, *A Mission in Kashmir*, Srinagar: Gulshan Publishing House, 2007: 30.

[32] 'Resolution on Land Reforms', Fifth Session, Second Committee, United Nations General Assembly (UNGA), 20 November 1950: 27.

[33] Indian Society of Agricultural Economics, *Agrarian Reforms in Western Countries*, Bombay: Vora and Co., 1946: 96.

[34] 'Naya Kashmir': 1.

[35] Wingate, 'Rules Regarding Grant of Waste Land for Cultivation': 27.

[36] M. Brecher, *The Struggle for Kashmir*, Toronto: Ryerson Press, 1953: 157.

[37] K. Gopal Iyer, 'Land Reforms in India: An Empirical Study, 1948–90', unpublished report, 1990: 112.

[38] 'Report of the Committee for Agricultural Reform', Government of Jammu and Kashmir, Srinagar: Government Press, 1949: 9.

[39] Ibid.

[40] P.S. Verma, *Jammu and Kashmir at the Political Crossroads*, New Delhi: Vikas Publishing House, 1994: 38.

[41] N.N. Raina, *Kashmir Politics and Imperialist Manoeuvres (1846–1980)*, New Delhi: Patriot Publishers, 1988: 163.

[42] Letter from Jawaharlal Nehru to Sheikh M. Abdullah dated 19 May 1948, cited in *Greater Kashmir*, 14 June 2008.

[43] Quoted in A. Murtaza, 'Sheikh Mohammad Abdullah: Victim of A Great Betrayal', *Greater Kashmir*, 14 June 2008.

[44] Ibid.

[45] For a detailed discussion on the effects of this on the Shia community, see the case study in Chapter Five of this book.

[46] On 13 July 1931, people demonstrated outside Central Jail Srinagar against the maharaja's decision to try Abdul Qadeer, a young Muslim, for sedition. The demonstration was brutally repressed, resulting in twenty-two people being shot dead by the maharaja's forces. The day is commemorated every year in Jammu and Kashmir as Martyrs' Day.

[47] Aslam, 'Land Reforms in Jammu and Kashmir': 61.

[48] Mirza Afzal Beg, 'Land Reforms in Jammu and Kashmir', *Mainstream*, vol. 15, 1 June 1976: 27.

[49] D.N. Dhar, *Socio-Economic History of the Kashmir Peasantry*, Srinagar: Centre for Kashmir Studies, 1989: 409.

[50] Jammu and Kashmir Big Landed Estates Abolition Act, 1950 promulgated by Shree Yuvaraj under section 5 of the Jammu and Kashmir Constitution Act, 1996 and published in the Government Gazette: 16.

[51] Iyer, 'Land Reforms in India': 112.

[52] Aslam, 'Land Reforms in Jammu and Kashmir': 61.

[53] Ibid.

[54] Ibid.

[55] Foreword to Beg, 'On the Way to Golden Harvests': 3.

[56] Daniel Thorner, 'The Kashmir Land Reforms: Some Personal Impressions', *The Economic Weekly*, 12 September 1953: 999–1002.

[57] Riyaz Punjabi, quoted in Rekha Chowdhary, 'Political Upsurge in Jammu and Kashmir: Then and Now', *Economic and Political Weekly*, vol. 30, no. 39, 30 September 1995: 2423; Prakash, 'Political Economy of Kashmir Since 1947': 2054.

[58] Wolf Ladjensky, 'Land Reforms: Observations in Kashmir', in L.J. Walinsky, ed., *Agrarian Reforms as Unfinished Business*, New York: Oxford University Press, 1977: 179–80.

[59] Ibid.

[60] Daniel Thorner, *The Agrarian Prospect in India*, second edition, Delhi: Allied Publishers, 1976: 50.

[61] Prakash, 'Political Economy of Kashmir Since 1947'.

[62] Ibid.: 2054.

[63] Aslam, 'Land Reforms in Jammu and Kashmir': 64.

[64] Rather, 'Agrarian Transformation in Rural Kashmir': 133.

[65] The author's field study interviews (in 2017) with erstwhile *jagirdar* families bear this out.

[66] Prakash, 'Political Economy of Kashmir Since 1947': 2054.

[67] United Nations Development Programme (UNDP), *Jammu and Kashmir Human Development Report*, UNDP, 2010: 200.

[68] Ibid.

[69] Ibid.

[70] J.B. Dasgupta, *Jammu and Kashmir*, The Hague: Matinus Nijhoff, 1968: 189.

[71] Census of India 1961.

[72] Author's interview with Peerzada Bilal Ahmed, Director, Department of Statistics, Government of Jammu and Kashmir, on 8 September 2017.

[73] Brecher, *The Struggle for Kashmir*: 157.

[74] UNDP, *Jammu and Kashmir Human Development Report*: 196.

[75] Author's interview with Peerzada Bilal Ahmed on 8 September 2017.

[76] M. Rashid, 'Women, Their Property and Economic Rights in Kashmir', *Greater Kashmir*, 22 June 2017.

[77] Data from village studies in both Budgam and Poonch bear this out (reported in Chapters Five and Six of this book).

[78] Figures from the Ministry of Statistics and Programme Implementation, Government of India.

[79] Census of India 2011.

[80] Ibid.

[81] Haseeb A. Drabu, 'Was Special Status a Development Dampener in J&K?', 8 August 2019, available at https://www.livemint.com/opinion/columns/

opinion-was-special-status-a-development-dampener-in-j-k-1565248797810. html, accessed 23 September 2019.

[82] Sheikh Mohammad Abdullah, 'Jammu and Kashmir 1947–1950', Department of Information, Government of Jammu and Kashmir, 1950: 4.

[83] R.A. Shaban, 'Testing Between Competing Models of Sharecropping', *Journal of Political Economy,* vol. 95, no. 5, October 1987: 893–920; Besley and Burgess, 'Land Reform, Poverty Reduction, and Growth'; Klaus Deininger, Songqing Jin and Vandana Yadav, 'Impact of Land Reform on Productivity, Land Value and Human Capital Investment: Household Level Evidence from West Bengal', selected paper at the American Agricultural Economics Association Annual Meeting, Orlando, FL, 27–29 July 2008.

[84] Drabu, 'Was Special Status a Development Dampener in J&K?'.

[85] Author's interview with Peerzada Bilal Ahmed, 8 September 2017.

[86] Robert Thorp, *Kashmir Misgovernment*, Srinagar: Gulshan Publishers, 1980.

[87] Mridu Rai, *Hindu Rulers, Muslim Subjects: Islam, Rights and the History of Kashmir*, Princeton: Princeton University Press, 2004: 7.

[88] P.N.K. Bamzai, *History of Kashmir*, vol. 1, Delhi: Metropolitan Book Co., 1962: 132.

[89] Address of Mahasha Nahar Singh, Jammu and Kashmir Legislative Assembly Debates, Budget Session, 6 May 1952: 25.

[90] See Asad Ashraf, 'Bihar's Land Reforms in Dustbin: Land Mafias Prevail', *The Citizen*, 19 January 2019.

CHAPTER FOUR

Impact of State Development Policy in Jammu and Kashmir

Introduction

The beginnings of the development process in Jammu and Kashmir were different from that in the rest of India. Land reforms, debt conciliation, improvements in public service delivery and investment in public works were all started under the aegis of the emergency administration of the National Conference. Since the emergency administration came to power just after the tribal invasion, it inherited several challenges, such as destruction of infrastructure, relief and resettlement of refugees and depleted revenues – the revenue for 1948–49 was reduced to just 50 per cent of that in 1946–47.[1] Land revenue alone suffered a loss of Rs 3.11 lakh as no revenue could be realized from lands expropriated from the landlords. The economy suffered another body-blow as 'the age-old economic ties of the people living in the state, particularly on its borders, with those living on the other side of the frontiers had been cut off, thereby shattering the entire economic structure which was so laboriously and diligently built through centuries'.[2]

With the natural supply route through Muzaffarabad being closed due to the fighting, there was an enormous shortage of essential commodities, particularly rice and salt, and 'people began to fall prey to [an] artificial famine'.[3] Since agriculture had to be suspended due to the tribal invasion, the government had to borrow Rs 50 lakh from the Government of India just to feed the people of the state, for which it hypothecated cash securities of

Rs 2.17 crore.[4] Another '94 and a half lakh rupees was spent by the state government on rations, medicines, blankets and other non-food aid to the refugees displaced by the invasion'.[5] The Government of India was dealing with a much bigger refugee crisis caused by the Partition, and therefore could offer very limited help for the Nagrota and other refugee camps.

These beginnings ensured that the focus of development planning was on the rebuilding of infrastructure. Recurrent natural disasters and political instability made it difficult for successive governments to switch tracks, and in the four decades that followed 1948, they continued with the same policy focus. Because of the infrastructure-heavy budget allocations (particularly for power, roads and irrigation), some development indicators like per capita income grew more rapidly than others like literacy (especially female literacy). The fee hike in educational institutions in the initial years of Sheikh Abdullah's government also had some effect on enrolment rates, till education was made free from primary school to university level by the Bakshi government.

But 'Naya Kashmir' remained a strong influence on state development policy. Its focus on Scheduled Castes, Scheduled Tribes, women, workers and a rights-based approach to development led the state to intervene directly to ameliorate economic and social inequalities through land reforms, restitution of mortgaged properties, debt reduction, etc., with the last of these redistributive measures coming to a conclusion only in 1979.

The interplay between these two distinct influences on state policy over time led to the evolution of a unique model of development in Jammu and Kashmir, with characteristics that are presented below.

Primacy of State Action

The development experience of Jammu and Kashmir was driven primarily by the state. A simple analysis of state policy and expenditure in any area of human development, and improvement in the same, would not be sufficient to understand this. What must be further grasped is that successive state governments gave priority to development as opposed to increasing the state's GDP (gross domestic product), quite unlike what most other Indian states were doing at the time. This was done in four ways.

1. *Sustained state commitment for 'nation-building activities'*
Power development, irrigation, road-building, education, health and industrialization were prioritized consistently in budget allocations. Successive elected governments retained these fiscal priorities despite political upheavals and natural disasters like the floods in 1950, 1953, 1959, 1963 and 1973, and a series of earthquakes in 1964–65. Even governments commonly acknowledged as corrupt and unpopular focused on public spending – for example, Bakshi Ghulam Mohammad's two terms saw education being made free till the university level, and the setting up of engineering colleges, medical colleges, agricultural colleges and schools.

2. *Increase in the state's efficiency to deliver public services*
The maharaja's government failed to provide adequate access to food, medical care and education for the people of the state. Perhaps no single event showed up the glaring lack of public service delivery than during the Great Famine of 1877–79, precipitated by government institutions like the Land Revenue Department when the state failed to mitigate the losses from crop failure through public distribution of foodgrains. No wheat or rice was procured for distribution to the starving people and 'when it was apparent that there was no food, barley from the state stores was sold to the people of Srinagar at Rs 1.40 per *kharwar*.[6] Even this barley was misappropriated by middlemen and sold at exorbitant prices.'[7] Two things are of particular note here – the priority of the government to feed the people of the city even though the bulk of the affected population was in the villages, and the lack of effort on the part of the government to distribute grains free of cost.

In the spring of 1878, the government ordered its officials to search and seize all grain stocks, such as rice left in the houses of villagers, as seed grain for the following year. People from the affected areas were actively prevented by government officials from leaving the state to look for work or food till the winter of 1878 under the old system of *rahdari*, whereby peasants were stopped from leaving so that they could be forced to cultivate the fields the following year and there would be no shortfall of land revenue due to a shortage of agricultural labour. The 'gaunt people then took to (eating) oil cake and rice chaff and this diet soon hastened the work of death'.[8] Though the famine started in 1877, it was only at the end of 1878 that almshouses were established and grain imported from the Punjab. The officials in charge adulterated the grain with dirt and 'sold it to the wealthy at rupees 25 per *kharwar*'.[9]

Contrast this with the situation in 1953 and 1957, when snow and heavy rains (respectively) destroyed the rice crop at the time of harvest, but the government set up an efficient public distribution system (PDS) to distribute rice and wheat flour at nominal rates and prevented loss of life due to starvation. The state government even provided forty-eight yards of cloth to every person on ration tickets till 1952, as against the 'Naya Kashmir' target of thirty yards per person per annum. 'The coverage under the Public Distribution System increased from less than 2 per cent in 1948 to 70 per cent till 1970-71.'[10] By 1980–81, the state was importing 1.42 lakh tonnes of cereals under the PDS to cover domestic shortfalls. On the demand side, the per capita PDS purchases by the rural poor were the highest in the country after Kerala during 1986–87.

Jammu and Kashmir continues to have one of the most efficient public distribution systems in the country,

> with a PDS-led reduction of 2.06 per cent in rural poverty and 4.31 per cent in urban poverty, both of which are significantly higher than the national average of 1.66 per cent and 1.71 per cent respectively. In the case of urban poverty reduction due to PDS, Jammu and Kashmir is ahead of top performer Kerala [at 3.62 per cent].[11]

Harsh Mander and his team undertook a survey of 50 villages and slum areas in ten districts of Kashmir valley in the summer of 2008 and found that:

> less than four per cent of the people said they had no ration card and most reported that they were regularly able to access subsidized grain. Given that this is a food deficit state, the contribution of PDS to food security of the residents of Kashmir cannot be over-stated. The study found gaps in the opening of ICDS centres in some remote locations, but the supply of hot cooked supplementary nutrition was heartening. The coverage of midday school meals was even better, with 98 per cent children reporting that they ate hot cooked meals regularly at school.[12]

Mander attributes the lack of widespread hunger to the land reforms. Clearly, Jammu and Kashmir does not suffer from anywhere near the kind of chronic hunger that plagues states like Jharkhand, Madhya Pradesh and Bihar, which is a considerable achievement of public policy, especially considering the widespread hunger and recurrent famines in the state prior to 1948.

Gains were also recorded in the state's efficiency and capacity to deliver public services in health and public infrastructure (see Table 4.1 for figures on increased coverage and human development index [HDI] gains therefrom).

3. *Redistribution as an essential element of state policy*

The primacy of state action in human development can be gauged by the state's focus on the people of the state, aiming to provide them a better standard of living through redistribution. Unique redistributive legislations were passed to reduce debt, return mortgaged properties and evenly distribute land right from 1948. More importantly, redistribution remained a continuing policy concern till the 1980s with regular reviews of initiatives like the Big Landed Estates Abolition Act, 1950, the Distressed Debtors' Relief Act, 1949, etc., and the shortcomings thereof being covered by new legislation (such as the Agrarian Reforms Act) or amendments (such as extension of the jurisdiction of Debt Conciliation Boards to 90 per cent of all debts below Rs 5,000).

4. *State priority to public spending*

Studies by Abhijit Sen and Gaurav Dutt and Martin Ravallion put forward the view that development outlays are a significant determinant of poverty reduction.[13] Jammu and Kashmir historically has had high levels of public spending despite recurring budget deficits. While the popular perception remains that the state is able to do this because of high levels of central financial assistance, this interpretation is simplistic. It ignores the fact that from 1948 to 1988, Jammu and Kashmir did not get its fair share of grants as a special category state. It received heavy loans instead.

There is another point worth noting here. The bulk of whatever resources the state did get from the centre was used by the government to fund the social sector, rather than give incentives for development of the private sector. Over time, this has led to a sustained increase in the state's human development index (HDI) indicators, although the private sector, particularly private industry, remained nascent. This is reflected in the current human development ranking of the state: with an HDI of 0.53, Jammu and Kashmir is much above the average national HDI of 0.47.[14] It has an HDI rank of ten out of the twenty-nine states in India, but an economic rank of twenty-one.[15] According to the *Jammu and Kashmir Human Development Report* of 2010, the low GDP growth is not because of low revenue receipts but because of consistently high levels of public spending.[16] This level of public spending is not found in many other states because of the continuous pressure from the central government on state governments to reduce budget deficits.

To understand these four dimensions, it is useful to employ the conception of the state as an ideological force or 'project', as put forward by Philip Abrams in relation to the actual 'state system', a formal power structure built of departments, personnel and rules, as defined by Ralph Miliband.[17] The state in Jammu and Kashmir, as in other parts of India was essentially a system that exercised power over the society. But unlike in most other Indian states (with the exception of Kerala and West Bengal), it was equally an ideological project with strong socialist ideals and goals. Over time, the interaction between these two defined the policies the state conceptualized and implemented, and hence the development experience of Jammu and Kashmir.

Having said that, it would be simplistic to believe that every policy of the state had a positive social impact or was implemented without corruption. Corruption and ill-conceived policies were rife in Jammu and Kashmir, as in many other states in India. A classic example of this is the Integrated Rural Development Programme (IRDP) of 1980, which aimed at providing productive assets to parts of the rural population. Due to imperfect knowledge of markets and prices, the beneficiaries of the programme were exploited by middlemen: 'villagers given Jersey cows [by the government] sold milk at depressed prices to the middleman, who sold it on at high prices, reaping profits as high as 66.6%'.[18] M.S. Bhat concludes that the implementation of the IRDP actually widened the gap between the poor and the poorest.[19] The failure of the programme clearly demonstrated the urban bias embedded in state policy, as the market system created by modernization actually worked against the rural poor by capitalizing on their lack of market knowledge even where the objective was to be of benefit to them.

According to the Development Committee Review's Report of

1975, power and drinking water subsidies were provided primarily to the urban centres, which comprised less than 20 per cent of the population.[20] The 80 per cent that lived in villages and contributed 60 per cent of the state's income secured only a small fraction of these benefits. The report pointed out: 'The ultimate burden of these subsidies falls on those sections of the community living in the rural areas, who are too poor to make use of electricity and have no access to filtered water supplies.'[21] Food for the urban population was also heavily subsidized. The subsidy meant that the government had to pay low prices to farmers when buying this grain and as a result, 'food farmers are left with depressed prices'.[22]

The state's forestry policy, similarly, is a study in lack of foresight and ineptitude. Jammu and Kashmir was once 'one of the most heavily forested states in India, home to a variety of Himalayan tree species and valuable medicinal herbs'.[23] The forests also supported 'valuable species like the Hangul and Snow Leopard, and contributed to soil and water conservation and flood mitigation'.[24] Traditional lifestyles did not interfere greatly with the forests though depending on them for fodder and fuel, since their capacity to impact was small. There was also a strong community-level oral tradition which stressed that the forests needed to be preserved to ensure continued supply of natural resources that supported livelihoods – an old Kashmiri Sufi proverb says, '*An poshyi telyi yeli wan poshyi*' (Food will last as long as the forest will). Upon his coronation in 1926, the maharaja had issued a proclamation that allowed timber from dead or fallen trees in an area to be used by the villagers free of charge, provided they did not sell it.[25]

But later the state government inserted itself into the relationship between communities that lived near the forests in two ways. First, it began exploiting forests commercially on a large scale, taking charge of forest management, forestry policy and sales from forest land from the 1940s onwards. Its policies were based on the commodification of forests and not on an appreciation of their ecological value. 'As urbanization increased demand for food, the forest department started to fell trees at an ever-increasing rate, taking the average to 116 lac trees felled per year. Not enough effort was put into regeneration of forests, resulting in the denudation of vast tracts of forest areas.'[26]

Second, the state initiated public encroachment upon forestland through developmental schemes like the Grow More Food scheme that was formulated in 1948, aiming to convert forest area to agricultural use. 'Initially, 5000 acres [40,000 kanals] were affected but now this area has been extended considerably: unofficial estimates place it at 14,000 hectare acres [1.12 lakh kanals].'[27] Thus, due to the cumulative effect of state policy and the pressures of modernization, the forests of Jammu and Kashmir are in a critical condition. This adverse impact on the environment has been exacerbated by a 'number of polluting industries like cement plants and leather tanneries in J&K province as well as brick kilns, stone crushers, etc., that pollute both air and water'.[28]

The social forestry policy was similarly misguided, and resulted in large tracts of the Wular (the largest fresh water lake in Asia), Aanchar and other lakes being planted over with poplar saplings by the people, with the state standing by as a mute spectator. This encroachment of the watershed gravely compromised the Kashmir valley's natural flood-water dispersal system.

The government's modernist stress on applying technology to mould nature led to high-cost large-scale projects with no regard for environmental sustainability. For example, road-building, deemed essential to furthering development, became so central to the state's conception of 'development' that it spent public funds to fill natural canals connecting the lake system in Srinagar and built roads on top of them. These canals not only had been the transport lifelines of the city, but also had provided natural outlets to the waters of lakes that formed 'important repositories of unique biological diversity'.[29] After the canals were filled up, with their self-cleansing linkage mechanisms broken down, the lakes (including the Dal, Aanchar and Nagin) began stagnating. Urbanization compounded the problem as increasing quantities of untreated sewage started being dumped into the lakes, leading to reduction of water depth, eutrophication and excessive macro-vegetation, threatening not only the survival of the lakes but also of important native species like the *Snow trout* and *Chara*. 'The number of *Chara*, an important native plant species, has fallen from 12 to only three in the period from 1953 to present.'[30] The government's practice of filling up natural water bodies, and building housing colonies, convention centres and hospitals over them, was an act that lacked vision and had multiple environmental ramifications.

All these problems with the development policy, i.e. imperfect information, corruption and lack of sustainability, essentially stemmed from *the highly centralized structure of government* in the state. Though it can be argued that this was the case across all Indian states, my analysis is that the degree of centralization was higher in Jammu and Kashmir because of the unfettered powers exercised by the interim government first, and then by unrepresentative, unelected governments imposed on the state by the centre from the 1950s onwards.

Continuous Obstruction of Democracy

Making concessions to the popular sentiment of Awami Raj (rule by the people) after the Glancy Commission Report, Maharaja Hari Singh established a Praja Sabha (People's Assembly) in 1934. With a limited electorate that included literate men and men with titles granted by the king or with property and annual income of four hundred rupees or more, the Praja Sabha was based on separate electorates for Hindus and Muslims. Estimates show that the number of people *actually* enfranchised was between 3 and 9 per cent of the total population. The Praja Sabha consisted thirty-three elected members and forty-two nominated members. The low levels of eligible voters and the fact that the number of nominated members exceeded the number of elected members meant that it was ineffective as a democratic institution in a fundamental sense.

With the dissolution of the monarchy, the people of the state looked forward to a truly democratic election on the basis of universal adult suffrage, as promised by the National Conference, but due to the complications and aftermath of the tribal invasion from Pakistan, this could not take place till 1951. As expected, the National Conference won hands down in this first democratic election. But it was marred by meddling from New Delhi and allegations of malpractice in some areas. Further, the long wait for the election compromised the foundational moment of democracy in the state.

The unfettered powers that devolved on the National Conference as it formed the interim government led it to pursue policies unilaterally, without the checks and balances of a normally functioning liberal democracy. Politically, the National Conference seemed unable to look beyond its anti-feudal campaign slogan, 'One leader, one party, one programme' (referring to Sheikh Abdullah, the National Conference and

'Naya Kashmir'). Over time, this led to concentration of power in the person (and later family) of Abdullah, and the suppression of political and social dissenters by the National Conference. The aftermath of the tribal invasion had given the interim government a convenient ploy for rounding up dissenters. A classic example of this was the Enemy Agents' Ordinance that was used to arrest and extern political leaders like Mohammed Abdullah Shopyani, Mohammad Nooruddin, Aga Showkat Ali, Jagar Nath Sathu, Khwaja Ghulam Nabi Gilkar, union leaders like Abdul Salam Yettu, and even a former supporter, Prem Nath Bazaz. The government also suppressed media critical of the government, the National Conference or Sheikh Abdullah himself – placing restrictions on the publication of certain papers and periodicals, and on Radio Pakistan.[31] This repression of dissent led many, including Sir Owen Dixon, the UN Representative assigned to South Asia after the Security Council's 1950 resolution on the Kashmir dispute, to be openly critical of the state government. Dixon observed that 'the state government was exercising vast powers of arbitrary arrest'.[32] The Panchayati Raj system was 'deprived of adequate administrative powers which were still exercised by the field level bureaucracy' and 'not granted adequate financial resources to discharge various functions'.[33]

As Sheikh Abdullah's personality cult grew to legendary proportions amongst the peasantry because of measures such as land reforms and debt conciliation,[34] the Congress government in Delhi imprisoned him in August 1953 on flimsy charges of political conspiracy. N.A. Baba observes: 'Abdullah's exit left the proposed plan for grassroots democracy in the state completely sidelined.'[35] Successive puppet governments were installed in the state, with the openly corrupt Bakshi government being the first of these: 'Bakshi's regime became the symbol of repression, nepotism and corruption. The two elections that took place during his reign in 1957 and 1962 were rigged'.[36] The financial independence of the state was subdued with massive cash inflows from Delhi. These funds were meant for the state's development, but ended up in the pockets of Bakshi and his relatives. Bakshi's income 'grew from Rs 10,000 in 1947 to Rs 1.25 crores in 1964'.[37] Systematic persecution of Sheikh Abdullah loyalists continued during this time. In 1964, Articles 356 and 357 of the Indian Constitution – which empowered the central government to dismiss elected state governments if a breakdown of law and order was perceived, and thereby also gave it *carte blanche* to dismiss any government that disagreed with them – were applied in Jammu and Kashmir. Bakshi was compelled to resign under the Kamaraj Plan.[38] From 1964 to 1975, many regimes were dismissed and others installed in their place by New Delhi, with none being given enough time to complete its term. Between 1953 and 1975, New Delhi issued '28 constitutional orders ratifying the integration of the state into the Union of India and 262 of the Union's laws were applied in Jammu and Kashmir', in complete subversion of the state's legal autonomy.[39]

Sheikh Abdullah returned to power in 1975 after the Indira–Sheikh accord, but on the basis of an understanding with the centre that he would not unilaterally pursue any radical policies. Even so, his government went ahead with enacting the Agrarian Reforms Acts 1 and 2, which led to establishing a land ceiling and redistribution of excess land to the tillers. His government also introduced the first step towards decentralized governance – the single line administration system. This unique system of planning and development divided each of the state's districts into *halqa*s comprising a certain number of villages.

> The twin objectives of the Single Line Administration were to secure a mechanism for developing the planning process at the district level to take full account of the resource endowments, the potentialities and need structure; and also initiate a process of equitable development of various areas within a district. But its effect was less extensive than it could have been because of lack of presence from [sic] Panchayat functionaries.[40]

Upon Abdullah's death in 1982, his son Farooq Abdullah came to the helm. But in 1984, his government was brought down from the inside as Indira Gandhi orchestrated the desertion of twelve National Conference legislators and the formation of a new party under Farooq Abdullah's brother-in-law, G.M. Shah. Jagmohan, the governor of the state, acting on instructions from New Delhi, refused to hold fresh elections; and it was not till 1986, when Farooq signed an accord with Rajiv Gandhi, that the path was paved for the election held the following year (in 1987) to be rigged in his favour with blessings from the centre. Experts are divided on whether the Muslim United Front (MUF), a conglomerate of parties which had emerged under the influence of the growing conservative Islamic movement, the Jamat-e-Islami, would have won the majority of the seats against the National Conference and Congress candidates in that election. However, the brazenness of the rigging, and the violence unleashed by the police on MUF candidates and their election agents on the orders of National Conference leaders, directly resulted in civil unrest that fed militancy from 1988 onwards.

In 1997, I was present at a private conversation where the National Conference minister Ghulam Mohiuddin Shah expressed regret about having Syed Yousuf Shah, the MUF candidate from Amirakadal, beaten up in front of him in a police lock-up after the 1987 election result and taunting him about daring to think he could win. Yousuf Shah went to Pakistan-administered Kashmir and became Syed Salahuddin, the leader of the feared militant group Hizbul Mujahideen. He is now on the US State Department's list of 'Specially Designated Global Terrorists'. His election agents were also beaten up by the police and some of them, including Yasin Malik, became members of the Jammu and Kashmir Liberation Front (JKLF), another militant group. This was not the exception but the general rule as the National Conference government cracked down on MUF candidates across the valley, most of whom crossed the border into Pakistan, received arms training and set up various militant organizations, resulting in violence and civil unrest from 1989 onwards. The compromised election of 1987 thus led directly to the militancy. To complete the vicious cycle of obstructing democracy, militancy led to the imposition of governor's rule in the state from 1990 to 1996. The trajectory of development that had started in 1948 was affected by the conflict as the security concerns of the centre gained precedence over development concerns of the state.

Gains across HDI Indicators

Despite the serious problems of obstruction of democracy, centralization of power and a great degree of opacity in governance, Jammu and Kashmir showed significant gains in human development index (HDI) indicators, mainly because of political commitment to the state as an 'ideological project'. In 1948, Jammu and Kashmir was one of the most deprived states in India, even amongst the princely states that were characterized by low levels of development. But from 1948 to 1988, HDI in the state improved significantly as compared to their imperial context, as is evident from Table 4.1. This sustained improvement enabled Jammu and Kashmir to move up from the special, i.e. backward, category of states to the general category of states in the 1970s.[41]

GDP Per Capita

As can be observed in Table 4.1, the state's GDP per capita rose from Rs 7,789 in 1948 to Rs 14,984 in 1988 (at constant prices). The birth rate was 32.60 per thousand in 1988 and by 2012, it was 18.3 per thousand. In 2015, Jammu and Kashmir, together with Tamil Nadu and West Bengal, recorded the lowest total fertility rate (TFR) in the country at 1.6.[42] The death rate came down to 8.30 per thousand in 1988[43] and 5.7 per thousand in 2012,[44] which reflects the improved access to health through

TABLE 4.1 *Selected Human Development Index (HDI) Indicators for Jammu and Kashmir, 1948 and 1988*

	HDI indicators	Unit	1948	1988	Source
1	GDP (at current prices)	Rupees crore	2,79,618	12,06,243	Ministry of Statistics and Programme Implementation, Government of India
2	GDP per capita (at constant 2004–05 prices)	Rupees	7,789	14,984	Ministry of Statistics and Programme Implementation, Government of India
3	Life expectancy	years	27	56.10	Registrar General of India
4	Poverty	per cent	NA	23.82	Planning Commission of India
5	Literacy rate	per cent	5*	45**	Census of India
6	Female literacy rate	per cent	NA	35**	Census of India
7	Birth rate	per 1,000 people	NA	32.60	Directorate of Economics and Statistics, Government of Jammu and Kashmir
8	Death rate	per 1,000 people	NA	8.30	Directorate of Economics and Statistics, Government of Jammu and Kashmir
9	Infant mortality rate	per 1,000 people	NA	81	*Jammu and Kashmir Human Development Report*, 2010

Notes: * Interpolated from the 1941 Census; **extrapolated figures from 1991 as the census could not be carried out in the state that year; NA: not available.

the establishment of more community-level dispensaries, employment of more doctors, vaccination drives in urban and rural areas, and an absence of famines.

Health

Perhaps the most impressive gain was recorded in life expectancy at birth, which increased from 27 years in 1948 to 56.1 years in 1988.[45] This trend has continued since. Life expectancy at birth in the state in 2010 was 72.6 years (Chart 4.1), which places it third in the country after Kerala and Delhi. Life expectancy for females, at 74.9 years, is higher than for men, which is 70.9 years. This places Jammu and Kashmir second in India after Kerala for female life expectancy. But if we look at life expectancy figures for different age-groups (published by the Registrar General of India), we can see that Jammu and Kashmir surpassed Kerala in terms of highest life expectancy for every age-group except for at birth.[46]

A 2014 study by the Institute for Social and Economic Change (ISEC) on health in India stated that the average healthy years lost to 'major groups

CHART 4.1 *Life Expectancy at Selected Ages: Jammu and Kashmir, and Kerala*

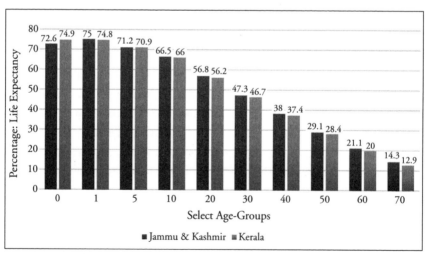

Source: Original data from Census of India 2016, Sample Registration System, https://docs.google.com/viewer?url=http://www.censusindia.gov.in/Vital_Statistics/SRS_Life_Table2.Analysis_2010-14.pdf , 2016, accessed 5 October 2020. Table reproduced from O.F. Kurien, 'Jammu and Kashmir Tops the Country in Life Expectancy – Except at Birth', *Indiaspend*, 23 October 2015.

of diseases' in Jammu and Kashmir was 9.1 for men and 10.8 for women, whereas for Kerala these were 19.7 and 24.6 years, respectively.[47] So Jammu and Kashmir leads Kerala in this regard. Most impressively, for the age-group 1–4 years, Jammu and Kashmir has the lowest percentage of deaths in India – 0.1 per cent of all deaths;[48] Kerala follows with 0.4 per cent.[49] The overall picture shows that Jammu and Kashmir is the healthiest state in India (in terms of physical health), despite the conflict and civil unrest.

Literacy

The state also witnessed an impressive growth in literacy, with the literacy rate rising from under 5 per cent in 1948 to 45 per cent in 1988, and female literacy going up from just over 4 per cent in 1961 to 35 per cent in 1988 (see Table 4.1). These gains came mostly from new enrolments – children going to school for the first time. Further gains in literacy could have been achieved with a vibrant adult education programme, but as interviews with government officials and field study respondents show, the adult education programme in cities and villages in the state remained mostly on paper. This was largely because the teachers in charge of adult education did not have sufficient training to overcome the reservations and negative attitude towards adult education across communities in the state.[50]

The state's literacy figures also suffered as a result of small budget allocations, with the government more focused on higher education than schooling. In the neighbouring state of Himachal Pradesh, which also started off with low literacy figures (19 per cent in 1951 according to the census), consistently high budget allocation and quality control by the government over school education brought about a revolution that boosted not only literacy figures (to 82.80 per cent in 2011), but also comprehension outcomes in children. Perhaps the need for better schooling would have been felt by the government if the electoral system had functioned normally. But without an empowered electorate that could have demanded otherwise, unrepresentative governments perpetuated the financial and administrative priorities given to large infrastructure projects. The armed conflict further debilitated the education system with low enrolment rates, high drop-out rates and the burning down or take-over of school buildings.

Even so, during the decade 2001–11, as Table 4.2 shows, literacy in Jammu and Kashmir went up by 11.62 percentage points from 55.52 to

TABLE 4.2 *Literacy Rates, 2001 and 2011, Age 7 and Above*

INDIA

Indicators	2001				2011			
	India		India Rural		India		India Rural	
	Male	Female	Male	Female	Male	Female	Male	Female
Literate								
Population	33,65,33,716	22,41,54,081	22,35,51,641	13,83,19,176	43,47,63,622	32,88,75,190	28,13,61,374	20,14,32,461
Literacy %	75.26	53.67	71.4	46.7	82.14	65.46	78.57	58.75
Total Percentage	64.83				74.04			

Jammu and Kashmir (J&K)

Indicators	2001				2011			
	J&K		J&K Rural		J&K		J&K Rural	
	Male	Female	Male	Female	Male	Female	Male	Female
Literate								
Population	30,60,628	17,46,658	20,69,618	11,22,460	42,64,671	28,02,562	28,91,749	18,56,201
Literacy %	66.60	43.00	61.65	36.74	78.30	58	73.76	51.64
Total Percentage	55.52				67.16			

Source: Census of India, 2001 and 2011.

67.16 per cent, as compared to just a 9.2 per cent increase (from 64.83 per cent to 74.04 per cent) in the national literacy rate for the same period. Also, female literacy rate in the state increased by 15 per cent, from 43 per cent to 58 per cent, whereas nationally, the increase was by 11. 79 per cent, from 53.67 to 65.46 per cent. This shows a clear acceleration in the literacy rate (as well as in the female literacy rate) in the state, despite the setbacks suffered from 1988 to 2002 (when an elected government came to power for the first time after the eruption of militancy). The high drop-out rates in the state during the militancy years have also reduced considerably, falling to just 5.66 per cent at the primary level and 4.18 per cent at the upper primary level in 2016.[51] In 1995–96, the figures were 48.36 and 59.24 per cent respectively.[52]

The largest number of children in India drop out after completing high school. And illiteracy is still a problem to contend with. In Jammu and Kashmir, illiteracy in the age-group 15–19 years reduced from 20.76 per cent in 2001 to 8.65 per cent in 2011 for males and by 19.46 percentage points, from 38.20 per cent in 2001 to 18.74 per cent in 2011, for females, whereas for India illiteracy reduced by 13.51 per cent during the same period. Even better, for girls in rural areas, illiteracy in this age group reduced by nearly 23 percentage points, from 44.69 per cent to 21.62 per cent, in this period. In rural India, this reduction was 17.18 per cent. These figures indicate that Jammu and Kashmir is on its way to closing the gender gap in education.

However, these gains in literacy have been achieved against the backdrop of chronic civil unrest, starting from the summer of 2007.

TABLE 4.3 *Illiteracy Rates, 2001 and 2011, Ages 15 to 19* (in per cent)

	2001		2011	
	India	India Rural	India	India Rural
Male	15.02	17.2	8.81	9.60
Female	27.34	27.34	13.83	16.26
	J&K	J&K Rural	J&K	J&K Rural
Male	20.76	23.54	8.65	9.22
Female	38.20	44.49	18.74	21.62

Source: Census of India, 2001 and 2011.

Cyclical bouts of street protests have seen young protestors being killed, maimed or blinded, and public and private property destroyed. Schools too have become targets of violence. In 2016, seventeen schools in Kashmir were set alight by unidentified perpetrators.[53] Students enrolled at all levels in the Kashmir valley lost entire years of teaching to curfews and strikes. Similarly, students living in border areas along the Line of Control (LOC) faced displacement, loss of teaching days and severe mental stress due to the increase in cross-border shelling.

To gain a better understanding of the overall development experience of Jammu and Kashmir, one needs to look at other indicators like infant mortality rate, nutrition, access to clean water and electricity, sanitation, etc. As data from the National Family Health Survey of 2015–16 (Table 4.4) show, Jammu and Kashmir is ahead of the national average in eighteen of these parameters.[54] It performs especially well in health-related indicators such as life expectancy (4.7 years more than the national figure), infant mortality and under-5 mortality rates, maternal health care, institutional delivery, and vaccination coverage; nutrition-based indicators such as nutritional deficiencies in children and adults, body mass index (BMI), etc.; and indicators related to household access to the necessities of life such as clean drinking water, sanitation and electricity. Remarkably, nutrition indicators show that the percentage of malnourished men and women (based on BMI) in the state is roughly half of the national figures. Considering the low access to food during the monarchical period, this is a notable achievement.

The Rapid Survey on Children conducted by the Government of India in 2013–14 indicates that factors like better access to nutrition, maternal health care, ante-natal care and vaccination have reduced child deprivation in Jammu and Kashmir. Its child deprivation index (CDI) figure by residence was 0.016, the lowest in India, which means that children in both rural and urban areas benefit almost equally from improved access to health and nutrition.[55] This figure looks even better when compared to the national CDI of 0.138. Similarly, the state ranks third in the protection development index (PDI) ranking among Indian states, meaning that it has a low proportion of ever-married girls between the ages 10 and 19.[56] Jammu and Kashmir ranks first among all Indian states in terms of the low incidence of child marriage within Scheduled Caste and urban communities.[57]

TABLE 4.4 *Selected Human Development Index (HDI) Indicators for India, and Jammu and Kashmir (J&K)*

Key HDI indicators	India	India rural	J&K	J&K rural
Population (female) aged 6 years and above who ever attended school (%)	68.8	63.0	65.6	63.0
Sex ratio of total population (females per 1,000 males)	991	1,000	972	978
Sex ratio at birth for children born in the last five years (females per 1,000 males)	919	927	922	928
Households with electricity (%)	88.2	83.2	97.4	96.3
Households with improved drinking water source (%)	89.9	89.3	89.2	85
Households using improved sanitation facility (%)	48.4	36.7	52.5	45.9
Mothers who had antenatal check-up in the first trimester (%)	58.6	54.2	76.8	74.1
Mothers who had at least four ante-natal care visits (%)	51.2	44.8	81.4	78.8
Average out-of-pocket expenditure per delivery in public health facility (Rs)	3,198	2,947	4,192	4,104
Children aged 12–23 months who were fully immunized (BCG, measles, and three doses each of polio and DPT) (%)	62	61.3	75.1	72.9
Children under 5 years who are stunted (height-for-age 12) (%)	38.4	41.2	27.4	28.8
Men who are literate (%)	85.7	82.6	87	86.5
Women who are literate (%)	68.4	61.5	69	65.4
Institutional births	78.9	75.1	85.7	82
Women with below-normal BMI (<18.5 kg/m2) (%)	22.9	26.7	12.1	14.1
Men with below-normal BMI (< 18.5 kg/m2) (%)	20.2	23	11.5	13.6
Anaemic children aged 6–59 months (<11 g/dl) (%)	58.4	59.4	43	44.1
Pregnant women aged 15–49 years who are anaemic (<11g/dl) (%)	50.3	52.1	38.1	39.4
Infant mortality rate (per thousand live births)	41		32	
Under-5 mortality rate (per thousand live births)	50		38	
Life expectancy at birth (in years)	67.9		72.6	

Source: 'National Family Health Survey 2015–16', International Institute for Population Sciences (IIPS), Mumbai, 2017.

In terms of education as well, even though the state had a much later start than the rest of the country, it does better than the national average in literacy figures for both men and women – 87 per cent and 69 per cent, as against the all-India figures of 85.7 per cent and 68.4 per cent, respectively. It does worse than the rest of the country only in terms of the sex ratio and percentage of females older than six years ever to have attended school (Table 4.4).

When comparing indicators across states, the most striking fact is that Jammu and Kashmir has one of the lowest levels of poverty in India. It also has the highest percentage of people who have their own houses – 96.7 per cent, just a little behind Bihar at 96.8 per cent.[58] In terms of life expectancy at birth, Jammu and Kashmir (at 72.6 per cent) is behind only two other Indian states – Kerala (at 74.9 per cent) and Delhi (at 73.2 per cent).[59] Jammu and Kashmir also has the fifth largest vaccination coverage in the country. It is behind only Mizoram and Karnataka in providing supplementary nutrition to children, outperforming even Kerala and Tamil Nadu in this regard.[60] It also has the seventh highest average wages in the manufacturing sector in the country.[61]

The above data show just how far Jammu and Kashmir has come on its unique developmental journey since 1948. And considering where it started from, its progress has been truly remarkable.

Equity of Development Gains across Social Groups

While the gains in HDI indicators are laudable, it is their equal spread across caste and region that is most noteworthy. For example, land redistribution has been equitable across caste and community (see Chapter Five). Poverty levels in the state are much lower than the rest of the country. This is not a recent phenomenon but part of a larger trend since the Planning Commission first started measuring poverty levels. In 1973–74, when the first phase of land reforms had already been carried out in the state, the percentage of poor people in Jammu and Kashmir was 40.83 per cent as against the all-India figure of 54.88 per cent.[62] By 1993, this figure had reduced to 25.7 per cent and the national figure was 36 per cent.[63] In 2004–05, the percentage of the population below the poverty line (using the Tendulkar methodology[64]) was 13.9 per cent as against an all-India figure of 37.2 per cent.[65] In 2011–12, this further decreased to 10.3 per cent with the corresponding all-India figure at 21.9 per cent.[66] What is even more interesting is the much lower incidence of rural poverty in the state – 11.5 per cent, as against the national figure of 25.7 per cent.[67] This suggests that land reforms in Jammu and Kashmir have had a significant effect on reducing poverty, a premise that presents a promising area for further research.

Moreover, the districts with the largest proportion of poor households, including Kishtwar, Ramban, Poonch and Kupwara, 'are all hilly areas with large expanses of barren land and unirrigated land, indicating that the existing poverty in the state has to do with lack of arable land and low employment opportunities away from agriculture'.[68] As far as the spread of poverty across social groups is concerned, in Jammu and Kashmir 'the Scheduled Caste poverty rates in rural and urban areas combined have now fallen below the national poverty rate for all groups'.[69] This is mostly because of land reforms, 'as a result of which a large number of landless Dalit labourers received plots of land of their own', leading to improved economic conditions and the formation of a small middle class among Dalits.[70] The government also passed legislation to give the Scheduled Castes the right to own property and pensionary benefits, which they had been denied till 1948. The Constitution of Jammu and Kashmir provided 8 per cent reservation to the Scheduled Castes in government services (direct recruitment), in line with their share in the total population of the state. Special scholarships were provided to Scheduled Caste scholars as early as 1955, whereas central sponsorship for scholarship schemes came only in 1997.

Similarly, 10 per cent reservation was provided to Scheduled Tribes in direct recruitment to government services. Though poverty figures for Scheduled Tribes in the state are not available, Jammu and Kashmir was one of only nine states that covers them under the centrally sponsored scheme to set up Scheduled Caste Development Corporations. The state government set up a Jammu and Kashmir Scheduled Caste, Scheduled Tribes and Backward Classes Corporation in 1986 to provide access to finance for all these social groups to set up their own business units. The Corporation also provided skills training to its beneficiaries, typically in nursing, electrical work, plumbing, computer maintenance, hand embroidery, etc. According to its website, 11,962 units were set up by Scheduled Tribes between 1993 and 2017 through bank financing facilitated by the Corporation, and 2,372 units were set up through direct financing by the Corporation. The state also had 10 per cent reservation for Scheduled Tribes in government services (direct recruitment), 3 per cent reservation for people living in border areas, 20 per cent for those living in backward (hard to reach) areas and 3 per cent for disabled persons.[71] Further, funds were allocated at the district level specifically for Scheduled Castes, Scheduled Tribes and Other Backward Classes under the District Development Boards (the decentralized planning system mentioned earlier). As Gujjars and Bakerwals (traditionally cattle-herders and shepherds) comprise the largest group among Scheduled Tribes in the state, a State Advisory Board for the Development of Gujjars and Bakerwals was set up in 1974 (though the Gujjars got recognition as a Scheduled Tribe only in 1991, they had already been identified as an underprivileged community by the state). This Board provided scholarships to Gujjar and Bakerwal children, and constructed hostels for students from these communities who were pursuing higher studies in major cities of the state. Care was taken to construct separate hostels for girls. As stated earlier, 1,85,583 kanals of land, mostly adjoining forests and lakes, were allotted to the landless in 1948–49. Though exact figures are not available, government sources say that most of the beneficiaries of this measure were the Scheduled Tribes who had been living as nomads in areas adjoining the forests.[72]

The only exception to the equal spread of developmental gains was in the case of women. Women fell behind all other social groups in accessing basic opportunities.

> Prior to 1931 the reins of Muslim society in the valley were in the hands of *Mullahs*, the Mirwaiz Jamia Masjid and the Mirwaiz Hamadani. . . . Both of them agreed that the minds of Muslims, *particularly the women*, were to be *saved* from the pollution caused by the impact of modern education and Western ideas. They upheld *purdah* and polygamy, opposed girls [sic] education and discouraged any change for the better.[73] (Emphasis added.)

In Jammu, the conditions were similar. In Ladakh, a matrilineal system operated and polyandry was practised but the state government declared it illegal in the 1950s. In 1934, the maharaja denied voting rights to women on the pretext that 'the inclusion of women voters would increase the administrative difficulties of the election'.[74] From 1931 to 1947, Kashmiri women (particularly Muslim women from poor backgrounds) joined the street protests against princely rule. Some of them were enlisted into the Women's Self Defence Corps but most did not play an active part in politics after that. It was only in 1952 that women got voting rights and in 1954 the National Conference started a women's wing, the first such body for women in the state. In 1975, Sheikh Abdullah's wife, Begum Akbar Jehan, started the Markaz-e-Behboodi Khawateen (Centre for the Welfare of Women). It provided marginalized or abandoned women skills training in embroidery, *papier-mâché* and other handicrafts, ran homes for 'destitute' children and women and provided them supplementary nutrition. But both these initiatives were essentially top–down. Instead of the women who had been active participants in the street protests organizing themselves into a credible movement, educated women from elite families within the anti-monarchical movement constituted the main actors in both these organizations. Even the celebrated Zoon Gujri of the Women's Self Defence Corps was not given a prominent place in the women's wing or in the State Assembly. Instead, 'harassed, persecuted and victimized, Zoon Gujri considered her safety and retired from politics'.[75]

'The first woman who contested the elections in Jammu and Kashmir in 1951 lost her security deposit' as no women voted.[76] It was not till 1972 that women were elected to the State Assembly for the first time. The six women who were elected then constitute the largest female representation in the Jammu and Kashmir Assembly till the present time. Though the Constitution of Jammu and Kashmir provided for the nomination of two 'prominent women in their chosen field', these positions went largely to women close to the ruling party who had made no significant contribution to society and had represented no larger societal interest or women's issues. The same goes for women nominated to the Legislative Council, the Upper House.

The gender gap in education and politics remained unaddressed but for token measures. After 1950, there was no involvement of women in grassroots-level activism either. For instance, there were no village-level bodies like the *mahila mandals* of Himachal Pradesh that have been active in ensuring better access to health care for their members, solving domestic disputes and tackling social problems like alcoholism. Development, filtered through a largely male-dominated, centralized power structure that was not based on democratic support from the grassroots, did not offer women the rapid opportunities for progress that it could have. Women's participation in public and political life remained low. As mentioned earlier, the government did try to make amends in the 1980s by reserving half of all the seats in medical and engineering colleges for women, but similar reservation for women in recruitment of teachers could have had a larger impact on girls' enrolment in primary schooling.

Militancy widened the gender gap in education,[77] mostly as a result of orphaned girls being forced to drop out of school.[78] According to the Census of India 2011, female literacy in the state, at 58.01 per cent, was much below the national figure of 74.4 per cent.

But from 2000 onwards, the state was well on the way to reducing this gender gap in education, with girls' enrolment rates catching up with that of boys. The school enrolment rate for girls aged 6–14 years in the state in 2004–05 was 85.7 per cent as compared to 89.7 per cent for boys, which was better than more economically well-off states like Gujarat, Maharashtra and even West Bengal.[79] The National Family Health Survey 2015–16 data showed that 69 per cent of all women in Jammu and Kashmir were literate as against the national average of 68.4 per cent. Though the fall in sex ratio was of great concern, this trend was reversed and the sex ratio improved from 883 females per 1,000 males in 2011[80] to 972 females per 1,000 males in 2016.[81] District-wise figures show that the largest reduction in sex ratio has been in Leh district – from 1,001 per 1,000 in 1951 to 690 per 1,000 in 2011 (also the lowest in absolute terms).[82] This huge reduction which has impacted the state-wide figures warrants more study, especially because this is not what one would expect in a traditionally polyandrous society with a higher literacy rate than the state average (77.2 per cent).[83] The sex ratio for the age-group 0–6 years is slightly better in Jammu and Kashmir (922 per 1,000) than the national figure (919 per 1,000).

With regard to other indicators of women's empowerment, the National Family Health Survey 2015–16 data (Table 4.5) show the state performing better than the national average in terms of violence against women, women having a bank account (7.3 percentage points ahead) and women's access to menstrual hygiene (8.9 percentage points ahead). Women's participation in decision-making within the household is in line with the national average. Perhaps the most significant indicator here relates to violence against married women, which is 9.4 per cent in Jammu and Kashmir as opposed to 28.8 per cent as the average in India. Even

TABLE 4.5 *Selected Gender Indicators, India, and Jammu and Kashmir* (in per cent)

Key indicators	India	Jammu & Kashmir
Currently married women who usually participate in household decisions	84.0 Rural 83.0	84.0 Rural 82.5
Women who worked in the last 12 months who were paid in cash	24.6 Rural 25.4	12.4 Rural 11.0
Ever-married women who have ever experienced spousal violence	28.8 Rural 31.4	9.4 Rural 10.6
Women owning a house and/or land (alone or jointly with others)	38.4 Rural 40.1	33.3 Rural 33.5
Women having a bank or savings account that they themselves use	53.0 Rural 48.5	60.3 Rural 55.4
Women aged 15–24 years who use hygienic protection methods during menstruation	57.6 Rural 48.2	66.5 Rural 60.2

Source: 'National Family Health Survey 2015–16', International Institute for Population Sciences (IIPS), Mumbai, 2017.

after accounting for under-reporting of domestic violence in the state and across the country, this low level of violence is significant. Jammu and Kashmir trails only in two indicators out of six – access to cash incomes and house/land ownership by women. These figures probably validate the fact that most of the agricultural work undertaken by women in the state is unpaid, and there is no widespread participation by women in manual labour (like in Bihar, for example).

The smaller social disparities in income, asset ownership, health care and other aspects of development in Jammu and Kashmir (when compared to the national average) are unique, especially when compared to states like Gujarat, Haryana and Uttar Pradesh where minorities, Scheduled Castes and women are largely left out of the development process or indeed the national scenario.[84]

Egalitarian Social Relations

Studies by Abhijeet Banerjee and Rohini Somanathan, Edward Miguel and Mary Kay Gugerty, Alberto Alesina, Reza Baqir and William Easterly, and others agree that ethnic diversity hinders the provision of public goods and services.[85] But of late, their findings have been critiqued for using ethnic diversity and not ethnic divisions as factors of study. In the Indian context, social inequalities and chronic religious or ethnic divides have led to confrontation and violent reprisals between social groups. P. Bardhan and Sudipta Kaviraj are of the view that highly unequal social settings make institutions of state action vulnerable to capture by vested interests and the social elite.[86] They can also systematically restrict the access of marginalized groups to social services, particularly health and education. For example, the persistence of caste inequalities in India constitutes a major obstruction to the processes of development, particularly redistributive measures. Land reforms in most states of India were rendered ineffective by powerful landlord (mostly higher-caste) lobbies that defeated legislation by exploiting its loopholes. As a result, the lower castes remained in much the same position as before. To invert this analysis would mean that social unity or lack of social schisms lead to higher levels of development. I argue that in Jammu and Kashmir, this was the case.

Jammu and Kashmir was a Muslim-majority state with 68.3 per cent Muslims.[87] The Ladakh and Kashmir regions of the state did not have Scheduled Caste populations as Ladakh is predominantly Buddhist, and in the Kashmir valley the only Hindus present are Brahmins (the remaining three caste groups having converted to Islam). The Hindu population has been historically concentrated mainly in Jammu, the only Hindu-majority region in the state.[88]

The share of the Scheduled Caste population, which is just over 9 per cent in the state as per the 2011 Census, is significantly lower than the national average of 16.6 per cent. Add to this a historically 'loose concept of caste'[89] according to which the 'lower castes used to exchange gifts with the higher classes and kings used to dine in the presence of workers',[90] and one gets a sense that schismatic social divisions that characterize social relations in most Indian states were not present here. P.N.K. Bamzai, a prominent Kashmiri historian, attributes this to the predominant influence of Buddhism (the state religion at one time) on caste rigidities.[91] An illustration of the Buddhist influence is seen in the prevalence of intermarriage between different castes in the post-Buddhist era. For instance, Kalhana mentions in *Rajatarangini* ('The River of Kings', a meticulous historical document on the kings of Kashmir) that

King Chakra Varman (923–33 CE) married an untouchable woman from the *doomb* community and 'made her the premier queen. She entered the famous sacred temple of Vishnu near Srinagar, to which, followed by feudatory nobles, she paid a visit in state. Her relatives held high posts and orders [issued by them] became like royal commands . . . and were not transgressed by anyone'.[92]

Later, a syncretic influence was also exerted by Shaivism and Sufism, the dominant schools of thought within Hinduism and Islam as practised in the Kashmir valley. In particular, the shared reverence for local shrines among Hindus and Muslims of the valley indicated social intermingling and a common belief system that coexisted with the two religions. R.L. Hangloo, an eminent Kashmiri Pandit scholar, describes it thus: 'Kashmiris have not questioned . . . the spiritual or religious philosophies of *rishis*, saints or other dervishes at the elite or the popular level in the light of organized religious ethics but . . . have consistently acknowledged the presence of their heretical traditions associated with *aastan*s (shrines) in their lives, individually and collectively.'[93] The fondness for Sufi poetry across religion in the Kashmir valley led to a rich poetic and musical tradition that exerted a negative influence on social divisions. For example, the poetry of the female mystics Lal Ded (a fourteenth-century female mystic) and Habba Khatoon (1554–1609, the last native Kashmiri queen turned mystic) was equally popular among Hindus and Muslims – a fact that speaks volumes not only about religious harmony, but also the acceptance of female agency by a largely patriarchal system. Though the Sufi and Bhakti movements flourished in other parts of India as well, their unique manifestation in the Kashmiri society was their ideological domination over potentially divisive readings of Islam and Hinduism – that is, to extend Hangloo's analysis, an acceptance of the heretic as the mainstream.

In the valley, the only Hindus were Brahmins; the rest of the population had converted to Islam, even though the local system of keeping surnames based on occupation (*kram*) meant that even as Muslims, the previous caste-group of a family could be identified. *Kram*s also functioned as endogamous social groups, though the system was not completely rigid. In terms of power structure, there was no enforced social separation even between *jagirdar*s (landlords) and *kashtkar*s (cultivators). In fact, there was a strong sense of interdependence within village communities wherein the landlords were 'expected to maintain a *langar* (public kitchen) where scores of people used to have their food daily. . . . In the evening besides food they would get shelter for the night.'[94] Often, 'the officials would monitor the peasants' dwellings to see that they had not taken away any grains for cooking (before the state's share of revenue was collected). The peasants, forced by hunger . . . would take away grain stealthily and cook it in the courtyard of Qadir Ganaie (the landlord)' as they knew the revenue officials would not bother them there.[95]

There was a larger sense of community, transcending religion, in Kashmir and Ladakh, with intermarriage between Muslims and Buddhists being common till the twentieth century in Ladakh, the largest geographical area of the state. Religious customs involved neighbours even if they belonged to other religions or castes. For instance, Kashmiri Pandits would offer walnuts as *prasad* (food offered as a part of worship rituals in Hinduism) after the *hyerath* (Shivratri puja, the biggest festival of Kashmiri Pandits) to their Muslim neighbours who would accept gladly, and Muslims would distribute *teher* (turmeric rice made on religious occasions) to the Pandits. These customs show an absence of caste-based taboos on sharing of food, which are typical of the caste system in the rest of India. Even in Jammu, where the caste system could be seen to be more prevalent than in other parts of the state, there was no restriction in moving between occupational groups – a large number of 'untouchables' worked as cultivators in the fields of upper-caste landowners.[96] Further, as among most hill communities in north India, sources of water, village playgrounds and grazing areas were common for all caste groups. Another practice common among hill communities across India is the participation of women in agricultural and non-agricultural tasks outside the household. Jammu and Kashmir is no exception; women in all three regions of the state work in the fields, harvest forest produce and take care of cattle.

The society in Ladakh, particularly in rural areas, was organized loosely along matrilineal lines because of the scarcity of arable land and the threat of parcellization through inheritance. As U. Gielen observes,

> Fraternal polyandry is most commonly practiced in western Tibetan societies such as . . . Ladakh. Although . . . actually outlawed since 1942 by Kashmir's Muslim-oriented state laws, polyandry continues to be practiced in the more remote regions of Ladakh. In these regions, an estimated 25–60 percent of all marriages were based upon polyandry during the late 1970s.[97]

But the ban did not end the practice of matrilineal inheritance immediately. It remained in existence into the 1990s especially among the elderly and the more isolated rural populations.[98] The practice of *magpa* marriages where the groom moves in with the bride's family was common.[99]

Sociologist B.A. Dabla believes that the low levels of spousal violence against women and the increased support women across the state get from their parental homes even after marriage is because of the widespread 'prevalence of endogamy that allowed women close contact with their parental families and kept ill treatment at the hands of the marital family in check'.[100] He also points out that *purdah* was only practised among women belonging to the religious, feudal and business elite. The majority of women were free from this practice as their labour was needed in the fields and forests. Most women in the state were not confined to the household and had a large degree of agency in this occupational model, often selling firewood, forest produce and milk for cash incomes.

However, in ancient times, women seem to have had more freedom. Kalhana's *Rajatarangini* records that 'women had emerged from the domestic into the political stage, were free, owned immovable property, managed their own estates and even fought at the head of their troops'.[101] There are a number of famous Kashmiri queens including Yashovati, Sugandha, Rani Didda, Kota Rani and Habba Khatoon, though for the most part power was concentrated in the hands of kings. During the Dogra rule, society was organized on patriarchal lines but women still had agency in household and agricultural matters.

Women were also a part of the anti-monarchical movement from the 1930s onwards.[102] In the beginning, this was mostly in the form of women protesting against rape or molestation of other women by soldiers. As these processions were fired upon and more and more women died, women's participation in street protests became larger. Women, particularly from the impoverished classes, were at the forefront of protest meetings led by the National Conference, probably because they constituted the majority of victims of molestation, rape and police firing. In comparison, educated women from elite classes joined the movement later. By the mid-1930s, 'processions of women were a common feature of the agitation in various localities of Srinagar and the towns of Baramulla, Sopore, Islamabad (Anantnag) and Shopian'.[103]

In 1947, the National Conference asked civilians to pool weapons for raising an armed volunteer corps to defend Kashmir against the tribal invaders. An armed Women's Self Defence Corps was also raised, and its members drawn from every social class included Zoon Gujri, a milkmaid and Mehmooda Ahmed Ali Shah, an eminent educationist.[104] The Corps played an important role in safeguarding public institutions and providing basic utilities in the refugee camps – it was a visible, emblematic representation and public symbol of women's empowerment.

The absence of rigid and violent social divisions in terms of caste and gender does not in itself mean that social relations were *completely* egalitarian. As mentioned earlier, power, money and education remained concentrated in the hands of the feudal elite, predominantly men, and the Dogra state itself was coercive and violent, particularly towards Muslims. Though there were no coercive social taboos regarding 'untouchability' in the Kashmir valley, there were practices carried on by Kashmiri Pandits that denoted their higher status, extended to their relationship with the Muslim community. For example, they would be referred to in honorific terms such as *mahra* (a local corruption of *maharaj*); and they would almost never eat at a Muslim's house (even if it was that of the local landlord) – this norm was relaxed to some extent, however, when they used utensils and ingredients from the Muslim host's kitchen to cook food for themselves while they were there.[105] Similarly, Muslims would normally not eat in Pandit houses, but these restrictions did not apply to weddings or other social gatherings. In my own village of Mattan in south Kashmir, the *Ramlila* was enacted every year till the 1980s and local Muslim boys would portray Ram, Sita and other prominent characters while Pandits directed the plays.

In the Jammu region, 'untouchables' are not allowed to wear white clothes, a turban or ride a horse during wedding processions, but there has been no *systematic* violence unleashed on them by the higher caste groups in their communities (though they did face discrimination from the Dogra state).

The absence of social polarization can be assessed from the comparatively low levels of violence in the state at the time of Partition, when violence was confined to the Jammu province. This led Gandhiji to call the state a beacon of light for the rest of India. The unity of people across religious and regional lines in resisting the tribal invasion from Pakistan in 1948 was further proof of this. The National Conference used this sense of common purpose to gain support for its development agenda and programmes. The absence of hard social divisions aided government-led redistribution post-1947. This is borne out by village studies (see Chapter Six) which show landowners cooperating with the land redistribution and even willingly foregoing their rights to land in excess of the ceiling limit (*bakshaish*), thus enabling it to be redistributed. Though most of the landowners may have done this out of compulsion, the absence of a united resistance indicates that they did place some value on not disrupting social relations predicated upon interdependence at the village level through violence or vocal protest.

The absence of communal riots in the state from 1948 to 1988 even in the face of serious provocations demonstrates the deep-rootedness of a sense of community. For example, the Parmeshwari Handoo case (where a Kashmiri Pandit girl eloped and married a Muslim boy) or the theft of the *Moi-e-Muqaddas* (the strand of Prophet Muhammad's hair kept at the Hazratbal shrine) did not see any escalation of street protests into large-scale communal violence.

Conclusion

A non-incremental rise in public spending on health, education and public infrastructure started only post-1948, which, along with land reforms, debt reduction and restitution of mortgaged properties, led to a corresponding increase in the HDI from 1948 to 1988. The fourth hypothesis regarding the improvement of HDI thus stands proven.

Having said that, there is another side to the story as well which should not be ignored. Political authoritarianism stemming from New Delhi increased the concentration of power in the hands of undemocratic governments in Jammu and Kashmir. This prevented the partnership of communities at the grassroots level in the twin processes of democracy and development. In this context of sustained obstruction of democracy in Jammu and Kashmir, the state's achievements in development, particularly redistribution, seem even more notable. But it cannot be denied that the lack of people's participation in institutions of governance has sullied the achievements of state development policy – democratic depth being a cornerstone of human development.[106] From 1988, militancy and the process of militarization directed by the centre to counter it shifted the focus of governance from development to security. The heavy death toll, the exodus of Kashmiri Pandits from the valley, the burning down of schools, the increase in the drop-out rates of schoolgoing children (particularly girls), the overburdening of hospitals and other public infrastructure, the destruction of public and private property, the internal displacement of villagers from violence-torn communities – all these affected the enabling social environment for development. Together, these constituted a 'decimation of [the institutional capacity] to deliver public services'[107] on the part of the state. Official apathy and growth of opacity in government functioning were other ill-effects of the armed conflict.

But here, a cautionary note. The development process anywhere is more than just the sum of the public services delivered by the system of governance and the political empowerment of the people. It is also comprised of the process of enhancing human capabilities – of individuals, families, social groups and communities, however marginalized; their ability to build a better life for themselves; and the agency of governance to help or hinder this process. So, when we look at this process in Jammu and Kashmir post-1988, it is apparent that even with the negative effects of armed conflict on public service delivery and political choice, progress in poverty reduction, decrease in income inequality, extension of health coverage and clean water supply continued in the state. Official figures on poverty – using the Lakdawala method of 1993, a technique of poverty estimation that used daily calorie intake as the primary method of determining poverty – show that reduction in poverty and income inequality in Jammu and Kashmir was fastest in the two decades between 1988 and 2008: from 23.82 per cent in 1987–88 to 3.48 per cent by 2000.[108] Though these figures were contested by the state government later, the growth in agricultural and horticulture incomes (particularly for apple and walnut growers), the rise in the establishment of shops and increased assistance from the central government were big positives. This indicates that armed conflict did not impact all sectors of the economy negatively, and in some cases, such as the marked increase in illegal land-grabbing (of government land), may even have contributed to an increase in asset and income at the household level. This is an important line of academic enquiry for the future.

NOTES AND REFERENCES

[1] Budget Address by G.L. Dogra, Jammu and Kashmir Legislative Assembly Debates, Budget Session, 6 May 1952: 29.

[2] National Council of Applied Economic Research (NCAER), *Techno-Economic Survey of Jammu and Kashmir*, New Delhi: NCAER, 1969: 14.

[3] Address by Mr Abdul Gani Trali, Jammu and Kashmir Legislative Assembly Debates, Budget Session, 6 May 1952: 20.

[4] Ibid.

[5] Ibid.: 31.

[6] A *kharwar* is an Afghan unit of measurement used in Kashmir since the Afghan rule in 1561. It is equal to 1,000 lb or 454.5 kg.

[7] W. Lawrence, *The Valley of Kashmir*, New Delhi: Kashmir Kitab Ghar, 1996: 214–15.

[8] Ibid.

[9] Ibid.

[10] United Nations Development Programme (UNDP), *Jammu and Kashmir Human Development Report*, UNDP, 2010: 61.

[11] Ibid.

[12] Harsh Mander, 'Hunger in the Valley: Report on the Implementation of Food and Livelihood Schemes of Government in Kashmir', 2010: 4, available at http://www.sccommissioners.org/Reports/Reports/JammuKashmir_FoodLivelihood Schemes_0809.pdf, accessed 2 August 2018.

[13] Abhijit Sen, 'Economic Reforms, Employment and Poverty: Trends and Options', *Economic and Political* Weekly, vol. 31, nos. 35–37, 14 September 1996; Gaurav Dutt and Martin Ravallion, 'Farm productivity and rural poverty in India', *Journal of Development Studies*, vol. 34, no. 4, 1998: 62–85.

[14] 'India Human Development Report', Planning Commission, Government of India, 2011.

[15] 'Gross State Domestic Product (GSDP) at Current Prices (as on 31-05-2014)', Planning Commission, Government of India, 2017, archived from the original (PDF) on 30 August 2017.

[16] UNDP, *Jammu and Kashmir Human Development Report*.

[17] Philip Abrams, 'Notes on the Difficulty of Studying the State', *Journal of Historical Sociology*, vol. 1, no.1, March 1988: 58–89; Ralph Miliband, 'State Power and Class Interests', *The Socialist Register*, vol. 1, 1977.

[18] Siddhartha Prakash, 'Political Economy of Kashmir Since 1947', *Economic and Political Weekly*, vol. 35, no. 24, June 2000: 2057.

[19] M.S. Bhat, 'Integrated Rural Development in J&K: Some Field Experiences', *Journal of Rural Development*, vol. 10, no 2, 1991: 34.

[20] 'Report of the Development Review Committee on Jammu and Kashmir, Part V: Agriculture and Irrigation', Government of Jammu and Kashmir, 1975.

[21] Ibid.: 1.

[22] Ibid.: 3

[23] G. Singh, 'Regeneration of Forests in Jammu & Kashmir State', in S.K. Chadha, ed., *Kashmir: Ecology and Environment*, New Delhi: Mittal Publications, 1991: 81.

[24] M.A. Wani, 'Degeneration of Environment in Kashmir Valley: Need for Immediate Awakening', in S. Bhatt, ed., *Kashmir Ecology and Environment: New Concerns and Strategies*, New Delhi: APH Publishing, 2004: 175.

[25] H.L. Saxena, *The Tragedy of Kashmir*, New Delhi: Nationalist Publishers, 1975: 89.

[26] 'Note on Environment and Development: Jammu and Kashmir Perspective', Planning Department, Government of Jammu and Kashmir, 2001: 2.

[27] Wani, 'Degeneration of Environment in Kashmir Valley': 175.

[28] 'Note on Environment and Development: Jammu and Kashmir Perspective': 2.

[29] D.P. Zutshi, 'Dal Lake: Environmental Issues and Conservation Strategy', in S. Bhatt, ed., *Kashmir: Ecology and Environment: New Concerns and Strategies*, New Delhi: APH Publishing, 2004: 18.

[30] Ibid.: 20.

[31] S. Butt, *Kashmir in Flames*, Srinagar: Ali Mohammed and Sons, 1981: 46–47.

[32] J. Korbel, *Danger in Kashmir*, Princeton: Princeton University Press, 1954: 208.

[33] 'Jammu and Kashmir State Development Report', Planning Commission, Government of India, 2003: 248.

[34] Some villagers of my own village in south Kashmir said they had heard from their grandparents that there were rumours of '*La Allah il Allah*, Sheikh Mohammad Abdullah' being found written on the leaf of a chinar tree in south Kashmir in the late 1950s, which shows that his cult of personality had reached a quasi-religious status.

[35] N.A. Baba, 'Democracy and Governance in Kashmir', in N.A. Khan, ed., *The Parchment of Kashmir: History, Society, and Polity*, New York: Palgrave Macmillan, 2012: 109.

[36] M.I. Khan, 'Evolution of My Identity vis-a-vis Islam and Kashmir', in Khan, ed., *The Parchment of Kashmir*, 2012: 17

[37] Ibid.

[38] Kumaraswamy Kamaraj belonged to the Congress party and was elected the Chief Minister of Tamil Nadu three times. On 2 October 1963, he resigned as Chief Minister in order to strengthen the party cadre in his state. In 1963, he suggested to Prime Minister Nehru that other regional Congress leaders too should resign from political office and work towards strengthening the party. This came to be known as the Kamaraj Plan. Although Bakshi was not a member of the party, he was prevailed upon by the Congress to hand in his resignation, and he did so in the hope of gaining a larger political role nationally. He was to be bitterly disappointed.

[39] N.A. Khan, 'Editor's Note', in Khan, ed. *The Parchment of Kashmir*, 2012: 121.

[40] Sushma Choudhary, 'Does the Bill Give Power to People?' in G. Mathew, ed., *Panchayati Raj in Jammu & Kashmir*, New Delhi: South Asia Books, 1990: 34.

[41] 'Jammu and Kashmir Digest of Statistics, 1960–1990', Department of Planning and Statistics, Government of Jammu and Kashmir, 1991.

[42] Figures presented in the Rajya Sabha, *The Times of India*, 29 May 2017.

[43] 'Abridged Life Tables, 1988', Registrar General of India, 1988.

[44] Figures provided by the Directorate of Economics and Statistics, Government of Jammu and Kashmir.

[45] 'Abridged Life Tables, 2010–2014', Sample Registration System Data Analysis Report, Registrar General of India, 2016: 6.

[46] Ibid.

[47] Thomas M. Benson, K.S. James and S. Sujala, 'Does Living Longer Mean Living Healthier?: Exploring Disability Free Life Expectancy in India', Working Paper 322, Bangalore: The Institute for Social and Economic Change, 2014.

[48] Sample Registration System (SRS) Statistical Report, Office of the Registrar General and Census Commissioner, Ministry of Home Affairs, Government of India, 2014: 1.

[49] Ibid.

[50] See case study in Chapter Five of this book.

[51] 'Jammu and Kashmir Economic Survey 2016', Department of Economics and Statistics, Government of Jammu and Kashmir, 2016: 55.

[52] 'Report on Economic Reforms of Jammu and Kashmir', Ministry of Finance, Government of Jammu and Kashmir, 1998; commonly known as the Godbole Committee Report. The Godbole Committee was appointed by the state government to recommend economic reforms in Jammu and Kashmir .

[53] A. Hussain, 'Education in Kashmir Faces Another Challenge: Almost 20 Schools Burnt in Unrest', *Hindustan Times*, 26 October 2016.

[54] 'National Family Health Survey 2015–16', International Institute for Population Sciences (IIPS), Mumbai, 2017.

[55] A.R. Chaurasia, 'Child Deprivation in India: Evidence from Rapid Survey of Children 2013–2014', *Indian Journal of Human Development*, vol.10, no.2, Delhi: Sage Publications, 2016: 201.

[56] Ibid.: 208.

[57] Ibid.

[58] Census of India 2011, Planning Commission, Government of India.

[59] United Nations Development Programme (UNDP), *Human Development Report 2011: India*, UNDP, 2011.

[60] 'Status of Effective Coverage of Supplementary Nutrition Programme for Children', Integrated Child Development Services (ICDS), Government of India, 2011, retrieved 20 April 2014.

[61] National Council of Applied Economic Research (NCAER), 'State Investment Potential Index', New Delhi: NCAER, 2016: 104.

[62] 'Poverty Line Survey', Planning Commission, Government of India, cited in *Jammu and Kashmir Economic Statistics*, Government of Jammu and Kashmir, 2008: 7, available at http://ecostatjk.nic.in/publications/BPL200809.pdf, accessed 5 October 2020.

[63] Ibid.

[64] The Tendulkar methodology is named after Suresh Tendulkar who was appointed head of a government committee to revise the criteria of poverty estimation in India. The committee recommended that the Government of India discontinue estimating poverty on the basis of the earlier calorie-based model and instead consider monthly spending on education, health, electricity and transport.

[65] 'Press note on poverty estimates in India based on the 66th Round of the National Sample Survey, 2009–10 data on Household Consumer Expenditure Survey', Planning Commission, Government of India, 19 March 2012: 7.

[66] 'Press note on poverty estimates in India based on the 68th Round of National Sample Survey, 2011–12 data on Household Consumer Expenditure Survey', Planning Commission, Government of India, 22 July 2013: 6.

[67] Ibid.: 2.

[68] L. Bhandari and M. Chakravarty, 'Spatial Poverty in Jammu and Kashmir', *LiveMint*, 24 February 2015, available at https://www.livemint.com/Politics/ qIhZeetYN 29chTZPq1s63N/Spatial-poverty-inJammu-and-Kashmir.html, accessed 5 October 2020.

[69] A. Panagariya and V. More, 'Poverty by Social, Religious and Economic Groups in India and Its Largest States: 1993–94 to 2011–12', Columbia University Working Paper Series, September 2013: 33.

[70] Yoginder Sikand, 'Dalits in Jammu: Demanding to Be Heard', available at https://www.countercurrents.org/dalit-sikand101104.htm, 10 November 2004, accessed 22 September 2017.

[71] 'The Jammu and Kashmir Reservation Rules', Social Welfare Department Notification, Service Rules Ordinance (SRO) 294, Government of Jammu and Kashmir, 21 October 2005: 3.

[72] Author's interview with Peerzada Bilal Ahmed, Director, Department of Planning and Statistics, Government of Jammu and Kashmir, on 8 September 2017.

[73] S. Akhter, *Kashmir: Women Empowerment and the National Conference*, Srinagar: Jay Kay Publishing House, 2011: 78.

[74] 'Elections in Kashmir', Franchise Commission, Government of India Papers, Government of India, 1934: 2.

[75] P.N. Bazaz, *Daughters of the Vitasta: A History of Kashmiri Women From Early Times to Present*, New Delhi: Pamposh Publications, 1959: 262.

[76] A. Masoodi, 'Kudos to Mehbooba Mufti but Where are Kashmir's Female Politicians?' *LiveMint*, 4 April 2016, available at https://www.livemint.com/

Politics/ThLJaAlCSB4bZmCKExFFIO/Kudos-to-Mehbooba-Mufti-but-where-are-Kashmirs-female-poli.html, accessed 3 January 2018.

[77] UNDP, *Jammu and Kashmir Human Development Report*: 53.

[78] T. Kawoosa, 'Over 60 Per Cent Leaving Midway', *Epilogue*, Issue 10, November 2008: 10.

[79] National Sample Survey, National Sample Survey Office (NSSO), Ministry of Statistics and Programme Implementation, Government of India, New Delhi, 2011.

[80] Census of India 2011.

[81] 'National Family Health Survey 2015–16'.

[82] Census of India 1981, Planning Commission, Government of India; and Census of India 2011.

[83] Census of India 2011.

[84] For a full discussion of disparities in development across class, caste and gender in India, see Jean Drèze and Amartya Sen, *An Uncertain Glory: India and Its Contradictions*, New Delhi: Allen Lane Books, 2013.

[85] Abhijit Banerjee and Rohini Somanathan , 'Political Economy of Some Public Goods: Some Evidence from India', *Journal of Development Economics*, vol. 82, issue 2, 2007: 287–314; Edward Miguel and Mary Kay Gugerty, 'Ethnic Diversity, Social Sanctions, and Public Goods in Kenya', *Journal of Public Economics*, vol. 89, 2005: 2325–68; Alberto Alesina, Reza Baqir and William Easterly, 'Public Goods and Ethnic Divisions', *The Quarterly Journal of Economics*, vol. 114, no 4, 1999: 1243–84.

[86] See Pranab Bardhan, *The Political Economy of Development in India*, Delhi: Oxford University Press, 1984; and Sudipta Kaviraj, 'Democracy and Social Inequality', in Francine R. Frankel, Zoya Hasan, Rajeev Bhargava and Balveer Arora, eds, *Transforming India: Social and Political Dynamics of Democracy*, New Delhi: Oxford University Press, 1997: 89–119.

[87] Census of India 2011.

[88] Ibid.

[89] M.K. Kaw, *Kashmir and Its People: Studies in the Evolution of Kashmiri Society*, New Delhi: APH Publishing, 2004: 92.

[90] Nila, *Nilmat Purana*, translated by Ved Kumari, vol. 1, Srinagar: Jammu and Kashmir Academy of Art, Culture and Languages, 1973: 38.

[91] P.N.K. Bamzai, *Culture and Political History of Kashmir*, vol. 2, New Delhi: M.D. Publications, 1994: 68.

[92] M.A. Stein, trans. ([1900] 1989), *Kalhana's Rajatarangini: A Chronicle of the Kings of Kasmir*, vol. 5, Delhi: Motilal Banarsidass: 325–30.

[93] R.L. Hangloo, 'Kashmiriyat: The Voice of the Past Misconstrued', in Khan, ed., *The Parchment of Kashmir*, 2012: 45.

[94] M. Shamsuddin Ganaie, *The Ganaies of Mattan* (self-published by author), 1999: 50.

95 Ibid.: 32.

96 M. Brecher, *The Struggle for Kashmir,* Toronto: Ryerson Press, 1953.

97 U. Gielen, 'Gender Roles in Traditional Tibetan Cultures', in L.L Adler, ed., *International Handbook on Gender Roles*, Westport, CT: Greenwood, 1998: 456.

98 Ibid.

99 Katherine Hay, 'Gender, Modernization, and Change in Ladakh, India', unpublished MA thesis, University of Waterloo, Ottawa, 1997: 9.

100 B.A. Dabla, *Gender Discrimination in the Kashmir Valley*, Delhi: Gyan Publishing House, 2000: 31.

101 Stein, trans., *Kalhana's Rajatarangini*: 528.

102 Dabla, *Gender Discrimination in the Kashmir Valley*: 19.

103 Shazia Malik, *Women's Development Amid Conflicts in Kashmir: A Socio-Cultural Study*, India: Partridge Publishing, 2014: 35.

104 For a comprehensive account of Kashmiri women and their role in the anti-monarchical movement, see N.A. Khan, *Islam, Women, and Violence in Kashmir: Between India and Pakistan*, New York: Palgrave Macmillan, 2010.

105 Author's interview with Mrs Nancy Bhat Munshi, a Kashmiri Pandit settled in Jammu, 12 May 2017.

106 See United Nations Development Programme (UNDP), *Human Development Report 2014: Sustaining Human Progress: Reducing Vulnerabilities and Building Resilience*, UNDP, 2014.

107 H.A. Drabu, 'Jammu and Kashmir Economy Reform and Reconstruction: A Report on Economic Needs Asessment', Srinagar: Asian Development Bank, June 2004: 3.

108 T. Rather, 'Progress in Conflict: Why poverty decreased measurably during militancy', *Kashmir Reader,* 3 January 2016, available at http://kashmirreader. com/2016/01/23/progress-in-conflict-why-poverty-decreased-measurably-during-militancy/.

CHAPTER FIVE

Harmony over Self-Interest

The Human Experience of Land Reforms in Kashmir

Introduction

In order to glean qualitative data relating to the impact of state development policy on people's lives in Jammu and Kashmir, I had previously intended to carry out two village studies of one month duration each, in the Jammu and Srinagar divisions. Through these village studies, I hoped to draw logical inferences regarding the linkages between land reforms, household income, expenditure, literacy, health care access, etc., as well as to compare these findings across the two divisions. According to the official records, the largest amount of land redistributed in the state was in Budgam district in the Kashmir division, and the smallest amount of redistribution was in Poonch district in the Jammu division. As my study deals in significant measure with the effect of land reforms on rural households, I thought it would be helpful to contrast the findings of the areas with the most and the least land redistribution. This rationale led me to choose Budgam and Poonch districts for sampling. After selecting the districts, one village in each district, namely Peth Kanihama village in Budgam and Nangali village in Poonch, were randomly selected for study.

Interviews with farmers in Peth Kanihama brought to light anecdotal evidence of Aga Yousuf's *fatwa* against land reforms. Since Shia Muslims constitute 14 per cent of the state's population,[1] the effect of the *fatwa* was likely to be substantial. This necessitated extension of the field study to the nearby Shia village of Sehpora, in order to study the differential effect of land reforms and other government policies on the Shia community. The study therefore eventually covered three villages instead of two, and was carried out in four-and-a-half months.

While this chapter focuses on the study villages in Kashmir, the focus of Chapter Six is on Nangali, a village in Poonch district in Jammu.

Nature of the Enquiry

This study approaches the development experience of the state of Jammu and Kashmir as the sum of the development experience of its communities. This perspective comes from development economics, particularly from the concept of human development that focuses on the individual as the subject of development and not on models based on the 'trickle-down effect' of economic growth. The approach sees merit in understanding the unique experience of communities at the micro level and the state at the macro level in order to gain prescriptive insight into the larger *process* of development. The objectives of the study are as listed below.

1. To study the specific development experience of three village communities in Jammu and in Kashmir under the state development policy;
2. To understand the differential development experience of communities that received the most and the least amount of land during agrarian reforms in the Jammu and Kashmir regions.

Methodology and Sampling Design

The entire state of Jammu and Kashmir constitutes the universe of the study. The study was carried out in one district each in Jammu and in Kashmir, namely Budgam and Poonch. Two villages, namely Peth Kanihama in Budgam district and Nangali village in Poonch district, were randomly selected for study from within the two districts. During the course of the study of the first village, the need was felt to extend the study to the neighbouring village of Sehpora. The sampling was thus a mix of random and purposeful methods.

Two preliminary visits were made to each selected village, to approach community elders, women and youth, to intimate to them the nature and

Getting consent from informant for interview – Peth Kanihama
(Photo by Omar Wani)

objectives of the study, and to conduct transect walks to understand the layout of the villages. Later, focused group discussions and key informal interviews were carried out in local mosques in Peth Kanihama and Sehpora, and in the local *panchayat ghar* (village committee office) in Nangali, to gather data on the implementation of government policy and key development indicators at the village level. Written permission was taken from informants for the use of their interviews and photographs.

This was followed by interviews conducted at the household level in each village, with the aim of covering at least 25 per cent of all the households. The sampling frame of 25 per cent was determined after giving due consideration to the number of households in the village and the paucity of time. Fifty per cent of all respondents were women. Data on land distribution were gathered from the local land records offices (*niabats*) in the villages studied.

The survey mostly used participatory rural appraisal (PRA) techniques including transect walks, focused group discussions, semi-structured interviews and triangulation. The use of these techniques ensured high levels of participation from the community as well as made data collection a two-way process. PRA, also known as rapid rural appraisal (RRA) and participatory learning and action (PLA), gained popularity as a decentralized, community-based research method from the late 1980s onwards, through the work of development practitioners in Asia and Africa, particularly Robert Chambers, a fellow of the Institute of Development Studies, University of Sussex, UK, who has been referred to as 'development's best advocate'.[2] A great deal of anecdotal evidence was used to reconstruct the condition of each village before 1948, and key informant interviews with elderly men and women were used to

Office of the *tehsildar* (executive magistrate), Beerwah, Budgam

glean valuable information where factual evidence was not available. The information so gathered was triangulated where possible with village records kept by *chowkidar*s (village record officers) or *tehsildar*s (executive magistrate at *tehsil* level).

While I acknowledge that human memory is not free from errors of bias or omission, I would not ignore personal accounts that provided me with vital details about the social and economic structures in their respective village communities. The process also empowered the people in the village communities to articulate their own experiences of the process of development initiated by government policy. Given this, recording their accounts became even more vital.

During the initial visits the PRA tool – daily activity schedule – was used to break the ice and move on to a general discussion with inhabitants on the history of the village. The focused group discussions that followed centred on the development context in the village before 1948, particularly regarding land ownership, livelihood, debt, health and education. They also discussed the post-1948 period including land reforms, debt conciliation, establishment of local schools and health centres, etc. Persons with the most information on these subjects, particularly among the elderly who had seen the reforms first hand, were identified during the course of these discussions and were approached later for key informant interviews. Key informant interviews were also carried out using a semi-structured interview structure with two representatives of erstwhile *jagirdar* families (one Muslim and one Pandit) and Aga Yousuf's son, Aga Mehmood. This interview structure was used because the flow of questions was determined more by the narration of experiences by the informant.

Thereafter, interview schedules were used in a village-wide, door-to-door survey. Both closed and open-ended questions were used to draw out detailed data. Observation was also used to find out more about the collective social dynamics of the village. This combination of research methods was employed to gain maximum in-depth information at the village level, and to help cover both literate and illiterate respondents. The door-to-door survey was deliberately used to talk to women, most of whom could not find the time to attend, or had reservations about attending, formal group discussions. I am happy to say that I achieved my goal of women comprising 50 per cent of all respondents in each village sample.

Data gathered from the village-level surveys were triangulated with

Women respondents, Peth Kanihama

official records from the *patwari* (village land records officer) and the district statistical record, where available, to ensure accuracy. Current land records are based on the records of the Permanent Settlement carried out between 1887 and 1905. The first of these settlements was carried out by A.A. Wingate in two (out of twenty-eight) *pargana*s (groups of villages). The second settlement was carried out by British civil servant Sir Walter Lawrence, who went on to survey the entire state using the same methods. In these surveys, the limits of a village were determined first, after which the village was given a number called *numbr-e-hadbast*, which indicated where the land belonging to one village ends and that of another begins. The total land in each village was then measured and ownership of the same recorded, detailing the type of land, measurements, sources of irrigation, etc. This basic record of rights/ownership (*misl-e-haqiat*) was entered in registers and plotted on detailed maps on cloth (*latha*), presumably for ease of transportation and durability. A copy of each village map (*masaevi*) was also recorded on paper and kept securely in the central record room (*muhafiz khana*) in Jammu or Srinagar. Every three years, the

Accessing land records in the offices of the *patwari*s, Budgam village records were updated by the village land records officer (*patwari*). This process was known as *jamabandi*. The changes in ownership that had occurred in the interim period were recorded by the *patwari* in a printed register known as the mutation register, or *misl-e-inteqal*, which is

> separately maintained for each village, consisting of normally [sic] 100 leaves. Each leaf has a foil and counterfoil and is duly numbered. The title page depicts the name of village, *Tehsil*, District and date of issue etc. The foil is known as '*Parat-Sarkar*' and counterfoil as '*Parat-Patwar*'. The *Parat-Patwar* has to be entered by the *Patwari* as per the existing entries of the *Jamabandi* and *Parat-Sarkar* are made as per the orders passed by the Revenue officers on mutations.[3]

In this study, I have used the information contained in the mutation registers at the time of land redistribution in the relevant village, depending on the legal provisions under which land was redistributed. In Peth Kanihama and Nangali, land was redistributed under the Big Landed Estates Abolition Act, 1950 as well as the Agrarian Reforms Act 2, 1976, so the mutation registers for 1950 and 1975 have been referred to. For Sehpora, the register for 1975 alone was referred to as land was redistributed only under the Agrarian Reforms Act 2. The mutation registers are large registers kept at the local land records office (*niabat*) in the safekeeping of the local *patwaris* who are the keepers of these records. Legally, these registers can be accessed only by the land records officers. An additional reason for the restriction of access to them, which would imply handling the registers physically, is that they are quite old and fraying and are only covered in thin brown paper, making them vulnerable to damage.

For the purposes of this study, special permission had to be obtained for access to the records from the divisional commissioners of both Jammu and Kashmir. I was denied permission to handle the records directly, but the local *patwaris* were directed to go through the old mutation registers and provide me with the information they contained. I sat with four *patwaris* (the record for Sehpora was divided between two *patwar halqas*) for a week each to understand how mutation registers were made and updated, and to double-check the relevant information against the registers.

Once all the information was compiled, I disaggregated the same by religion and by sex.

Comparative Experiences

My experience of working in Kashmir was vastly different from working in Poonch, Jammu. As expected, the topography and layout of the villages in Kashmir and in Poonch were vastly different. In Kashmir, both the villages were clustered and the houses were close to each other. This and the common religious beliefs made the mosque and the *imambara* (a Shia religious centre) natural congregation points, and fostered a close sense of community. The houses were mostly located close to the road and access was easy. In Nangali, Poonch, the houses were scattered on both sides of the river and the adjacent mountainside, and could often be accessed only via narrow footpaths. The spread of the village was also much greater. There was a fierce spirit of independence among the households even though the community cooperated in seasonal activities like harvesting grass from the hillside in summer and harvesting crops in autumn. The religious communities congregated at their respective places of worship, but the bazaar and the *panchayat ghar* saw mixed gatherings in a familiar and friendly atmosphere.

The attitudes of the respondents were also different across the two regions. For example, assuming the study to be for 'official' purposes, the inhabitants of both the villages in Budgam were initially reticent and guarded. It took two to three meetings to convince them that the data was being gathered for an academic study that would echo their concerns and be a reflection of their lives. Cynicism was also prevalent amongst the middle-aged male population – they were particularly hard to convince of the *value* of such a study. But once these concerns were discussed openly in the village mosque and *imambara*, there emerged a larger consensus on cooperating with the author.

On my visits to the local *niabat* (land records office), I noticed a disconnect between the people and the officers – an overwhelming suspicion of officialdom, particularly as represented by village-level officials, and a dogged determination on the part of the people (especially the women) to get their work done *despite* the officials. This was in sharp contrast to their behaviour during the door-to-door survey, when they were open, welcoming and hospitable to a fault with repeated offers of refreshments and conversation in a family atmosphere. In Poonch, the villagers were more open publicly and interacted on a more equal footing with officials. They were interested in knowing how they could benefit from the study and were proactive in looking through the interview schedule forms to discuss what the questions meant.

This differential behaviour across communities in the Poonch and Kashmir regions reflects their differential experiences of armed conflict. In Poonch, the village community relies on the official machinery for evacuation and relief provision in times of cross-border shelling (as the entire district falls more or less within a distance of 10 kilometres or less from the Line of Control); so the relationship between the two is more symbiotic. In Kashmir, because of the heavy army presence and personal violence faced by some respondents during anti-militancy operations, there exists a gap between the state as represented by government offices and officers on the one hand, and the village community on the other. But despite this, the Kashmiri village community approaches government offices in a resolute and not servile manner.

The civil unrest in Kashmir impacted my research as well; stone-pelting often made going to the villages or government offices difficult. To recount one instance, while accessing land records at the *niabat* office in Beerwah in April 2017, there was a rumour of the office being burnt down as an angry mob of protesting youth was teargassed by paramilitary forces. The local *patwari* acted quickly by shutting all the doors and windows. All of us present held our breath and pretended not to be there. Luckily, the mob went running into another street.

Findings from Village Studies

Village Study 1: Peth Kanihama, Block S.K. Pora, Tehsil Magam, District Budgam

Peth Kanihama is a picturesque village situated 2 kilometres from the bustling market town of Magam on the Srinagar–Gulmarg road. It consists of five *mohalla*s (neigbourhoods) on both sides of the Sukhnag river.

The people are mostly agriculturists or small shopkeepers with a few government employees. They belong to the Sunni Muslim community but are differentiated by *kram* – surnames based on traditional occupations. Even after conversion to Islam, communities across Kashmir retained surnames denoting occupations under the traditional caste system they

TABLE 5.1 *Broad Demographic Profile of Peth Kanihama, Budgam District*

Number of households	222
Total population	1,465 (737 males, 728 females)
Religion	Muslim (Sunni)
No. of literates	816 (456 males, 360 females)
No. of illiterates	649 (281 males; 368 females)
Total land area	666.96 kanals
Cropped area	521.28 kanals
SC/ST population	Nil

Source: 'Constituency-wise Amenity Directory, 2011–12', District Planning and Statistics Officer, Budgam, Government of Jammu and Kashmir, 2013.

had been following when they were Hindu. These surnames correspond to social groups – *grees* (agriculturalists), *peer* (priests), *pahayl* (shepherds), *tilwaiyn* (oil extractors) and *doomb* (servants) – but no social discrimination or restriction applies to the occupation one chooses because the caste system as it exists in Hinduism is not practised. There is an absence of some occupational groups that are common to Kashmiri villages, such as *kaandyir* (bakers), *puj* (butchers), *aaryim* (vegetable cultivators) and *waatal* (sweepers), but the villagers explain that this is because of the lack of a *jagirdar* in the village (typically *jagirdar*s would employ butchers, bakers, sweepers and the like). Till the mid-1990s there were twenty Kashmiri Pandit families in Peth Kanihama, but they migrated after the onset of militancy. Most of the land in the village belonged to the Pandit families. Some of them were educated and socially mobile, with houses in Srinagar's posh Karan Nagar and Dewan Bagh neighbourhoods. They included the prominent socialist radio broadcaster Master Zinda Kaul and the famous doctor Shambhunath Qasba.

The agricultural land is mixed: *aabi* (irrigated land) using the traditional *khul* (gravity-based canals using stream water) system for growing rice, and *khushki* (unirrigated land), mostly used for apple orchards. Most families have a small *vaed* (vegetable patch) for domestic use. Focused group discussion with the elders in the village brought to light that, till 1948, most households in the village were tenant cultivators for Muslim and Pandit landowners. Though there was no *jagirdar* in the village, in the neighbouring village of Nowlara, there was a Shia landlord, Khwaja Abbas

Boat on the Sukhnag river, Peth Kanihama

Shah, whose land was cultivated by nine families of the village. Poverty was rife and most people subsisted on the cultivator's portion of rice, which was so meagre that it would last them only from the harvest in November to May. From May to November, they subsisted on boiled vegetables, particularly bottle gourds and turnips from their vegetable patches, lotus roots from the nearby lakes and forest greens. There was a moneylender in the village named Jagan Nath, s/o Sod Bhat; till the 1950s most people in the village would borrow money from him in advance of the next harvest. Later, they started taking loans from banks or cooperatives.

In the 1940s, there were only six educated people (from 121 households) in the village. Of these three were Muslims – the brothers M. Sultan Dar and Haji Ali M. Dar, and M. Sultan Bhat – and none of them had studied beyond the fifth standard. The other three were Pandits – Badrinath who had passed the eighth standard; Gash Lal, a matriculate; and Hakeem Prem Nath, a matriculate of Lahore University who taught at the school in the nearest town of Beerwah. None of the women were educated. Smallpox and cholera were rampant till the late 1940s. There was no health-care facility in or near the village, but there were two local *hakeems* who used herbs as medicine and practised the *Unani* system of medicine.

The elders said that there was a great degree of social unity in the village from 1948 to 1988, not just between different occupational groups, but also between Muslims and Pandits. They attributed this to the absence of the caste system and common respect for Sufi shrines. They said that even Pandits would visit the prominent Sufi shrines (*aastans*) including the one in the village and tie threads to the lattice of the *aastan* for fulfilment of wishes, a practice common among Muslims across the valley.

Peth Kanihama: Post-1947 to the Present

In 1947, the Shia landlord Abbas Shah left for Pakistan and his land came under the office of the Custodian of Evacuee Properties. In 1948, the nine families who cultivated his 50 kanals of land applied for, and were promptly granted by the government, *qabz-e-kaash* (inheritable cultivator's rights to possession of land and produce therefrom). Significantly, all these families were from the *doomb* community who historically had been servants in the landlord's household and later had been allowed to move to Peth Kanihama to cultivate his land.

The Big Landed Estates Abolition Act came into force in 1950 and land all across the valley started being redistributed to the *kashtkars*. The villagers of Peth Kanihama heard from their neighbours in the Shia village of Sehpora that the famous Shia scholar, Aga Syed Yousuf, had issued a *fatwa* denouncing the reforms as un-Islamic and asking his followers to return the land if they could not pay for it. The land in their village did not fall under the purview of the Act as there was no religious or feudal estate there.

The Agrarian Reforms Act 2 was passed in 1976, and a land ceiling imposed on all large landholdings. The *tehsildar* and the *patwari* arrived at the house of one of the big landowners in the village Lassa Bhat (a corruption of the name Ghulam Rasool Bhat) and set up camp there. Every landowner and cultivator had to present themselves at the camp and give details regarding their ownership and cultivation of the agricultural land. This was verified against the land records (*latha*/ledgers) that the officials had carried with them. Land in excess of the ceiling was given to the cultivators. There were a few cultivators who did not want to take the allotted land because of the Aga Yousuf's *fatwa*. Prominent among them was Lal Dar, a pious man who cultivated a Pandit landowner's paddy land. He declared that he would not take the land if the landowner did not forego his rights to it voluntarily and through a public declaration (*bakshaish*). The Pandit landowner smiled and made the declaration before all those present. Only then did Lal Dar put his thumb impression on the land-title document.

This was narrated to us by Mohammed Ramzan Dar, Lal Dar's 62-year-old son who, as a 20-year-old, had been an eyewitness to the incident. When I asked him why the landowner had given *bakshaish* so easily, he said it was because even the landowners were in favour of the agrarian reforms being implemented quickly and easily: many like Master Zinda Kaul and Shambunath Qasba were convinced of the worth of socialist ideas, and others like the Bhats did not want to get involved in long drawn-out land disputes.

Mohammed Ramzan Dar, son of Lal Dar,
key informant, Peth Kanihama

Many other farmers in the village followed Lal Dar's example and obtained *bakshaish*. Out of 571.28 kanals of agricultural land held by forty-four large landowners, 506 kanals reverted to the government. Of this, 344 kanals of land were redistributed amongst 92 families (see Table 5.2). Fourteen families were left out, which included *peers*, *tilwaiyns* and *pahayls* who did not have any agricultural land. The *peers* and *tilwaiyns* had access to cash incomes from their respective professions – namely, teaching children the Quran and extracting oil from the mustard crop. *Pahayls* or shepherds used to get a portion of the *grees*' rice yields at harvest time in exchange for taking their animals to pasture. The villagers said

TABLE 5.2 *Land Data, Peth Kanihama, Budgam District*

1	Total agricultural land cultivated by the villagers (in 1975)	571.28 kanals (including 50 kanals from the *jagir* of Khwaja Abbas Shah, Shia landlord from another village – Nowlara, Gund Khwaja Qasim)
2	Number of households (in 1975)	121
3	Land resumed by government under land ceiling (under the Agrarian Reforms Act)	506 kanals
4	Land redistributed under land reforms post-1948	394 kanals – 344 kanals under Agrarian Reforms Act 2 (1976) and 50 kanals under Evacuee Properties Act (1950)

5	Number of beneficiaries	100, out of which
		a. Muslims: 99
		  Pandits: 1
		b. Males: 90
		  Females: 10
		c. Benefited under Agrarian Reforms Act 2: 92
		  Benefited under Evacuee Properties Act: 8

6	Number of landowners whose land was redistributed	44 out of which
		a. Muslim: 40
		  Pandits: 4
		b. Male: 40
		  Female: 4

Source: Village Land Records Office (*patwar halqa*), Beerwah, Budgam.

that over time, some of these families bought land from the *grees* families.

One hundred and twelve kanals of land were used by the government for various development initiatives including building a school and a dispensary, and a vibrant social forestry programme under which poplars are grown for commercial purposes. I pointedly asked all the key informants in separate interviews if the *patwari, tehsildar* or other minor officials from the revenue department had asked them for bribes, misappropriated any agricultural land from them, or allowed the big landowners to retain more than the ceiling limit. All of them answered in the negative. They attributed this to the strict vigil kept on these officials by the district administration, particularly M. Shafi Pandit, the then district collector.

At the time this research was carried out, 185 households belonged to the above poverty line (APL) category, twenty-four to the below poverty line (BPL) category and thirteen to the Antodaya Anna Yojana (AAY – the poorest of households in the BPL category) category. No one in the village was without a house. The door-to-door survey revealed that four AAY households have land, access to good cash incomes and wield considerable political influence, and had paid bribes to Consumer Affairs and Public Distribution officials to get AAY cards so that they can access free rations. The village headman (*numberdar*) heads one such household. The comparative analysis of findings that follows has therefore removed these four households from the AAY category and added them to APL category to remove factual errors from the sample. Out of the genuine AAY households, six are headed by widows, and the remaining seven are distributed across old occupational groups including *chopan, ganie* and *war* – shepherds and agriculturalists respectively.

A government primary school was set up in the village in 1952 and it was upgraded to a middle school in 1969. In 2016, it was further upgraded to a high school. Most families started sending their children to school from 1960 onwards. Haji Shaban Dar, a tailor who worked for families of British civil servants and businessmen in the summer resort of Gulmarg, took the lead in educating his daughters, Azi and Raja, who graduated from higher secondary school and college respectively by 1970. However, all key informants were unanimous in saying that the adult education programme (NAEP – National Adult Education Programme) in their village was a sham. The local teacher, who was given the additional responsibility for the programme in addition to his regular teaching duties,

Young girls returning home from school, Peth Kanihama

did not make any effort to approach or teach the adult population. When officials from the education department came for inspection visits, till the 1980s, the teacher (and his successors) would gather already literate adult villagers and pass them off as NAEP beneficiaries. This suggests a degree of complicity on the part of the inspecting officials, for they surely would not have fallen for the same gag multiple times. According to Sarva Shiksha Abhiyan figures, Peth Kanihama had 55.69 per cent overall literacy and 49.45 per cent female literacy in 2011.

Mass vaccinations were started from the 1950s. Vaccination teams led by doctors would camp at the school in Magam (2 kilometres from Peth Kanihama) and tour the nearby villages, vaccinating all the children. Cholera and smallpox, rampant in the village till the late 1940s, were phased out in 1950 and 1975 respectively. A dispensary was set up in Magam in 1954, which was upgraded to a sub-district hospital by 1970. It had facilities for out-patients, an operation theatre for minor surgeries and a well-equipped gynaecology ward. The staff strength was ten doctors, six medical assistants and four nurses. Another health sub-centre was set up in Hanjibuk, less than half a kilometre from Peth Kanihama, in 1991. This centre had one medical assistant and one ANM (auxillary nurse midwifery) with facilities for basic first-aid. Free basic medicines were provided. Respondents said that the staff was regular in attendance and helpful.

Books and the Poplar Tree

While trying to find a link between land reforms and education I came across the story of Ghulam Nabi Dar, son of Ghulam Rasool Dar, now a minor official in the Forest Department. His father was a poor cultivator working for one of the Pandit families, but he was very keen that his son should study. Education was free in the government school in Beerwah where Ghulam Nabi went, walking 4 kilometres every day to and from school. In 1975, when he reached class 9, his father had no money to pay for his books. It seemed unlikely that he would be able to finish high school. But then the unthinkable happened. His father got ownership of the six kanals of land that he had tended for the Kauls, a Pandit family.

On the land was a row of poplar trees. His father borrowed an axe from his neighbour and chopped down one of them. It took him a whole day to accomplish this. He sold the tree for eighty rupees, which helped Ghulam Nabi buy books for classes 9, 10 and 11. Eventually, after finishing class 11, he applied and was selected for a job in the forest department.

Village Study 2: Sehpora, Block S.K Pora, Tehsil Magam, District Budgam

Sehpora is a picturesque little village located 5 kilometres from Peth Kanihama and populated entirely by one sect of Shia Muslims. The village is partly situated on a hillside and partly on the valley floor. The agricultural land is both *aabi* and *khushki* with most households having vegetable patches near their homes. Fifty per cent of the households are dependent on agriculture, 41 per cent are engaged in shawl embroidery, and the remaining 9 per cent run small businesses or work as labourers in the nearby town (based on personal communication with the village teacher).

Only five households have members who are engaged in government service. The main social groups include *gilkar* (masons, carpenters), *rofgar*

TABLE 5.3 *Broad Demographic Profile of Sehpora, Budgam District*

Number of households	149
Total population	1,203 (609 males, 594 females)
Religion	Muslim (Shia)
No. of literates	578 (323 males, 255 females)
No. of illiterates	625 (286 males, 339 females)
Total land area	734.88 kanals
Cropped area	560 kanals
SC/ST population	Nil

Source: 'Constituency-wise Amenity Directory, 2011–12', District Planning and Statistics Officer, Budgam, Government of Jammu and Kashmir, 2013.

Elderly man and disabled woman embroidering shawls: Sehpora, Budgam

(shawl embroiderers), *wovur* (shawl weavers), *chopan* (cattle herders) and *malik* (landowners). The *imambara* forms the heart of the village community and the *imam* (priest) is revered as an authority to whom all social, legal and religious problems are referred. In this respect Sehpora's village community is more inward-looking; hardly any dispute from the village ends up in court. Disputes that cannot be solved in the village are referred to the *aga* (Shia religious leader) in Budgam.

In 1948, there was no *jagirdar* in the village, but a lot of the land adjacent to the village was owned by big landowners (both Muslims and

Pandits). Prominent among these were two Muslim landowners – Haji Jaffer Malik and Haji Jawad Malik, and three Pandit landowners – Pandit Trilokinath Bakshi, Pandit Ved Lal Bakshi and Pandit Jankinath Bakshi. Most of the people worked as kashtkars to these landowners while some worked as labourers in Punjab. No school or health centre existed in the village. Till 1950, there were only two educated people in Sehpora – Haji Hassan Bhat, who had completed a Master's degree from Lahore, and Ghulam Hassan Mir, who had studied till the ninth standard. None of the women were educated. There were frequent outbreaks of smallpox and cholera till the 1940s, especially cholera, which most often came from Punjab, carried by labourers returning to the village to celebrate festivals with their families. According to the villagers, there was a strong sense of social solidarity due to the high degree of interdependence and social interaction. For example, only six households had cows but they gave milk free of cost to all those who came asking for it in the morning – no money or labour or favour was expected in return. The villagers also attributed the lack of social friction to the vertical structure of social control exercised by the Aga family of Budgam who were acknowledged by all as the ultimate spiritual, political and legal authority.

Sehpora: Post-1947 to the Present

In 1975, the *tehsildar, patwari* and some minor officials of the revenue department set up camp in the neighbouring village of Bon Mokhama, Adina. All landowners and cultivators were called there, and their rights to land verified by the *latha* carried by the *patwari*. Seventy cultivators were allotted 170 kanals of land. Ten of them did not take possession of the land redistributed to them in accordance with Aga Yousuf's *fatwa*, as they could not pay compensation to the owners. Thus, despite 400 kanals of land falling in excess of the land ceiling limit, twenty-eight households in the village failed to gain any land. Even among the 60 cultivators that did get 104.19 kanals of land, two paid for it at one time and the others over decades.

At the time of the survey, there were twelve landless families in Sehpora, but all the families owned houses. In 2012, there was one family that did not own a house, but even this household received five marlas of land and financial assistance under the Indira Aawas Yojana (IAY) to build a house.

The respondents said there was no school in Sehpora till 1969. They

TABLE 5.4 *Land Data, Sehpora, Budgam District*

1	Total agricultural land cultivated by the villagers (in 1975)	560 kanals
2	Number of households (in 1975)	88
3	Land resumed by government under land ceiling (under Agrarian Reforms Act 2, 1976)	400 kanals
4	Land redistributed under land reforms post-1948 (under Agrarian Reforms Act 2, 1976)	104.19 kanals

5	Number of beneficiaries	60, out of which
		a. Muslims: 60
		    Pandits: 0
		b. Males: 49
		    Females: 11

6	Number of households that did not take possession of the land allotted	10
7	Number of households that paid for the land allotted to them	2

6	Number of landowners whose land was redistributed	103 out of which
		a. Muslim: 99
		    Pandits: 4
		b. Male: 91
		    Female: 12

Source: Village Land Records Officer (*patwar halqa*, Bon Mokhama), Budgam.

generally agreed that the village was slow to send children to school, starting only in the mid-1970s. There was also social resistance to sending girls to school because of the presence of male teachers and students. There was no adult literacy programme in the village. This was reflected in the literacy figures, with 46.9 per cent of men and 58 per cent of women being illiterate. Of the literate female population, only two were employed in government service. Peth Kanihama fared better in this regard with only 38.12 per cent male illiterates, 50.5 per cent female illiterates and thirty-two women in government service. Though this comparison suggests a positive relationship between the amount of land redistributed on the one hand, and literacy (especially female literacy) and salaried employment

House built with IAY assistance, Sehpora

Household survey in progress, Sehpora

on the other, further research is needed to substantiate this. Significantly, 69 households in the village fell in the BPL category and six in the AAY category, as against 74 in the APL category.

The village had access to two medical sub-centres, one at Mokhama (0.5 kilometre away) and another at Hanjibuk (3.5 kilometres away). Since the Mokhama centre had just one medical assistant, people preferred to go to the one at Hanjibuk. Sehpora is dependent on the Sub-District Hospital in Magam (7 kilometres away) for referrals and maternal health. Respondents interviewed said that good road access meant that they can reach the hospital well in time for emergencies.

Aga Sahab's Fatwa: Compliance and Innovation

After land was redistributed to 70 households under the Agrarian Reforms Act in 1976, Aga Syed Yousuf renewed the stress on his earlier *fatwa*. He said that taking anyone's property without compensation was *haraam* (unlawful) in Islam, and instructed his followers to either return the land allotted to them or to pay the original owners compensation from their own pockets. The amount and method of compensation was left undefined but had to be acceptable to both the original landowner and the allottee.

Only two families in Sehpora could afford to pay the compensation: that of Ghulam Hassan Malik Asadullah and Akbar Malik Talib. They entered into negotiations with the landowners Ved Lal Bakshi, Jankinath Bakshi and Trilokinath Bakshi, and paid them a mutually agreed price for their *khushki* (unirrigated) land. Ten allottees including eight women did not take possession of the land allotted to them; this land stayed with the government which used it to build a school and a water-supply scheme. The remaining 60 allottees hit upon a novel way to keep the land and comply with the stipulations of Aga saheb. They retained land ownership but gave a share of the produce to the original landowners. The amount of produce and duration of payment varied and was decided after negotiation.

Of these, three households continue to send a share of the produce to Pandit landowners in Jammu even now.

NOTES AND REFERENCES

[1] Census of India 2011, Planning Commission, Government of India.

[2] A. Cornwall and I. Scoones, eds, *Revolutionizing Development: Reflections on the Work of Robert Chambers*, London: Earthscan, 2011: 13.

[3] Official Website of Regional Director of Survey and Land Records, Jammu and Kashmir Records, http://rd-slrj.nic.in/, accessed 28 November 2017.

CHAPTER SIX

From Tenants to Leaders

The Human Experience of Land Reforms in Jammu

Introduction

The findings from the village study in Nangali, Poonch, Jammu division form the bulk of this chapter. It also includes the specific conclusions drawn from the village studies.

Historically, Poonch was famous for its strategic position on the Mughal route to Kashmir, for its scenic beauty and for the tales of valour of its people, including their contribution of nearly 60,000 soldiers towards the British war effort in the Second World War.[1]

Before 1947, Poonch was an independent principality within the princely state of Jammu and Kashmir, ruled over by the maharaja's paternal cousins, designated the rajas of Poonch. There were very few *jagirdars* in Poonch till 1947, but religious institutions including temples, gurdwaras and Muslim shrines owned huge estates which were cultivated by tenant farmers.[2] The Shahdara Sharief shrine alone owned nearly 2,500 kanals of agricultural and non-agricultural land. Out of the four *tehsils* that comprised Poonch principality before 1948, only one-and-a-half remain in Poonch now, the rest falling in Pakistan-administered Kashmir. The Nangali village falls in Haveli *tehsil*. This makes Poonch the smallest district in the state in terms of area, which is why the least amount of land has been redistributed here.

Mughal Road, Poonch

Glimpses of Nangali Village

Village Study 3: Nangali, Block Poonch, Tehsil Haveli, District Poonch

Nangali village is situated on the banks of the Drungali *nallah* and is 4 kilometres from the town of Poonch, which is the district headquarters. The village has unirrigated land mostly, and maize and wheat are grown widely, though there is some irrigated land on which rice is grown. The landscape is dominated by the beautiful Nangali Sahib gurdwara, from which the village gets its name.

The gurdwara, originally granted land by Maharaja Ranjit Singh's durbar in Lahore in 1814, owned most of the cultivable land till 1950, with over 60 *kashtkars* (cultivators), both Muslim and Sikh. All these cultivators had to pay half their crop to the gurdwara after the harvest. Mostly maize and some rice were cultivated as most of the land was unirrigated. There were a number of Sikh landowners including Laiq Singh, Kartar Singh, Bhagat Singh, Kalyan Singh and Beedi Singh, who had been granted land by Ranjit Singh as well, but no *jagirdar*. There were also a few independent farmers who were granted land later by the raja of Poonch for services rendered to him, including Sain Jat, Faqir Shah, Nawab and the *numberdar* (village headman) Pooran Singh, who was the raja's chauffeur.[3] Pre-1947, the majority of the villagers worked as labourers in Poonch town or in Rawalpindi for wages as low as 25 paise a day, or as cattle herders carrying butter and ghee in animal hides to sell in the small market town of Aliabad, now in Pakistan.[4]

TABLE 6.1 *Broad Demographic Profile of Nangali, Poonch District*

Number of households	315
Total population	1,565 (818 males, 747 females)
Religion	Islam, Sikhism, Hinduism
No. of literates	962 (552 males, 410 females)
No. of illiterates	603 (266 males, 337 females)
Total land area	2,016 kanals
Cropped area	648 kanals
SC/ST population	SC: 0, ST: 40

Source: 'Constituency-wise Amenity Directory, 2017', District Planning and Statistics Officer, Poonch, Government of Jammu and Kashmir, 2017.

Elders from the Gujjar (ST) community at a focus group discussion, Panchayat Ghar, Nangali village

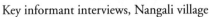

Key informant interviews, Nangali village

Focused group discussions and key informant interviews with elderly members of the village community in Nangali revealed that there was a collusory network of moneylenders in the village before 1947. The brothers Mohan Singh Khatri and Sant Singh Khatri, who lived in Baoli locality on the far side of the river, and the *numberdar* Pooran Singh lent money to the villagers. The repayment terms of the credit were based on both monetary amounts and physical labour, with three days of labour being the regular addition to the monetary interest for a loan of one silver coin. The credit terms were often exploitative, especially for the illiterate majority.

There was a primary school established by the raja 10 kilometres from the village; it had one teacher, Mohammad Akbar. The village had only four literate persons before 1948: Sain Jat, a Muslim, and Kirpal Singh, Beedi Singh and Pooran Singh, all Sikhs. But none of them had studied beyond class 5. The most literate person was Harbans Kaur, a matriculate from Lahore University who married Beedi Singh in the 1940s and became a schoolteacher in 1954.[5] She was also the only literate female in Nangali.

Sixteen Kanals for Fourteen Rupees

During a key informant interview with Baba Abdul, an elderly man from the Gujjar community in Nangali, I came upon an instance that showed the exploitation of village moneylenders in Nangali in detail. In 1945, Abdul's father Mira, and his uncles Kaka, Kalu and Baru, took a loan of fourteen rupees from the *numberdar* Pooran Singh. They had earlier approached the Khatri brothers in Baoli but had been turned down. They needed the money as two of their sisters were getting married in the spring and arrangements needed to be made for relatives coming from outside the village.

The rate of interest for the loan was so high that despite their best efforts they could not repay the sum within the period agreed upon. Pooran Singh took over sixteen kanals of their land in lieu of repayment of the loan. With all their agricultural land gone, they were forced to become landless labourers. This impoverished condition of the family took its toll on the next generation as well. Abdul had to leave the village as a sixteen-year-old to work as a labourer in Rawalpindi in the autumn of 1949.

Smallpox and malaria were rampant in the village and its surrounding areas till the 1950s. According to the villagers, they had approached the raja several times during the outbreaks but apart from organizing *yajnas* (religious ceremonies to propitiate the gods) he did not render any help. Mortality was high and the villagers had to depend on *hakeems* (traditional doctors practising herbal medicine) in Poonch town, carrying the affected on their shoulders if the *hakeem* could not find time to visit the village.

Nangali: Post-1947 to present

According to village inhabitants, in the summer of 1950, a camp was set up on the banks of the river Suran by the *tehsildar* of Haveli with the *patwari* and other revenue officials. The *mahant* (head priest) of the gurdwara provided food and firewood to those encamped. The revenue officials told the villagers that all cultivators would have to present themselves at the camp so that their claims could be verified as per the *latha*. According to land records, the Nangali Sahib gurdwara had the largest estate in the area at the time, nearly 330 kanals of land. Despite hosting the officers of the revenue department, the gurdwara lost 299.10 kanals of land to forty-five cultivators, which probably points to the honesty of the officers in charge.

In 1976, another camp was organized at the local school in Baoli, where another 23.03 kanals of land were taken from ten landowners (including Pooran Singh) and distributed to sixteen cultivators. This might look like an insignificant amount of land but, as mentioned earlier, there is a scarcity of arable land in the village because of its location on the mountainside, and with the gurdwara land already having been redistributed, there were very few large estates that fell in excess of the land-ceiling limit.

In total, 61 beneficiaries received land, of whom thirty-nine were Gujjars, a Scheduled Tribe community. One of these was Pehalwan Shah, who had been a tenant of the gurdwara till 1951. He educated his son Ameer Hussain who passed his matriculation exam in 1973 and is now the *sarpanch* (headman) of the village. The villagers reported that girls started going to school only after the 1950s. At the time of my survey, four schools operated in Nangali, the oldest in Bandi Cheechian having been established in the 1960s. A dispensary was also established in Bandi Cheechian in 1965, and a metalled road connects the village to the District Hospital in Poonch.

TABLE 6.2 *Land Data, Nangali, Poonch District*

1. Total agricultural land cultivated by the villagers (in 1951)	648 kanals
2. Number of households (in 1951)	142
3. Land resumed by government under land ceiling (under the Agrarian Reforms Act, 1976)	25 kanals
4. Land redistributed under land reforms post-1948	322.13 kanals: 299.10 kanals (under the Big Landed Estates Abolition Act 1950); 23.03 kanals (under the Agrarian Reforms Act 1976)

5. Number of beneficiaries	61 out of which
	  a. Muslims: 48, of whom 39 belonged to the Gujjar (ST) community
	    Hindus: 6
	    Sikhs: 7
	  b. Males: 98
	    Females: 2

6. Number of landowners whose land was redistributed	11, out of which
	  a. Muslims: 2
	    Hindus: 1
	    Sikhs: 8 (including the Nangali Sahib gurdwara)
	  b. Males: 10
	    Females: 0
	    Religious Institution: 1

Source: Village Land Records Officer (*patwar halqa*, Mandi), Poonch, from old land record *latha*s (ledgers).

At the time of the survey, 167 households fell in the APL category, 100 households in the BPL category and 48 in the AAY category. This means that 47 per cent of the households in the village live in poverty, which is a matter of concern. Six households have no agricultural land though they all own houses. Another concern is that, out of 603 village inhabitants who are illiterate, 337 are women, which means that every household has at least one illiterate female member.

On the health front, the village has access to a primary health centre (the dispensary mentioned above has been upgraded over the years) at

Bandi Cheechian (3.2 kilometres from Nangali) with one doctor and a support staff of four. The health centre has five beds, one operation theatre and a defunct x-ray machine. The respondents said that except for Pulse Polio[6] and vaccination coverage, they do not depend much on the centre which is usually understaffed. They prefer to go to the Poonch District Hospital, six kilometres away, for maternal health care and other major health issues. The good condition of the road makes the trip easy for those who live near the village bazaar. Those who live in scattered houses on the adjacent hills travel by foot carrying the more serious patients to the village bazaar, from where they hire a taxi to Poonch.

Comparative Analysis

Data from the three village studies in Peth Kanihama, Sehpora and Nangali (from Chapter Five and the present chapter) are analysed together in what follows. These village studies and first-person interviews have enabled me to record the collective experiences of those directly affected by state development policies from 1948 to 1988. To gain a nuanced understanding of the social experience of development in the villages of Jammu and Kashmir, the data from all three case studies need to be looked at comparatively. This will help in making linkages (if any) between key indicators such as land redistribution, poverty, indebtedness and literacy.

The most land was redistributed in Peth Kanihama and the least in Sehpora. The average size of landholding per household is the largest in Peth Kanihama (2.77 kanals per household) and the smallest in Nangali (0.19 kanal per household). This is because of the scarcity of cultivable land in Nangali – only 648 kanals out of 2,016 kanals in Nangali constitute arable land, the rest being rocky and unsuitable for cultivation.[7] In Nangali and Peth Kanihama, no individual or institution owns more than 35 kanals of land; the same is not true in Sehpora where the Malik family and its extended clan still dominate land ownership, the largest holding being 48 kanals.

The incidence of poverty decreases with an increase in the amount of land redistributed. The largest amount of land redistributed was in Peth Kanihama, which has the lowest percentage of BPL+AAY households (14.86 per cent). Nangali comes after Peth Kanihama in terms of land redistributed and in poverty estimates as well, with 47 per cent of its

TABLE 6.3 *Comparative Data of Key Indicators in the Three Study Villages*

Name of village	Total land redistributed (kanals)	Total cultivated land redistributed (per cent)	Average land-holding size (kanals)	BPL+AAY households (per cent)	Average household income (Rs/per month)	Average household expenditure (Rs/per month)	Indebted households (per cent)
Peth Kanihama	394.00	68.9	2.77	14.86	15, 982	13, 027	0.45
Nangali	322.13	49.7	0.19	47.00	8, 321	7, 619	1.00
Sehpora	104.19	18.6	1.65	50.3	6, 392	5, 176	11.00

Source: Sehar Iqbal, 'Social Impact of State Development Policy in Jammu and Kashmir: 1948 to 1988, unpublished PhD thesis, University of Kashmir, Jammu and Kashmir, 2018.

households living below the poverty line. Sehpora, where the least amount of land was redistributed, has the highest proportion of poor households (50.3 per cent). This relationship between land redistribution and the percentage of poor households remains consistent when applied to indebtedness as well. Again, only 0.45 per cent of Peth Kanihama's households is indebted, as against 1 per cent in Nangali and 11 per cent in Sehpora. The percentage of indebted households in Sehpora could be high also because 41 per cent of them work as shawl embroiderers. Typically, embroiderers take loans from middlemen while completing their allotted work (i.e. shawl embroidery) to cover their household expenditure in the meantime.

The amount of land redistributed also correlates positively to both household income and household expenditure, with Peth Kanihama leading both categories at Rs 15,982 per household per month and Rs 13,027 per household per month, respectively. Nangali follows with an average household income of Rs 8,321 per month and average household expenditure of Rs 7,619 per month. Sehpora shows an average monthly income of Rs 6, 392 and an average monthly expenditure of Rs 5,176 per household.

According to Census 2011 data, Nangali leads the three villages in literacy rates with 61.4 per cent of its population being literate. Peth Kanihama follows with 55.69 per cent and then Sehpora with 48.04 per cent. In terms of female literacy rates, Peth Kanihama leads with 49.45 per cent of its women literate, followed by Nangali with 45 per cent and

TABLE 6.4 *Comparative Literacy Data for the Three Study Villages*

Name of village	No. of literates*	Literacy rate*	Female literacy rate*	Percentage of children (aged 6–14 years) currently in school**	Percentage of girls (aged 6–14 years) currently in school**
Peth Kanihama	394.00	55.69	49.45	98.27	96.2
Nangali	322.13	61.04	45.00	98.00	89.0
Sehpora	104.19	48.04	42.9	90.33	87.5

Source: * Census of India 2011.

　　** Sarva Shiksha Abhiyan figures, 2013–14: for Budgam, http://www.ceobudgam. in/SSA.aspx, accessed 13 October 2020; for Poonch, from the office of the Chief Education Officer, Poonch.

Sehpora with 42.9 per cent. Sarva Shiksha Abhiyan figures on school attendance show that Peth Kanihama has the highest percentage of children of schooling age attending school (98.27 per cent), followed by Nangali (98 per cent) and Sehpora (90.33 per cent). This means that literacy is positively correlated to income and the amount of land redistributed – Peth Kahinama has the maximum amount of land redistributed, followed by Nangali and Sehpora in that order (Table 6.3). This relationship also holds for the correlation of land redistributed to school attendance in the case of girls, with over 96 per cent of girls of school-going age attending school in Peth Kanihama, 89 per cent in Nangali and 87.5 per cent in Sehpora, though factors like community attitudes towards education (particularly girls' education), distance from school and distance from water sources also play a role in school enrolment and attendance. For instance, girls have to walk nearly 2 kilometres (to and fro) every day to collect water from a spring in Nangali village. This makes them more likely to miss school than their counterparts in Peth Kanihama who have access to piped water in their homes. Attitudes towards girls' education are also more conservative in Nangali and Sehpora than in Peth Kanihama, and this is reflected in the literacy and school attendance figures.

Conclusion

The objective of the three village studies was to understand the effect of state development policy on village communities, and to find out how the experiences of village communities differed across regions. The collected data looked at land redistribution within villages in great detail, taking into account the intersectionality of religious belief and land reforms. The study of Peth Kanihama and Sehpora particularly showed how religious leaders influenced their followers to give up or pay for the land that the government was giving them free of cost. In Peth Kanihama, Sunni peasants came up with the concept of *bakshaish* to accommodate religious concerns and still get the land. This gives an interesting insight into the process of land reforms and how it was shaped uniquely by the village communities it interacted with as well as the government.

Overall, land redistribution had a positive effect on income, expenditure, literacy and school enrolment, and a negative effect on rural poverty and indebtedness. This explains why, despite the conflict generally taking a heavy toll on the public infrastructure and the economy of Jammu and Kashmir, poverty – especially rural poverty – has remained consistently low in the state as compared to other Indian states.

The common perception that land redistribution in Jammu and Kashmir was marred by the corruption of implementing officials of the land revenue department was also disproved in the case of the three study villages through first-person interviews with elderly agriculturists who themselves had been part of the process of redistribution. Not only did the revenue officials distribute land to all cultivators, they showed no favour to landowners even if they stayed with them and ate their food – the Nangali gurdwara being a case in point. In Peth Kanihama, some minor officials asked for bribes, but strict action by higher officials prevented any serious wrongdoing. The fact that, overall, land was redistributed fairly, is borne out by the low levels of landlessness.

From key informant interviews, it became clear that in the pre-1948 period, the village communities were indebted to a large degree and exploited by powerful moneylenders, especially in Nangali. This had largely disappeared post-1948, because of state legislation on indebtedness and easier access to institutional credit. Even in Sehpora, which had the highest proportion of indebted households (11 per cent, see Table 6.1), no debt was over Rs 1 lakh, which indicates the low level of rural indebtedness.

Land fragmentation, commonly perceived as an evil after-effect of agrarian reforms, was highest in Nangali and lowest in Peth Kanihama, demonstrating that the pressure of population on limited agricultural land also has a role to play, not just the amount of land redistributed *per se*; otherwise the figures would have been the other way round.

Inhabitants of all three villages have access to health facilities within or close to their village, and to sub-district hospitals nearby. But the health sub-centres near Peth Kanihama and Sehpora were cleaner and better staffed. Shorter road distances in the valley mean that villagers from Beerwah can access specialty and super-speciality referrals in Srinagar much quicker (a two-hour journey by car) than their counterparts in Poonch (an eight-hour journey by car to Jammu). Among those interviewed, vaccination was almost universal. Out-of-pocket expenditure on health formed an important component of overall household expenditure, with the highest expenditure on medicines at 18 per cent of household income being recorded in Sehpora, and the lowest expenditure at 10 per cent of household income in Peth Kanihama. This shows that the villagers view their health as important and they do have access to medicines.

On the whole, the data show that state development policy during the four decades from 1948 to 1988 has had a positive impact on the lives of village communities. The most beneficial outcomes are land redistribution, debt conciliation and extension of health coverage.

Notes and References

[1] For a comprehensive history of Poonch, see K.D. Maini, *Poonch: The Battlefield of Kashmir*, Srinagar: Gulshan Publishers, 2012.

[2] Author's interview with K.D. Maini on 22 May 2017.

[3] Key informant interview with Baba Abdul, aged 84, s/o Mira in Nangali, on 24 July 2017.

[4] Ibid.

[5] Key informant interview with Raj Kaur, w/o Ghar Singh, on 24 July 2017.

[6] A nationwide immunization campaign by the government to eliminate polio in India by vaccinating all children under the age of five.

[7] According to official figures from the records in the *latha*s (ledgers) of the land revenue office, Nangali.

CHAPTER SEVEN

The Greater Relevance

The Development Experience of Jammu and Kashmir

Introduction

In 1948, Jammu and Kashmir was considered one of the most backward princely states with one of the lowest per capita incomes, literacy rates and life expectancy in India. As we have seen in the previous chapters, by 1988, the state's progress with regard to human development index (HDI) indicators like per capita income, literacy, reduction in death rate, etc., was remarkable, and in areas like reduction of poverty (especially rural poverty), life expectancy and access to health care, better than the national average. Further, the progress in HDI indicators was largely similar across social groups. The major drawbacks were the slow growth of elementary education and the low participation of women in education and employment between 1948 and 1988.

According to Pranab Bardhan, the capitalist class, rich farmers and bureaucrats play a major role in influencing public policy in India, and the process of development is heavily coloured by their class interests.[1] In Jammu and Kashmir post-1948, there developed unique circumstances that enabled government policy to break out of this restrictive model. The resultant policy, process and public experience of development in the state were unique. I argue that this was a direct result of certain fatures unique to Jammu and Kashmir. These are discussed in the following sections.

The Constitution and 'Naya Kashmir'

The fact that Jammu and Kashmir had its own Constitution was the main reason why radical policy measures of the state government could not be challenged legally by the Supreme Court of India or legislation relating to these be nullified by deficiencies in central legislation. The unique character of the state's Constitution, evolved from the underlying principles of 'Naya Kashmir', ensured a legislative commitment to ending exploitation and a firm grounding of the principles of equity (embodied in a policy preoccupation with redistribution) and equality (demonstrated in the legislative and policy provisions). This essentially *human-centred* conception of development enshrined in 'Naya Kashmir' was, in many ways, a precursor to the concept of human development in economics. This constitutional foundation ensured that redistribution asserted itself periodically as a key goal of government policy from 1948 till the 1980s, and could not be challenged legally either within or outside the state.

Committed Political Leadership

P.R. Dubhashi attributes the ineffectiveness of land reforms to a lack of 'will to implement the policy' where 'political power was closely tied to agrarian power structure'.[2] Sheikh Abdullah went ahead with implementing the Big Landed Estates Abolition Act, 1950 knowing full well that it was a big political risk. This shows his level of commitment to 'Naya Kashmir' as well as the unqualified support for this from his party. It also reflects Abdullah's belief that the redistributive measures envisaged in 'Naya Kashmir' would guarantee more public support for the National Conference in a future election.

Not just Abdullah but even other politicians like Mir Qasim (earlier in the National Conference who then joined the Congress party), who was the chief minister of the state from 1971 to 1975, were of the belief that land reforms were the key to popular support. Qasim promulgated the Agrarian Reforms Act 1, 1972 to make up for the deficiencies of the first agrarian reforms legislation, but this was repealed and replaced by the Agrarian Reforms Act 2 in 1976 by Sheikh Abdullah who had by then returned to power after a long period of incarceration. The Act imposed a stricter land ceiling and redistributed more land from big landowners to tillers. But neither Abdullah nor Qasim could have pushed through legislation to achieve these aims if not for the provisions of Article 370 of the Indian Constitution that gave protected status to Jammu and Kashmir.

Abrogation of Articles 370 and 35A

With the recent abrogation of Article 370 that gave Jammu and Kashmir protected status, the debate around its impact has intensified and it is being argued that it was a hurdle in the development of the entire region. This is patently wrong, for it was the precisely *the legislative freedom* granted by Article 370 that *allowed* the leadership in the state to experiment with radical legislations like the Big Landed Estates Abolition Act, the Distressed Debtors' Relief Act and the Agrarian Reforms Acts while similar legislation for asset redistribution was successfully rendered toothless by landlord and moneylender lobbies in the rest of India.

According to A.G. Noorani, 'The state of Jammu and Kashmir is the *only* state in the Union of India that *negotiated* the terms of its membership with the Union. The Constituent Assembly merely put the imprimatur of its approval, on 17 October 1949, to a draft agreed between the Union and the State' (emphasis added).[3] Article 306-A (later to become Article 370) of the Indian Constitution was envisaged by the political leadership in Jammu and Kashmir as a measure to protect the legal autonomy of the state and grant freedom of agency to the state government. Both these had been important constituents of the discussions between Nehru and Sheikh Abdullah immediately before and after the Accession. Abdullah's popularity meant that he was crucial to the public's acceptance of the validity of the Accession to India within the state and as an advocate of the same internationally. Abdullah, for his part, wanted a free hand in implementing 'Naya Kashmir' without interference from New Delhi.

Article 370 gave the state of Jammu and Kashmir a unique legal standing within the Union of India by guaranteeing that:

1. It would have its own Constitution;
2. The Central government could legislate directly on only the three categories of subjects within its competence namely defence, communications and foreign affairs. Even this was to be 'in consultation with the Government of Jammu and Kashmir state'. Any other legislation on the union list was not

applicable to the state of Jammu and Kashmir until it was ratified by the State Assembly.[4]

Through these provisions, Nehru secured Abdullah's support and was able to get him to speak at the United Nations in support of India and the Accession. Abdullah made sure that there could be no legal hurdle in implementing legislation to achieve his party's economic and social goals. Thus, Article 370 ensured complete legal authority to the state government for carrying out its radical reforms. Such freedom was not available to any other state government in India. Interestingly, Abdullah opposed the adoption of the Directive Principles of the Constitution of India into the Constitution of Jammu and Kashmir. Instead the Directive Principles of the Constitution of Jammu and Kashmir were based verbatim on the aims of 'Naya Kashmir'. This in turn ensured that redistribution became a key policy aim for the state government.

The state already had its own penal code constituted by Maharaja Ranbir Singh in the 1800s, known as the Ranbir Penal Code. It later came to have its own civil procedure code, thus cementing a unique legal identity within the Union of India. This identity helped in shaping the development process.

Article 35A of the Indian Constitution enabled the state legislature of Jammu and Kashmir to define its permanent residents, as well as provide rights and privileges of citizenship for these residents. As former finance minister Haseeb Drabu points out,

> Contrary to hampering J&K's development, Article 35A enabled the transformation of the economic structure . . . [of the state]. What prevented the J&K Big Landed Estates Abolition Act 1950 from being annulled on the grounds of infringing the fundamental right to property under Article 19(1), was Article 35A(B). It is because of those land reforms that our poverty ratio is 10%, which is less than half of the all-India level, our income inequality coefficient of 0.221 is the lowest in India; our indebtedness at 12.67, is nearly one-third of the national average. There is a near absence of landless labour; less than 2% of our work-force.[5]

Drabu further says that the lack of foreign investment in Jammu and Kashmir is because of 'the UN-sanctified "disputed status" . . . and not because of special status accorded by Article 35A'.[6]

Absence of Schismatic Social Divisions

Constitutional provisions could not in themselves have led to the implementation of revolutionary government policies like land redistribution, writing off private debts on a mass scale and affirmative action for women in professional education if they had met with strong social resistance. Jammu and Kashmir historically has displayed a great degree of harmony in social relations in spite of hierarchies and divisions within communities, particularly in the valley where there is an absence of a caste system.

The fact that feudal beneficiaries like the Jammu Chamber of Commerce or the Hindu Maha Sabha failed to gather popular support for blocking debt conciliation and land reforms shows that despite differences in religion, region and caste, there was overall social harmony amongst social groups in the state from 1948 to 1988. The sense of commonality can be gauged from many incidents, with the same pattern repeating itself before and after 1948.

In 1946, Sheikh Abdullah enjoyed a high degree of state-wide public support, so much so that even his biggest political rival in Kashmir, Ghulam Abbas of the pro-Pakistan party, Muslim Conference, appealed to the maharaja to release him and his colleagues from prison.[7] Similarly, common opposition to the oppressive character of monarchical rule prompted support for the National Conference's agenda even from privileged social groups like the Kashmiri Pandits, the Dogras of Jammu and some landlords. This can be demonstrated by the key roles played in the National Conference's anti-monarchical movement by Girdharilal Dogra, Sat Pal Sawhney, Pandit Jia Lal Kilam, and landlords such as Ghulam Mohammed Mir of Salar and Malik Ghulam Qadir of Nowgam, Verinag. Malik Ghulam Qadir was imprisoned by the maharaja for his role in the freedom struggle but he refused to abandon his political affiliation. This shows that his commitment to the anti-feudal cause was not incremental. The lack of effective opposition to agrarian reforms post-1950 is also telling. Not only did the *jagirdar*s in Jammu and Kashmir fail to unite against the land reforms, but those landlords who were part of the Land to the Tiller Committee formed by the National Conference's interim government backed its resolution of not providing compensation to landowners for the land that was redistributed.

This is not to say that all Kashmiri Muslims, Dogras, Pandits, Ladakhis and other ethnic groups in the state extended full support to the National Conference's agenda, but simply to point out that there was a critical mass of support across these groups that enabled the enactment and implementation of redistributive legislation. This was further facilitated by a remarkable lack of effective opposition.

Traditional Structures of Mutual Aid and Interdependence in Local Communities

In all three regions of the state of Jammu and Kashmir – Jammu, Kashmir and Ladakh – there existed a strong tradition of mutual aid, with communities in villages and cities coming together to help each other in times of need. This could have been because of the inaccessibility of the state especially during the winter months and the resultant scarcity of labour that combined to strengthen interdependence among local communities. For example, in the Kashmir valley, villagers came together in spring to clean the *zamindari khuls* (channels of the local, gravity-based irrigation system), removing clay, weeds, stones and other obstructions so that water for the summer rice crop could flow uninterrupted. Similarly, those who owned cattle distributed milk free of cost to anyone from the village who asked for it every morning. To refuse was considered a sin. The transplantation and harvest of rice was an all-village affair, with men and women working together in the fields and special food prepared in common for them. Harvest songs and a festive atmosphere further helped to bind the village together. The rural and urban communities came together in a similar way at the time of marriages, with neighbours taking up a part of the responsibilities in the arrangements as well as providing financial assistance to the parents of the bride or groom on the wedding day. The same community mechanisms provided aid to families at the time of funerals as well, with neighbours taking turns to bring cooked food to the bereaved family and helping with the burial and funeral prayer arrangements.

Tareak Rather, an eminent Kashmiri sociologist, observes that mutual aid of this kind is a 'display of social coherence of the highest order, typical of traditional mountain societies where people have similar daily tasks and strong roots in culture'.[8] G.M. Wani calls it 'a strong sense of internal solidarity and external exclusiveness . . . [with its own] norms of social behaviour'.[9] Pirzada Amin emphasizes the role of religion in strengthening this social solidarity, particularly through the syncretic influence of shrines in Kashmir, arguing that public worship at these shrines brought together people of different faiths.[10] What lends further credence to this view is the function of shrines and mosques as institutions providing not just spiritual unity but actual aid to the marginalized across communities. Shrines in the Kashmir valley like Baba Reshi have acted as social centres where wayfarers, the poor and the abandoned received food and shelter, according to the basic tenets of Sufism.[11] In some cases the shrine itself had public kitchens (langars) where free food was distributed, as in Baba Reshi near Tangmarg. In others, devotees brought rice and other food items for the poor or mentally ill who congregated outside the shrines.

From the 1990s onwards, when mosques asserted themselves as the new focal points of the Muslim community, the bait ul maal system that was commonplace in many Muslim countries came into vogue in the Kashmir valley. A bait ul maal (lit. 'house of money') is a public treasury (in this case based in the local mosque) to which members of the community make monetary contributions according to their means. From these funds, it provides grants to the poor, the ill, and widows and orphans within the local Muslim community. This system formalized more abstract norms of social solidarity or mutual aid into a continuously functioning, local social security system in the Kashmir valley

The Jammu region also demonstrated informal systems of solidarity and mutual aid during marriages and funerals, with one member from each household in the village helping out in the house where the wedding or funeral took place. Harvest time would see the same system in practice for cutting and storing crops. Interestingly, this practice extended also to Scheduled Caste households, where members of the upper castes would go to help out (but not eat anything).[12] Similarly, in Ladakh,

> [community] cooperation is formalized in various ways: shared agricultural work, such as neighbours combining to harvest each of their crops in turn, has a special name (bes), as does the practice of collectively taking animals to the phu (pasture). The distribution of water is determined by a time honoured system overseen by people on a rotational basis.

In addition, there is the paspun, small groupings of families, sometimes from different villages, that provide mutual support, especially at times of stress, such as illness and death.[13]

Such interdependence and cooperation is not found in most of north India (states like Haryana, Rajasthan, etc.), where the caste system makes intermingling and, by extension, common action almost impossible, and mobility of labour leaves little scope for interdependence. In Jammu and Kashmir, mutual support and interdependence resulted in a lack of societal confrontation even when state development policy went against class interests. The lack of violence between landowners and tillers in the wake of agrarian reforms is a clear example of this. Most other experiments with land reforms in Asia were doomed to failure as violence escalated during their implementation; for instance, Gunnar Myrdal's *Asian Drama: An Enquiry into the Poverty of Nations*[14] showcases just how divisive and violent land reforms were in Vietnam, during the same period. In India, Uttar Pradesh, Punjab and other states saw entrenched social divisions and the threat of violence by upper-caste landowners defeat land reform proposals after Independence in 1947.

Sudden Collapse of the Apex of the Feudal State

The sudden collapse of the top strata of the feudal structure offered a rare historical opportunity to implement radical reforms in the state of Jammu and Kashmir. The migration of the maharaja left the feudal system disunited and weakened the resistance to radical redistribution in the form of land reform and debt eradication. The establishment of the emergency administration in the backdrop of the first Indo–Pak war of 1947 gave sweeping powers of legislation and action to the National Conference that had no parallel with that in any other Indian state. Till the first elections held in 1952, Sheikh Abdullah's administration was not constrained by electoral concerns which could have meant being beholden to powerful feudal functionaries who might have lent electoral support in hard-to-win areas.[15] This left the government free to implement radical reforms and garner mass support for the coming election, in contrast to other states where 'the composition of state legislatures, the existence of a strong rich farmers' lobby and the strategic position the rich agriculturists occupied both in political as well as economic life of the rural sector, made the implementation of radical land reforms very difficult'.[16]

In this way, ideological commitment, constitutional independence, social synergy and historical opportunity worked together to create a unique developmental context and process in Jammu and Kashmir.

The Greater Relevance of Jammu and Kashmir's Developmental Journey

The data generated during this study at state and village levels demonstrate that the social impact of the state's policies and programmes was largely positive, sometimes even transformative, for those crushed under the burden of poverty, debt and disease. Though there were imperfections in the implementation of policy over time because of the old administrative machinery, the data at both macro and micro levels bear out the real improvement to the lives of the people of Jammu and Kashmir. But the concentration of power in the interim administration and the person of Sheikh Abdullah proved detrimental to the foundation of democracy in the state. The National Conference's interim government used its unfettered powers for arbitrary arrests and suppression of dissent, particularly in the Kashmir valley. This was repeated by successive regimes till 1988 as elections were systematically rigged, barring that of 1977, which is widely held to be the only free and fair election between 1948 and 1988. The space for a genuine and thriving democracy was shrunk considerably, culminating in the openly rigged election of 1987 that triggered the armed insurgency – as some of the defeated candidates left for Pakistan and gave calls to their supporters and youth in general for armed struggle. Political expediency thus uprooted genuine democracy. The highly centralized, linear policy framework created by the interim government, and continued by later governments, worked in a top–down manner and, over time, squeezed out the potential for growth of a genuine grassroots democracy in the state. Looking at these processes, it is easy to see that whereas the state provided economic empowerment to the people, it failed to protect them from political disempowerment over generations, or, at worst, colluded with the central government in a systematic denial of the citizens' political rights. Political disempowerment despite economic empowerment by the state government from 1948 to 1988 led directly to the eruption of armed insurgency.

Negative effects on the environment, particularly deforestation, shrinkage of water bodies, reduction in biodiversity and recurrence of man-made disasters, also resulted from the linear model of development. However, the full exploration of that aspect is beyond the scope of this study.

HDI gains in poverty reduction, income inequality per capita income, maternal and child health, life expectancy and household assets continued even after the start of the conflict and continue till the present time. The conflict did take a toll on some indicators, especially literacy rates, as schools were burnt down by militants or occupied by security forces. However, enrolment rates have picked up in recent years and are in line with national averages. The changes in HDI indicators post-1988 and the reasons for these comprise an important research area for the future.

Perhaps the most important lesson from Jammu and Kashmir is the continuous positive effect of land reforms on poverty reduction and access to food. By all accounts, the record of the princely state of Kashmir on both these counts was dismal, but radical, timely and decisive legislations implemented from the 1950s to the end of the 1970s gave landless labourers and tenant farmers means of subsistence and access to cash incomes. This is the single largest factor responsible for the low poverty figures and better access to nutrition in the state.

According to the Agricultural Census of 2011–12 and the 2011 Socio-Economic Caste Census, 41.7 per cent of India's people still depend on agriculture. The same sources state that 4.9 per cent of rich (typically upper-caste) farmers own more than 32 per cent of all agricultural land, and that 56.4 per cent of the country's rural households do not own any agricultural land. Rural poverty has been difficult to weed out in this scenario and India has fallen to the 100th place among 119 countries in the Global Hunger Index as of 2017. These stark facts are largely due to the failure of the central and state governments to act decisively on land reforms, and they could well take a leaf out of Jammu and Kashmir's book in this regard to alleviate the people's suffering.

As three-fourths of South Asia's population lives in India, the lessons learnt from Jammu and Kashmir could be of great importance in the larger South Asian context. Out of these, the endurance of HDI indicators over time based on real asset redistribution and eradication of debts is especially important. As South Asian nations try to find more locally sensitive and long-lasting solutions to the problems of poverty and inequality, studying the development experience of the state can be very useful. The flip-side of the systematic obstructions of democracy in the state from 1948 to 1988 is also worthy of study in a world where democracy and development are often portrayed as substitutes and not complements. The denial of political rights and its relation with civil unrest and violence is of equally great relevance in the contemporary world. Whichever way one looks at it, the development experience of Jammu and Kashmir has valuable lessons for India in particular and the world at large.

NOTES AND REFERENCES

[1] For more details, see Pranab Bardhan, *The Political Economy of Development in India*, Delhi: Oxford University Press, 1984.

[2] P.R. Dubhashi, 'Land Reforms: Intention, Implementation and Impact', *Kurukshetra*, vol. 35, no. 1, October 1986: 14.

[3] A.G. Noorani, *Article 370: A Constitutional History of Jammu and Kashmir*, Delhi: Oxford University Press, 2011: 3.

[4] Shiva Rao, *The Framing of Indian Constitution: Selected Documents*, vol. 4, New Delhi: IIPA, 1968: 556.

[5] 'Article 35A Enabled the Transformation of the Economic Structure', Dr Haseeb A. Drabu's interview in *Kashmir Life*, available at https://kashmirlife. net/article-35a-enabled-the-transformation-of-the-economic-structure-issue-02-vol-11-206987/, accessed 14 August 2019.

[6] Ibid.

[7] M. Brecher, *The Struggle for Kashmir*, Toronto: Ryerson Press, 1953: 18.

[8] Interview with Professor Tareak A. Rather, Department of Central Asian Studies, University of Kashmir, on 16 November 2017.

[9] G.M. Wani, 'Political Assertion of Kashmiri Identity', in N.A. Khan, ed., *The Parchment of Kashmir: History, Society, and Polity*, New York: Palgrave Macmillan, 2012: 137.

[10] Pirzada M. Amin, 'Hazratbal: A Crescent of Faith', in K. Warikoo, ed., *Cultural Heritage of Jammu and Kashmir*, New Delhi: Pentagon Press, 2009: 168.

[11] For the origin of public feeding at shrines, see M.I. Khan, *Kashmir's Transition to Islam: The Role of Muslim Rishis*, New Delhi: Manohar Publishers, 1994.

[12] Interview with Shri Sohan Singh, resident of village Chamba, Katra, on 12 October 2017.

[13] N. Wilson, 'Cold, High and Dry: Traditional Agriculture in Ladakh',

Permaculture News, 6 February 2009, available at https://permaculturenews. org/2009/02/06/cold-high-and-dry-traditionalagriculture-in-ladakh/, accessed 18 October 2017.

[14] G. Myrdal, *Asian Drama: An Enquiry into The Poverty of Nations*, London: Allen Lane, The Penguin Press, 1968.

[15] As has happened in many other states like Rajasthan, Bihar and Madhya Pradesh where the structure of feudalism remained intact.

[16] M. Dandavate, 'Land Reforms in Free India', *Mainstream,* vol. 11, nos. 1 and 2, 1972–73: 33.

CHAPTER EIGHT

Insult and Injury

Development in and as a Union Territory

Introduction

On 5 August 2019, the home minister of India, Amit Shah, read out a draft of the Jammu and Kashmir Reorganization Bill in the Lok Sabha, the lower house of the Indian Parliament. The introduction of the controversial Bill followed a presidential order under Article 370 of the Indian Constitution, which replaced a presidential order from 1954 which specified that only some provisions of the Constitution of India would apply to the state of Jammu and Kashmir (according to the stipulations of the Instrument of Accession). This presidential order thus revoked the special status the state had. The 1954 order had legally established that Article 3 of the Indian Constitution, which allows the Union to make alterations to the area, boundaries and names of Indian states, would not apply to Jammu and Kashmir. Its substitution made possible the introduction of the Reorganization Bill. The new presidential order made all provisions of the Constitution of India applicable to Jammu and Kashmir, including Article 3. The process of changing Jammu and Kashmir's constitutional status without the approval of its state assembly has been questioned by legal experts in India and abroad. But it is the narrative that the Indian government pushed across the world to explain the need for its drastic act that is more germane.

It has been reported that Amit Shah's hand shook slightly while reading out that the state of Jammu and Kashmir was to be partitioned into two Union territories. For all his outward calm, he must have been acutely aware that this move was unprecedented in the constitutional history of India – also of how deeply unpopular the move would be in Kashmir valley, the epicentre of an armed insurgency against India since 1988. The Indian home minister had sent extra forces of 35,000 to supplement the already present 3,08,000 armed forces personnel in Jammu and Kashmir, to contain the street protests that have become one of the regular ways of expressing dissatisfaction and anger against both the state and central governments. The Indian government made sure no one in the Kashmir valley could come out of their homes and be counted. Groups of heavily armed soldiers placed barbed wire across exit points of neighbourhoods; internet services were snapped; and restrictions were imposed on movement by invoking Section 144.[1] The silencing of Kashmiris was complete. This gave the government a free hand to create a narrative nationally and globally to explain why it needed to introduce the controversial Bill.

This narrative centred around the fabricated claim that Jammu and Kashmir is racked with underdevelopment because of its special legal status within the Union of India. The Indian home minister declared that Article 370[2] had 'ruined Jammu and Kashmir, stalled its development, prevented proper healthcare and education and blocked industries'.[3] All the statistics and data quoted thus far in this book refute these claims. We have seen in the earlier chapters that Jammu and Kashmir does far better than India's national average figures in terms of the percentage of its population living in poverty, and that it has a remarkably low *rural poverty rate* at a time when poverty is driving thousands of Indian farmers to suicide year after year. It also has better life expectancy than the national average, better nutrition levels for women and children of all ages, and far fewer hungry and homeless people. Jammu and Kashmir has also caught up with the national average on literacy rates.

All these milestones in human development have been achieved despite the devastating armed conflict and brutal repression by the state and government machinery. When one looks at the rocky start Jammu and Kashmir had in 1947, with a raging war, abysmally low literacy rates and a shockingly low life expectancy, these development achievements need to be lauded and appreciated all the more.[4]

This book has attempted, through a comprehensive study of facts and statistics, to debunk the myth that 'underdevelopment' has been the root of conflict in Jammu and Kashmir. Now, it would be worthwhile to look at how this myth of underdevelopment is being spread so systematically to justify the political disempowerment of the disputed state.

Binary Constructs and Othering: Liberal and Conservative Approaches to Kashmir

In an interview published in the *Los Angeles Review of Books* in 2018, the Indian historian Pankaj Mishra elaborated his theory of 'emancipatory imperialism' in the modern Indian context.[5] He described it as liberal India's historical approach to the Kashmir problem which is essentially seen as a 'civilizing mission'. He explained that by looking at Kashmir through the lens of emancipatory imperialism, an Indian 'civilizer' feels that it is his duty to 'show Kashmir's overwhelmingly religious Muslims the light of secular reason – by force, if necessary'.[6] He identified this as the same kind of public narrative that 'the liberal internationalists who helped adorn the Bush administration's pre-emptive assault on Iraq with the kind of humanitarian rhetoric about freedom, democracy, and progress that we originally heard from European imperialists in the 19th century'.[7]

This construct aptly describes the approach of successive Indian governments headed by liberals (mainly the Congress and other centrist and left parties) to the Kashmir problem from 1947 to 2014: a persistent fear of the Kashmiri Muslim political identity; the systematic disabling of free political choice (through rigged elections) and the use of force to quell dissent. Though some of the governments that instituted these measures were headed by conservatives, the Indian right wing (led by the Bharatiya Janata Party [BJP]) did not have an absolute electoral majority till 2014, when they got the full opportunity to pursue their own Kashmir agenda.

It is important to understand that the ideology of Indian conservatives vis-à-vis Kashmir is different from that of Indian liberals, even if they use versions of the same policy measures. The territory of Jammu and Kashmir is to them central to India's sovereignty and national identity. This approach sees Kashmir primarily as an unruly frontier state that needs to be forced into capitulation through armed force and targeted legislation. The ruling Bharatiya Janata Party's concept of Hindu nationalism employs a different version of the same binary construct that Mishra describes – that of Indian Hindus as civilized and Kashmiri Muslims as the dangerous, uncivilized 'other' in need of being controlled. This reductionist binary has been the basis of various strong-arm policies pursued by the Indian government ever since it withdrew support from the elected coalition government it was a part of, in June last year. The stripping away of the special constitutional provisions that gave the state a measure of legal autonomy and economic protection was the biggest step in advancing the conservative agenda in Kashmir. But it needed to be rationalized to public opinion in India and the world – which saw this as a stifling of dissent in the world's largest democracy. Hence the picture that is painted of Jammu and Kashmir as a sick, underdeveloped state thrown into chaos because of Article 370.

Wrong on Every Count: The False Narrative of Underdevelopment Deconstructed

In his speech to the Parliament on 5 August 2019, the home minister declared that the special legal autonomy Jammu and Kashmir had enjoyed was the reason it was 'underdeveloped'; that is why it needed to be removed. He referred to all mainstream political leaders in the state as corrupt and self-centred, accusing them of lining their pockets with overgenerous development grants from the centre, something they were only able to do because of Article 370: 'Only 3 families[8] benefited from Article 370, the rest of the people suffered.'[9] That corruption among politicians is rife in India is no secret; with a score of 41 out of 100 (100 being the best score in terms of controlling corruption and 0 implying the country has no control over corruption), India's position is 80 in the list of corrupt countries according to the global Corruption Perceptions Index.[10] And it has slipped two places in the list since the BJP came to power in 2014, a fall that international experts attribute directly to an increase in opaque political financing and corporate lobbying over government. So the home minister's idea that a disabling of the legislative apparatus in the state (by reducing it to a Union Territory that cannot hold elections) and an increase in investment in the state by Indian corporates would help to end corruption is unrealistic, to say the least.

In his speech, Amit Shah kept repeating that Jammu and Kashmir was plagued by poverty because of Article 370: 'Kya mila 370 se, kya mila?

Gareebi ke ilava kucch nahi mila!' (What did you get from Article 370 – nothing but poverty!). He offered no figures, however, to back his claim, when even a casual reading of the macro-statistics would have told him that Jammu and Kashmir has one of the lowest poverty rates in India.

> In J&K, the absolute level of poverty – households living below the poverty line – is 10%, against the all-India average of 22%. The relative inequality, the distribution of income as well as consumption in J&K are all much more evenly spread across the population. The income inequality coefficient for rural households in J&K is 0.221, making it one of the most egalitarian sub-national economies in the country.[11]

These figures make it clear that not only is poverty in Jammu and Kashmir not as high as the all-India average, it is also *less unequal in terms of incomes* with a Gini coefficient of 0.24,[12] indicating that the inequality in incomes between the rich and the poor is very low (a score of 0 means that there is no inequality in these incomes). Compare this with the all-India Gini coefficient of 0.339[13] – India is now one of the eleven most unequal countries in the world, according to the Commitment to Reducing Inequality (CRI) Index.[14] India's rank is 147 out of 157 countries in this index because of the failure in collecting taxes from the richest, in extending public spending and in providing entitlement to the millions who work in the agricultural and unorganized sectors. In its report on CRI globally, Oxfam International described India's neglect in addressing inequality as 'a very worrying situation given that it is home to 1.3 billion people, many of whom live in extreme poverty'.[15]

Another indicator of the well-being of any economy is the level of indebtedness of households. In Jammu and Kashmir, the percentage of indebted households in 2017 was estimated to be 29.5 per cent in rural areas and 17.9 per cent in urban areas, whereas it was 31.4 per cent for rural areas and 22.3 per cent for urban areas at the all-India level.[16] 'Households in J&K have the second lowest incidence of indebtedness in the country. Combining the incidence of indebtedness and the average value of assets per household, J&K, with a debt-to-asset ratio of less than one, is one of the best in the country.'[17]

As we have seen in the previous chapters, all these indicators – the low levels of poverty, low level of indebtedness, high levels of household assets and low inequality – are directly linked to the radical redistribution of land and scaling down of debt that took place in Jammu and Kashmir, kickstarting a development trajectory that was unique in India. And it was the legal autonomy enjoyed by the state, granted by Article 370, that made these radical policies and their implementation possible. As Drabu observes,

> When the J&K government initiated land reforms and divested the landed aristocracy of their land, the right to property was a fundamental right under Article 19. What prevented the J&K Big Landed Estates Abolition Act, 1950 from being annulled on the grounds of infringing Article 19(1)(f) was sub-clause (b) of Article 370A.[18]

Jammu and Kashmir also scores higher than the all-India average on social indicators such as life expectancy at birth, infant mortality rate, maternal mortality rate, household access to clean drinking water, household access to sanitation, nutrition, and prevention of homelessness and child marriage. So clearly, the people of Jammu and Kashmir have benefited enormously from Article 370, using their legal autonomy for public good rather than private gain. The portrayal of Jammu and Kashmir as an underdeveloped state is, no doubt, wrong. But what has done more serious damage to the economy of Jammu and Kashmir is the BJP government's unilateral dismantling of its constitutional competence.

The Jammu and Kashmir Reorganization Bill: Dagger to the Throat of J&K's Development

The introduction of the Jammu and Kashmir Reorganization Bill on 6 August 2019 created an uproar in the Lok Sabha. The only two Kashmiri Members of Parliament tore copies of the Indian Constitution on the floor of the house, calling the Bill a historical blunder. Among political parties in the opposition, Janata Dal (United) and the All India Trinamool Congress staged a walk-out in protest, while the Indian National Congress, Samajwadi Party and Nationalist Congress Party opposed the Bill. The BJP and its allies pushed the Bill through both the Lok Sabha and the Rajya Sabha on the strength of their parliamentary majority. The government had picked a state that was one of the best performers in terms of providing a good quality of life to its citizens, constructed an unsubstantiated narrative of the state's underdevelopment, and, for the first time in India's constitutional history, downgraded a state to a Union Territory. This made the central government's control over the state absolute – unchecked by any legislative structure chosen by the people of Jammu and Kashmir.

The BJP government then approved the Jammu and Kashmir Reorganization Order, a set of legal provisions that allowed citizens from other states to become permanent residents of the Union Territory of Jammu and Kashmir. Article 370 had stipulated that only 'permanent residents' of Jammu and Kashmir would have the right to own land and apply for government jobs. The new order stated that all persons who had been residing in Jammu and Kashmir for at least fifteen years, their children and central government officials who had served in the region for at least ten years (and their children) would be provided domicile status. Under Section 96 of the Jammu and Kashmir Reorganization Act, referred to as the Jammu and Kashmir Civil Services (Decentralization and Recruitment) Act, a migrant registered by the Relief and Rehabilitation Commissioner of the Union Territory can also apply for domicile, and anyone with domicile status can apply for gazetted or non-gazetted jobs. The Ministry of Home Affairs at the centre initially limited domicile eligibility for jobs to entry-level non-gazetted posts and Group D posts (offering low pay scales). After political parties across the board criticized the move, on 3 April 2020, the Home Ministry issued orders extending this eligibility to all posts in government, including senior positions (Group A and B posts).

As of early September 2020 the Indian government has granted domicile to more than 1.2 million people in Jammu and Kashmir, many of whom were not permanent residents earlier.[19] This has triggered fear amongst the local population about their access to employment and land ownership being reduced.[20] Ostensibly, the domicile laws were changed to bring private investment into Jammu and Kashmir, which, it was claimed, had not come to J&K previously because of the restrictions that Article 35A imposed on land ownership by non-residents. Again, this is patently incorrect. Even before 5 August 2019, land was available to industry on a 90-year lease (renewable further) and on easy terms set by the Jammu and Kashmir government, much like other state governments across India. The reasons for the reluctance of private investors to invest in Jammu and Kashmir were security concerns due to the long-standing conflict and the lack of cheap transportation linkages for manufacturing. Both reasons still exist. In fact, the security situation has worsened: 'Ceasefire violations on the Line of Control doubled in 2019 from the year before. Militant violence continued. . . . The first six months of 2020 have been one of the most lethal periods in recent years, killing 118 militants and 26 security forces.'[21] Fresh recruitment to militancy has continued among Kashmiri youth, signalling the falsity of the 'Article 370 as the wellspring of militancy' theory put forward by the India's home minister in the Parliament.

And more recently, an international dimension has been added to the existing security concerns. The Chinese military has used the abrogation of Article 370 to make targeted incursions into the Line of Control in Ladakh and now holds around 1,000 square kilometres of Indian territory.[22] The stand-off in Galwan valley that killed at least fifteen Indian soldiers on 15 June 2020 was a visible manifestation of the new Chinese military policy in the region. The Chinese foreign ministry had issued a statement a day after the abrogation of Article 370, saying that India's decision to unilaterally change its domestic laws and administrative divisions was illegal and invalid because a large part of Ladakh is under Chinese actual control. According to seasoned defence analyst Ajai Shukla, China saw the change in the legal status of the state of Jammu and Kashmir as a challenge to its sovereignty and reacted accordingly.[23] Hence, both internally and externally, the worsening security situation in Jammu and Kashmir and Ladakh is a direct fall-out of the Jammu and Kashmir Reorganization Act.

Dismantling Entitlements in Jammu and Kashmir: The Aftermath of 5 August 2019

The abrogation of Article 370 also meant the dismantling of many independent statutory bodies that dealt with the rights of the vulnerable in Jammu and Kashmir. Eight such independent bodies that dealt with cases of women, children, the disabled, human rights and public accountability have been dissolved. The cases they were addressing have not been passed on to their national counterparts, resulting in appellants not being able to pursue the cases and get redressal for their complaints. This constitutes a serious denial of the legal rights of the people of Jammu and Kashmir.

As stated earlier, Jammu and Kashmir was the only state in India to reserve half its medical seats for women, resulting in a huge increase in women's access to health. But the legal ramifications of August 2019 threaten these gains in women's health too. The Board of Professional Entrance Examinations (BOPEE) that has thus far conducted medical examinations based on this law, is in danger of being dissolved. If this happens, it could signal the end of affirmative action for women in medical education and pose a grave threat to women's access to health care in the erstwhile state.

As it is, over the last couple of years (2019–20), it has been much harder for women to access medical treatment in Jammu and Kashmir. Pregnant women, women requiring dialysis, chemotherapy and emergency surgeries found it very difficult to reach hospitals for check-ups and treatments because of the blanket restrictions on individual and vehicular movement, and the ban on mobile phones that came into effect after the abrogation of Article 370 in August 2019. According to the *British Medical Journal*, life-threatening situations were created 'due to unavailability of transport, ambulance services, shortage of medical staff, and dwindling supplies of life-saving medications'. Rural women living in remote areas were the worst affected; cases of stillbirths due to pregnant women having to walk unusually long distances, and miscarriages due to lack of timely communication with gynaecologists were recorded at Lad Ded Hospital, the main maternity hospital in Srinagar. With 1.6 million cases of chronic ailments that require daily medication,[24] the restrictions on movement also led to an alarming lack of access to medicine in the Kashmir valley. All this points to a serious disruption in people's access to health care in a region that has been lauded for its health-care coverage previously.

The renewed use of pellet guns to quell protests since 5 August 2019 is another violation of the right to health for the people of Jammu and Kashmir, causing as it does widespread injuries, blindness and, in some cases, death. Public health experts point out that 'the use of pellet guns is not only a gross violation of human rights, but also a serious violation of the right to health. People in Kashmir have been subjected to fatal consequences and permanent disabilities as a result of the use of pellet guns.'[25] The recent firing of pellets on a religious procession in Bemina, Srinagar, led Meenakshi Ganguly, South Asia Director, Human Rights Watch, to issue a statement emphasizing that 'Indian leaders who claim that their policies are improving the lives of Kashmiris cannot disregard that security forces are maiming, blinding and killing people. The Indian government should cease the use of shotguns firing metal pellets and review its crowd-controlling techniques to meet international standards.'[26]

The restrictions on the internet have similarly affected the prospects of education for school, college and university students – 'students have struggled to catch up on classes due to internet restrictions . . . the audio-visual content and course material put up online by the schools and colleges could not be accessed on low speed connections'.[27] The easing of the internet ban in a few districts in August 2020 has not done much to ameliorate this problem.

Conclusion

The abrogation of Article 370 has caused severe damage to the economic health of Jammu and Kashmir. Rather than helping, the change in the legal status of Jammu and Kashmir from being a full-fledged state to a Union Territory has hampered development in Jammu and Kashmir considerably. This is exacerbated by the large-scale restrictions put in place by the Indian government. According to a report by the Kashmir Chamber of Commerce and Industry (KCCI), in the Kashmir valley alone, the economy has suffered huge losses to the tune of Rs 40,000 crore since 5 August 2019. The trade body also estimates that 5,00,000 Kashmiris have lost their jobs due to the private sector being paralysed by the shutting down of shops and businesses in the tourism and transportation sector. The internet ban has hit tech start-ups and the handicrafts industry the hardest. Due to a complete disruption in digital payments and lost access to markets outside Jammu and Kashmir, both these sectors suffered heavy losses. Hundreds of businesses have closed, leading to massive job losses. Covid-19 restrictions are expected to cause further economic distress and unemployment.

The much-hyped announcements by the Government of India that Union Territory status would serve as a development panacea for Jammu and Kashmir have proven false. It is clear that the abrogation of Article 370 was just another exercise to deepen state control, disempower the people of Jammu and Kashmir politically and open up the resources of the erstwhile state to corporate plunder. The sad thing is that the entire exercise was justified in the name of development.

NOTES AND REFERENCES

1 A legal provision first used during British colonial rule in India that prevents the gathering of more than four people in one place. Section 144 of the Criminal Procedure Code (CrPC) of 1973 authorizes the executive magistrate of any state or territory to issue an order in urgent cases of nuisance or apprehended danger to prohibit the assembly of four or more people in an area. Over the years, it has been used indiscriminately in Jammu and Kashmir to stifle dissent.

2 A legal provision that gave the erstwhile state some measure of constitutional authority within the Union of India.

3 Amit Shah's speech in the Lok Sabha, 5 August 2019. Right-wing commentators and social media users in India regularly employ versions of these arguments when discussing youth protests and militancy in the Kashmir valley.

4 As against the national literacy rate of 18.39 per cent, the literacy rate in the princely state of Jammu and Kashmir was a miserable 5 per cent (see Administration Report of Jammu and Kashmir State, 1893–94) and life expectancy was just 27 years (see R.C. Bhargava, 'Economic Background', in Baghwan Sahay, ed., *Jammu and Kashmir*, Srinagar: Universal Publications, 1969: 119). A government estimate had put 70 per cent of the state's rural population as indebted (B.J. Glancy, 'Enquiry Commission Report submitted to His Highness the Maharaja', Jammu and Kashmir State Archives, Jammu, 1932).

5 Francis Wade, 'The Liberal Order is the Incubator for Authoritarianism: A Conversation with Pankaj Mishra', *Los Angeles Review of Books*, 15 November 2018, available at https://lareviewofbooks.org/article/the-liberal-order-is-the-incubator-for-authoritarianism-a-conversation-with-pankaj-mishra/, accessed 17 October 2020.

6 Ibid.

7 Ibid.

8 Implying the Abdullahs, the Muftis and the Azads.

9 Amit Shah's speech in the Lok Sabha, 5 August 2019.

10 'India Slips Two Places on Global Corruption Perception Index', *The Hindu*, 23 January 2020.

11 Haseeb A. Drabu, 'Was Special Status a Development Dampener in J&K?', *LiveMint*, 8 August 2019, available at https://www.livemint.com/opinion/columns/opinion-was-special-status-a-development-dampener-in-j-k-1565248797810.html, accessed 1 October 2020.

12 National Sample Survey, 71ˢᵗ Round, Schedule 25, Research and Publication Unit, National Sample Survey Office (NSSO), Ministry of Statistics and Programme Implementation, Government of India, New Delhi, 2016.

13 Ibid.

14 The CRI is an index of indicators that measures government action on social spending, tax and labour rights – the three areas international experts say are critical to reducing inequality.

[15] Max Lawson and Matthew Martin, 'The Commitment to Reducing Inequality Index 2018', Oxfam International, 8 October 2018: 10, https://oxfamilibrary. openrepository.com/bitstream/handle/10546/620553/rr-commitment-reducing-inequality-index-2018-091018-en.pdf, accessed 3 September 2020.

[16] National Sample Survey, 70th Round Report: Debt and Investment Survey in Jammu and Kashmir, Directorate of Economics and Statistics, Government of Jammu and Kashmir, 2017: 2.

[17] Drabu, 'Was Special Status a Development Dampener in J&K?'.

[18] Ibid.

[19] '12 lakh Issued Domicile Certificates, Most Hold PRC, says J&K Admin', *The Indian Express*, 6 September 2020, https://indianexpress.com/article/india/12-lakh-issued-domicile-certificates-most-hold-prc-says-jk-admin-6584858/, accessed 1 October 2020.

[20] Thomson Reuters Foundation, 'Kashmir Domicile Law Raises Fears of Losing Land, Culture', *Deccan Herald*, 28 July 2020, https://www.deccanherald.com/national/north-and-central/kashmir-domicile-law-raises-fears-of-losing-land-culture-866559.html, accessed 2 September 2020.

[21] Ipsita Chakravarty, 'What Exactly Did the August 5 Decisions Achieve in Jammu and Kashmir?', *Scroll.in*, 5 August 2020, https://scroll.in/article/969452/what-exactly-did-the-august-5-decisions-achieve-in-jammu-and-kashmir, accessed 14 October 2020.

[22] Vijaita Singh, 'China Controls 1,000 sq. km of Area in Ladakh', *The Hindu*, 31 August 2020, https://www.thehindu.com/news/national/china-controls-1000-sq-km-of-area-in-ladakh-say-intelligence-inputs/article32490453.ece, accessed 17 October 2020.

[23] Ajai Shukla, 'Withdrawal From Galwan Valley Puts Indian Troops Further From LAC', *Business Standard*, 9 July 2020, https://www.business-standard.com/article/current-affairs/withdrawal-from-galwan-valley-puts-indian-troops-further-from-lac-120070900008_1.html, accessed 17 October 2020.

[24] 'Kashmir Communications Blackout is Putting Patients at Risk, Doctors Warn', *The British Medical Journal*, 366: l5204, 19 August 2019: 1, doi: https://doi.org/10.1136/bmj.l5204.

[25] Sarojini Nadimpally, 'Use of Pellet Guns Has Caused a Public Health Crisis in Kashmir', *The Wire*, 29 March 2017, https://thewire.in/health/pellet-guns-kashmir-public-health, accessed 14 October 2020.

[26] Human Rights Watch estimated that 17 people had been killed and 139 people including children blinded by pellets between 2015 and 2017 alone. See https://www.hrw.org/news/2020/09/04/india-stop-using-pellet-firing-shotguns-kashmir, accessed date 17 October 2020.

[27] Khalid A. Shah, 'Students in Kashmir Attended Regular Classes for Only Two Weeks in the Last One Year', *The Print*, 8 August 2020, https://theprint.in/opinion/students-in-kashmir-attended-regular-classes-for-only-two-weeks-in-the-last-one-year/477782/, accessed 14 October 2020.

Bibliography

Primary Sources

Pamphlets/Information Leaflets/Official Letters

Henvey, F., 'Condition and Prospects of Kashmir on the 1st of June, 1880', letter to Secretary to Government of India, Jammu and Kashmir State Archives, Jammu.

Letter from Jawaharlal Nehru to Sheikh M. Abdullah dated 19 May 1948, cited in *Greater Kashmir*, 14 June 2008.

'Modern Jammu and Kashmir', information leaflet, His Highness's Government, 1941, Jammu and Kashmir State Archives, Jammu.

'Naya Kashmir', published by All Jammu and Kashmir National Conference, Lahore, 1945, Jammu and Kashmir State Archives, Jammu.

Central and State Government Reports

'Abridged Life Tables, 1988', Registrar General of India, 1988.

'Abridged Life Tables, 2010–2014', Sample Registration System Data Analysis Report, Registrar General of India, 2016.

Administration Report of Jammu and Kashmir State of His Highness's Government, 1893–94.

Annual Administration Report (General), Medical Department, His Highness's Government, 1934.

Annual Administration Report (General), Medical Department, His Highness's Government, 1936–37.

Beg, Mirza Afzal, 'On the Way to Golden Harvests: Land Reforms in Jammu and Kashmir', Land Reforms Office, Government of Jammu and Kashmir, Jammu: Government Press, 1952.

'Budget 1948', His Highness's Government, Jammu and Kashmir, Srinagar: Sri Ranbir Government Press.

Census of India, selected years.

'Constituency-wise Amenity Directory, 2011–12', District Planning and Statistics Officer, Budgam, Government of Jammu and Kashmir, 2013.

'Constituency-wise Amenity Directory, 2017', District Planning and Statistics Officer, Poonch, Government of Jammu and Kashmir, 2017.

'Draft of Third Five-Year Plan, 1961–66', Planning Department, Government of Jammu and Kashmir, 1966.

Economic Review of Jammu and Kashmir, 1973–84, Directorate of Economics and Statistics, Government of Jammu and Kashmir, 1984.

Economic Review of Jammu and Kashmir, 1984–85, Directorate of Economics and Statistics, Government of Jammu and Kashmir, 1985.

'Elections in Kashmir', Franchise Commission, Government of India, 1934.

'First Five-Year Plan Document', Department of Planning and Development, Government of Jammu and Kashmir, 1951.

Glancy, Bertrand J., 'Enquiry Commission Report submitted to His Highness the Maharaja', 1932, Jammu and Kashmir State Archives, Jammu.

'Government of Jammu and Kashmir Commission of Inquiry Report' (also known as the Ayyangar Committee Report), 1965.

'Gross State Domestic Product (GSDP) at Current Prices (as on 31-05-2014)', Planning Commission, Government of India, archived from the original (PDF) on 30 August 2017.

'In Ninety Days: A Brief Account of Agrarian Reform Launched by Sheikh Abdullah's Government in Kashmir', Ministry of Information and Broadcasting, Government of Jammu and Kashmir, Srinagar, (n.d.).

'India Human Development Report', Planning Commission, Government of India, 2011.

'J&K Review of Progress', Department of Planning and Statistics, Government of Jammu and Kashmir, 1961.

'Jammu and Kashmir: A Review of Progress', Department of Information, Government of Jammu and Kashmir, 1969.

'Jammu and Kashmir Digest of Statistics', Department of Planning and Statistics, Government of Jammu and Kashmir, 1981.

'Jammu and Kashmir Digest of Statistics', Department of Planning and Statistics, Government of Jammu and Kashmir, 1988.

'Jammu and Kashmir Digest of Statistics, 1960–1990', Department of Planning and Statistics, Government of Jammu and Kashmir, 1991.

'Jammu and Kashmir Digest of Statistics, 2000–01', Department of Planning and Statistics, Government of Jammu and Kashmir, 2002.

'Jammu and Kashmir Economic Survey 2016', Department of Economics and Statistics, Government of Jammu and Kashmir, 2016.

Jammu and Kashmir: Fifty Years, Srinagar: Department of Information, Government of Jammu and Kashmir, 1998.

'Jammu and Kashmir State Development Report', Planning Commission, Government of India, 2003.

Kashmir Information Series: Education, Government of Jammu and Kashmir, Srinagar: Government Press, 1951.

National Sample Survey, National Sample Survey Office (NSSO), Ministry of Statistics and Programme Implementation, Government of India, New Delhi, 2011.

National Sample Survey 71st Round, Schedule 25, Research and Publication Unit, National Sample Survey Office (NSSO), Ministry of Statistics and Programme Implementation, Government of India, New Delhi, 2016.

'National Sample Survey 70th Round Report: Debt and Investment Survey in Jammu and Kashmir', Directorate of Economics and Statistics, Government of Jammu and Kashmir, 2017.

'Note on Environment and Development: Jammu and Kashmir Perspective', Department of Planning and Statistics, Government of Jammu and Kashmir, 2001.

'Poverty Line Survey', Planning Commission, Government of India, cited in *Jammu and Kashmir Economic Statistics*, Government of Jammu and Kashmir, 2008, available at http://ecostatjk.nic.in/publications/BPL200809.pdf, accessed 5 October 2020.

'Press note on poverty estimates in India based on the 66th Round of the National Sample Survey, 2009–10 data on Household Consumer Expenditure Survey', Planning Commission, Government of India,19 March 2012.

'Press note on poverty estimates in India based on the 68th Round of National Sample Survey, 2011–12 data on Household Consumer Expenditure Survey', Planning Commission, Government of India, 22 July 2013.

'Relief and Rehabilitation in Kashmir', Kashmir Bureau of Information, Government of Jammu and Kashmir, May 1949.

'Report of the Committee for Agricultural Reform', Government of Jammu and Kashmir, Srinagar: Government Press, 1949.

'Report of the Development Review Committee on Jammu and Kashmir, Part V: Agriculture and Irrigation', Government of Jammu and Kashmir, 1975.

'Report on Economic Reforms of Jammu and Kashmir', Ministry of Finance, Government of Jammu and Kashmir, 1998.

'Report on J&K Government Achievements', Government of Jammu and Kashmir, 1954, Jammu and Kashmir State Archives, Jammu.

'Sample Registration System (SRS) Statistical Report', Office of the Registrar General and Census Commissioner, Ministry of Home Affairs, Government of India, 2014.

'Status of Effective Coverage of Supplementary Nutrition Programme for Children', Integrated Child Development Services (ICDS), Government of India, 2011.

The Constitution of Jammu and Kashmir, Government of Jammu and Kashmir, Srinagar: Government Press, 1956.

'The Constitution of Jammu and Kashmir and Plan Documents of the Jammu and Kashmir Government', Government of Jammu and Kashmir, 1956, Jammu and Kashmir State Archives, Jammu.

'The Jammu and Kashmir Reservation Rules', Social Welfare Department Notification, Service Rules Ordinance (SRO) 294, Government of Jammu and Kashmir, 21 October 2005.

Wingate, A.A., 'Rules Regarding Grant of Waste Land for Cultivation as Sanctioned by His Highness the Maharaja Sahib Bahadur', Jammu and Kashmir State Archives, Jammu, 1917.

Speeches and Debates

Address by Mahasha Nahar Singh, Jammu and Kashmir Legislative Assembly Debates, Budget Session, 6 May 1952.

Address by Mr Abdul Gani Trali, Jammu and Kashmir Legislative Assembly Debates, Budget Session, 6 May 1952.

Address by Mr G.L. Dogra, Jammu and Kashmir Legislative Assembly Debates, Budget Session, 1952.

Address by Sheikh Abdullah to the Educational Reorganization Committee, Jammu and Kashmir Legislative Assembly Debates, Jammu, December 1950.

Jammu and Kashmir Legislative Assembly Debates, Budget Session, 1952–1954, Jammu and Kashmir State Archives, Jammu.

Praja Sabha Debates, 1944, Jammu and Kashmir State Archives, Jammu.

Speech by Mirza Afzal Beg in the State Legislative Assembly, 1951, Jammu and Kashmir State Archives, Jammu.

Interviews

Aga Mehmood, key informant, at Budgam, 5 June 2017.

Baba Abdul, s/o Mira, key informant, at Nangali, 24 July 2017.

Haseeb Drabu, from the landlord family of Rajpora Pulwama, at Srinagar, 6 June 2017.

K.D. Maini, historian and author, at Poonch, 22 May 2017.

M. Shamsuddin Ganaie, from the landlord family of Mattan, Anantnag, at Jammu, 11 May 2017.

Nancy Bhat Munshi, a Kashmiri Pandit living in Jammu, at Jammu, 12 May 2017.

Peerzada Bilal Ahmed, Director, Department of Statistics and Planning, Government of Jammu and Kashmir, at Srinagar, 8 September 2017.

Raj Kaur, w/o Ghar Singh, at Srinagar, 24 July 2017.

Sohan Singh, resident of village Chamba, Katra, at Jammu, 12 October 2017.

Tareak A. Rather, Department of Central Asian Studies, University of Kashmir, at Srinagar, 16 November 2017.

Secondary Sources

Aaradhana, P.S., *Himalayan Ecology*, New Delhi: Rajat Publications, 1998.

Abdullah, Sheikh Mohammad, 'Jammu and Kashmir, 1947–1950', Department of Information, Government of Jammu and Kashmir, 1950.

Abrams, Philip, 'Notes on the Difficulty of Studying the State', *Journal of Historical Sociology*, vol. 1, no.1, March 1988: 58–89.

Agarwal, P.K., *Land Reforms in India: An Unfinished Agenda*, Delhi: Concept Publishing, 2010.

Aggarwal, J.C. and S.P. Agrawal, *Modern History of Jammu and Kashmir*, Delhi: Concept Publishing, 1995.

Akhter, S., *Kashmir: Women Empowerment and the National Conference*, Srinagar: Jay Kay Publishing House, 2011.

Alesina, Alberto and Dani Rodrik, 'Distributive Politics and Economic Growth', *The Quarterly Journal of Economics*, vol. 109, no. 2, May 1994: 465–90.

Alesina, Alberto, Reza Baqir and William Easterly, 'Public Goods and Ethnic Divisions', *The Quarterly Journal of Economics*, vol. 114, no. 4, 1999: 1243–84.

Ali, S. and K.K. Singh, eds, *Role of Panchayati Raj Institutions for Rural Development*, New Delhi: Swarup and Sons Publishers, 2001.

Amin, Pirzada M., 'Hazratbal: A Crescent of Faith', in K. Warikoo, ed., *Cultural Heritage of Jammu and Kashmir*, New Delhi: Pentagon Press, 2009.

Anand, A.S., *The Constitution of Jammu and Kashmir: Its Development and Comments*, seventh edition, Delhi: Universal Publications, 2017.

Arakotaram, Karan, 'The Rise of Kashmiriyat: People-Building in 20th Century Kashmir', *The Columbia Undergraduate Journal of South Asian Studies*, Fall 2009.

Ashraf, Asad, 'Bihar's Land Reforms in Dustbin: Land Mafias Prevail', *The Citizen*, 19 January 2019.

Aslam, Mohamed, 'Land Reforms in Jammu and Kashmir', *Social Scientist*, vol. 6, no. 4, November 1977: 59–64.

Baba, N.A., 'Democracy and Governance in Kashmir' in N.A. Khan, ed., *The Parchment of Kashmir: History, Society, and Polity*, New York: Palgrave Macmillan, 2012.

Bajwa, Kuldip Singh, *Jammu and Kashmir War, 1947–1948: A Political and Military Perspective*, New Delhi: Har Anand Publications, 2003.

Balasubramanyam, V.N., *The Economy of India*, London: Weidenfeld and Nicholson, 1984.

Bamzai, P.N.K., *History of Kashmir*, vol. 1, Delhi: Metropolitan Book Co., 1962.

——, *Culture and Political History of Kashmir*, vol. 2, New Delhi: M.D. Publications, 1994.

Banerjee, Abhijit and Rohini Somanathan, 'Political Economy of Some Public Goods: Some Evidence from India', *Journal of Development Economics*, vol. 82, no. 2, 2007: 287–314.

Banerjee, Abhijit V., Paul J. Gertler and Maitreesh Ghatak, 'Empowerment and

Efficiency: Tenancy Reform in West Bengal', *Journal of Political Economy*, vol. 110, no. 2, April 2002: 239–80.

Banerji, J.K., 'Agrarian Revolution and Industrialization in Jammu and Kashmir', in S.R. Bakshi, ed., *History of Economic Development in Jammu and Kashmir*, Srinagar: Gulshan Publishers, 2002.

Bardhan, Pranab, *The Political Economy of Development in India*, Delhi: Oxford University Press, 1984.

Bazaz, P.N., *The History of Struggle for Freedom in Kashmir*, New Delhi: Kashmir Publishing Company, 1954.

——, *Daughters of the Vitasta: A History of Kashmiri Women from Early Times to the Present*, New Delhi: Pamposh Publications, 1959.

——, 'Land Reforms in Jammu and Kashmir', *Mainstream*, vol. 15, 1 June 1976.

——, *The History of Struggle for Freedom in Kashmir*, reprint, Srinagar: Gulshan Publishers, 2003.

Benson, M. Thomas, K.S. James and S. Sujala, 'Does Living Longer Mean Living Healthier?: Exploring Disability Free Life Expectancy in India', Working Paper 322, The Institute for Social and Economic Change, Bangalore, 2014.

Besley, Timothy and Robin Burgess, 'Land Reform, Poverty Reduction, and Growth: Evidence from India', *The Quarterly Journal of Economics*, vol. 115, no. 2, May 2000: 389–430.

Bhagwati, J., *India in Transition*, Oxford: Clarendon Press, 1993.

Bhalla, G.S., 'Agrarian Transformation: Interaction between Tradition and Modernity', *Yojana*, vol. 37, nos. 14 and 15, August 1993: 36–44.

Bhandari, L. and M. Chakravarty, 'Spatial Poverty in Jammu and Kashmir', *LiveMint*, 24 February 2015, available at https://www.livemint.com/Politics/qIhZeetYN29chTZPq1s63N/Spatial-poverty-inJammu-and-Kashmir.html, accessed 5 October 2020.

Bhandari, L., B. Debroy and R. Saran, 'India's Best and Worst States', *India Today*, 16 August 2004.

Bhargava, R.C., 'Economic Background', in Baghwan Sahay, ed., *Jammu and Kashmir*, Srinagar: Universal Publications, 1969.

Bhat, Ashiq Hussain, 'Pratap Singh's British Rule', *Kashmir Life*, 3 March 2014.

Bhat, M.S., 'Integrated Rural Development in J&K: Some Field Experience', *Journal of Rural Development*, vol. 10, no 2, 1991.

Bhat, M.S. and S.N. Alam, 'Agricultural Growth Performances in Jammu and Kashmir State', *Agricultural Situation in India*, vol. 42, no. 8, November 1987: 701–06.

Bhatnagar, I., 'Planning in Kashmir', *Kashmir Today*, vol. 4, no. 3, Srinagar: Department of Information, Government of Jammu and Kashmir, November 1959.

Bhatt, S., *Kashmir: Ecology and Environment: New Concerns and Strategies*, New Delhi: APH Publishing, 2004.

Bhattacharjea, A., *Kashmir: The Wounded Valley*, New Delhi: UBS Publishers, 1994.

Binswanger, Hans, Klaus Deininger and Gershon Feder, 'Power, Distortions,

Revolt, and Reform in Agricultural Land Relations', in Jere Behrman and T.N. Srinivasan, eds, *Handbook of Development Economics*, Amsterdam: Elsevier, 1995: 2659–772.

Bose, Sumantra, *Kashmir: Roots of Conflict Paths to Peace*, Cambridge, MA: Harvard University Press, 2003.

Brecher, M., *The Struggle for Kashmir*, Toronto: Ryerson Press, 1953.

Burki, Shahid Javed, *Kashmir: A Problem in Search of a Solution*, Washington, D.C.: United States Institute of Peace, 2007.

Butt, S., *Kashmir in Flames*, Srinagar: Ali Mohammed and Sons, 1981.

Chadha, S.K., ed., *Kashmir: Ecology and Environment*, New Delhi: Mittal Publications, 1991.

Chakravarty, Ipsita, 'What Exactly Did the August 5 Decisions Achieve in Jammu and Kashmir?', *Scroll.in*, 5 August 2020, https://scroll.in/article/969452/what-exactly-did-the-august-5-decisions-achieve-in-jammu-and-kashmir, accessed 14 October 2020.

Chaurasia, A.R., 'Child Deprivation in India: Evidence from Rapid Survey of Children 2013–2014', *Indian Journal of Human Development*, vol.10, no. 2, 2016.

Chenery, Hollis, Montek Ahluwalia, Clive Bell, John Duloy and Richard Jolly, *Redistribution with Growth*, Oxford: Oxford University Press, 1970.

Chohan, Amar Singh, *Health Services in Jammu and Kashmir, 1858–1947*, New Delhi: Atlantic Publishers, 1994.

——, *Development of Education in the Jammu and Kashmir State, 1846–1947*, New Delhi: Atlantic Publishers, 1998.

Choudhary, Sushma, 'Does the Bill Give Power to People?' in G. Mathew, ed., *Panchayati Raj in Jammu and Kashmir*, New Delhi: South Asia Books, 1990.

Chowdhary, Rekha, 'Political Upsurge in Jammu and Kashmir: Then and Now', *Economic and Political Weekly*, vol. 30, no. 39, 30 September 1995.

Common, M.S. and D.I. Stern, 'Economic Growth and Environmental Degradation: The Environmental Kuznets Curve and Sustainable Development', *World Development*, vol. 24, no. 7, 1996: 1151–60.

Cornwall, A. and I. Scoones, eds, *Revolutionizing Development: Reflections on The Work of Robert Chambers*, London: Earthscan, 2011.

Dabla, B.A., *Gender Discrimination in the Kashmir Valley*, Delhi: Gyan Publishing House, 2000.

Dandavate, M., 'Land Reforms in Free India', *Mainstream*, vol. 11, nos. 1 and 2, 1972–73: 31–33.

Dasgupta, J.B., *Jammu and Kashmir*, The Hague: Matinus Nijhoff, 1968.

Deininger, Klaus, Songqing Jin and Vandana Yadav, 'Impact of Land Reform on Productivity, Land Value and Human Capital Investment: Household Level Evidence from West Bengal', selected paper at the American Agricultural Economics Association Annual Meeting, Orlando, FL, 27–29 July 2008.

Dhar, D.N., *Socio-Economic History of the Kashmir Peasantry*, Srinagar: Centre for Kashmir Studies, 1989.

Directorate of Health Services in Jammu and Kashmir, 'History of Modern Healthcare in Kashmir', *Kashmir Health Line*, vol. 2, 2010.

Drabu, Haseeb A., 'Jammu and Kashmir Economy Reform and Reconstruction: A Report on Economic Needs Assessment', Asian Development Bank, June 2004.

——, 'Was Special Status a Development Dampener in J&K?', https://www.livemint.com/opinion/columns/opinion-was-special-status-a-development-dampener-in-j-k-1565248797810.html, 8 August 2019, accessed 23 September 2019.

Drèze, J. and Amartya Sen, *An Uncertain Glory: India and Its Contradictions*, New Delhi: Allen Lane Books, 2013.

Dubhashi, P.R., 'Land Reforms: Intention, Implementation and Impact', *Kurukshetra*, vol. 35, no. 1, October 1986.

Dutt, Gaurav and Martin Ravallion, 'Farm Productivity and Rural Poverty in India', *Journal of Development Studies*, vol. 34, no. 4, 1998: 62–85.

Foster-Carter, A., *The Sociology of Development*, Ormskirk: Causway Books, 1985.

Ganaie, M. Shamsuddin, *The Ganaies of Mattan*, self-published by author, 1999.

Gielen, U., 'Gender Roles in Traditional Tibetan Cultures', in L.L. Adler, ed., *International Handbook on Gender Roles*, Westport, CT: Greenwood, 1998: 413–37.

Goli, S., L. Singh, K. Jain and L.M.A. Pou, 'Socio-economic Determinants of Health Inequalities among the Older Population in India: A Decomposition Analysis', *Journal of Cross-Cultural Gerontology*, vol. 29, no. 4, 2014: 353–69, available at https://doi.org/10.1007/s10823-014-9251-8.

Gunder Frank, A., 'Crisis and Transformation of Dependency in the World System', Development Studies Discussion Papers, No. 113, University of East Anglia, Norwich, 1983.

Gupta, N.S. and A. Singh, *Agricultural Development of States in India*, vol. 1, New Delhi: Seema Publications, 1979.

Gupta, S., *Kashmir: A Study in India–Pakistan Relations*, Bombay: Asia Publishing House, 1967.

Habibullah, Wajahat, *The Political Economy of Kashmir Conflict: Opportunities for Economic Peace Building and for U.S. Policy*, Washington, D.C.: United States Institute of Peace, 2004.

Hangloo, R.L., 'Kashmiriyat: The Voice of the Past Misconstrued', in N.A. Khan, ed., *The Parchment of Kashmir: History, Society, and Polity*, New York: Palgrave Macmillan, 2012.

Hay, Katherine, 'Gender, Modernization, and Change in Ladakh, India', unpublished MA thesis, University of Waterloo, Ottawa, 1997.

Hoff, Karla and Andrew B. Lyon, 'Non-leaky Buckets: Optimal Redistributive Taxation and its Costs', *Journal of Public Economics*, vol. 53, 1995: 365–90.

Hussain, A., 'Education in Kashmir Faces Another Challenge: Almost 20 Schools Burnt in Unrest', *Hindustan Times*, 26 October 2016.

Indian Society of Agricultural Economics, *Agrarian Reforms in Western Countries*, Bombay: Vora and Co., 1946.

Iqbal, Sehar, 'Social Impact of State Development Policy in Jammu and Kashmir: 1948 to 1988', unpublished PhD thesis, University of Kashmir, Jammu and Kashmir, 2018.

Iyer, K. Gopal, 'Land Reforms in India: An Empirical Study, 1948–90', unpublished report, 1990.

Jayadev, Anishia and Huong Ha, 'Land Reforms in Kerala: An Aid to Ensure Sustainable Development', in Huong Ha, ed., *Land and Disaster Management Strategies in India,* New Delhi: Springer, 2015.

'Kashmir Communications Blackout is Putting Patients at Risk, Doctors Warn', *The British Medical Journal*, 366: l5204, 19 August 2019: 1, doi: https://doi.org/10.1136/bmj.l5204.

Kaviraj, Sudipta, 'Democracy and Social Inequality', in Francine R. Frankel, Zoya Hasan, Rajeev Bhargava and Balveer Arora, eds, *Transforming India: Social and Political Dynamics of Democracy*, New Delhi: Oxford University Press, 1997: 89–119.

Kaw, M.K., *Kashmir and Its People: Studies in the Evolution of Kashmiri Society*, New Delhi: APH Publishing, 2004.

Kawoosa, T., 'Over 60 Per Cent Leaving Midway', *Epilogue*, issue 10, November 2008.

Khan, M.I., *Kashmir's Transition to Islam: The Role of Muslim Rishis*, New Delhi: Manohar Publishers, 1994.

——, 'Evolution of My Identity vis-a-vis Islam and Kashmir', in N.A. Khan, ed., *The Parchment of Kashmir: History, Society, and Polity*, New York: Palgrave Macmillan, 2012.

Khan, N.A., *Islam, Women, and Violence in Kashmir: Between India and Pakistan*, New York: Palgrave Macmillan, 2010.

Khan, N.A. ed., *The Parchment of Kashmir: History, Society, and Polity*, New York: Palgrave Macmillan, 2012

Korbel, Joseph, *Danger in Kashmir*, Princeton: Princeton University Press, 1954.

Krueger, A.O., 'Political Economy of Rent Seeking Society', *The American Economic Review*, vol. 64, no. 3, 1974: 291–303.

Kurien, O.F., 'Jammu and Kashmir Tops the Country in Life Expectancy – Except at Birth', *Indiaspend*, 23 October 2015.

Ladjensky, Wolf, 'Land Reforms: Observations in Kashmir', in L.J. Walinsky, ed., *Agrarian Reforms as Unfinished Business*, New York: Oxford University Press, 1977.

Lamb, A., *A Disputed Legacy: 1846 to 1990*, Karachi: Oxford University Press, 1991.

Latham, Michael E., *Modernization as Ideology*, Chapel Hill: University of North Carolina Press, 2000.

Lawrence, Walter, *The Valley of Kashmir*, New Delhi: Kashmir Kitab Ghar, 1996.

Lawson, Max and Matthew Martin, 'The Commitment to Reducing Inequality Index 2018', Oxfam International, 8 October 2018, available at https://oxfamilibrary. openrepository.com/bitstream/handle/10546/620553/rr-commitment-reducing-inequality-index-2018-091018-en.pdf, accessed 3 September 2020.

Lipton, M., 'Agriculture, Rural People, the State and Surplus in Asian Countries', in J. Breman and S. Mundle, eds, *Rural Transformation in Asia*, Oxford: Oxford University Press, 1991.

Maini, K.D., *Poonch: The Battlefield of Kashmir*, Srinagar: Gulshan Publishers, 2012.

Malik, Iffat, *Kashmir: Ethnic Conflict, International Dispute*, Karachi: Oxford University Press, 2005.

Malik, Shazia, *Women's Development Amid Conflicts in Kashmir: A Socio-Cultural Study*, India: Partridge Publishing, 2014.

Malaviya, H.D., *Land Reforms in India*, New Delhi: Sri Gauranga Press, 1954.

Mander, Harsh, 'Hunger in the Valley: Report on the Implementation of Food and Livelihood Schemes of Government in Kashmir', 2010, available at http://www.sccommissioners.org/Reports/Reports/JammuKashmir_Food LivelihoodSchemes_0809.pdf, accessed 2 August 2018.

Masoodi, A., 'Kudos to Mehbooba Mufti but Where are Kashmir's Female Politicians?' *LiveMint*, 4 April 2016, available at https://www.livemint.com/ Politics/ThLJaAlCSB4bZmCKExFFIO/Kudos-to-Mehbooba-Mufti-but-where-are-Kashmirs-female-poli.html, accessed 3 January 2018.

Messervy, Frank, 'Kashmir', *Asiatic Review*, vol. 45, no. 161, 1949.

Miguel, Edward and Mary Kay Gugerty, 'Ethnic Diversity, Social Sanctions, and Public Goods in Kenya', *Journal of Public Economics*, vol. 89, 2005: 2325–68.

Miliband, R., 'State Power and Class Interests', *The Socialist Register*, vol. 1, 1977.

Misri, M.L. and M.S. Bhat, *Poverty, Planning and Economic Change in Jammu and Kashmir*, New Delhi: Vikas Publishing House, 1994.

Moorcroft, William and George Trebeck, *Travels in the Himalayan Provinces of Hindustan and the Punjab in Ladakh and Kashmir in Peshawar, Kabul, Kunduz and Bokhara: From 1819 to 1825*, vol. 1, New Delhi: Asian Educational Press, 1837.

Murphy, J., 'Ecological Modernization: The Environment and the Transformation of Society', Oxford Centre for the Environment, Ethics and Society (OCEES) Research Paper No. 20, Mansfield College, Oxford, 2001.

Murtaza, A., 'Sheikh Mohammad Abdullah: Victim of A Great Betrayal', *Greater Kashmir*, 14 June 2008.

Myrdal, G., *Asian Drama: An Enquiry into The Poverty of Nations*, London: Allen Lane, 1968.

Nadimpally, Sarojini, 'Use of Pellet Guns Has Caused a Public Health Crisis in Kashmir', *The Wire*, 29 March 2017, available at https://thewire.in/health/ pellet-guns-kashmir-public-health, accessed 14 October 2020.

National Council of Applied Economic Research (NCAER), *Techno-Economic Survey of Jammu and Kashmir*, New Delhi: NCAER, 1969.

——, 'State Investment Potential Index', New Delhi: NCAER, 2016.

'National Family Health Survey 2015–16', International Institute for Population Sciences (IIPS), Mumbai, 2017.

Nila, *Nilmat Purana*, translated by Ved Kumari, vol. 1, Srinagar: Jammu and Kashmir Academy of Art, Culture and Languages, 1973.

Noorani, A.G., *Article 370: A Constitutional History of Jammu and Kashmir*, Delhi: Oxford University Press, 2011.

Norberg-Hodge, H., *Ancient Futures: Learning from Ladakh*, Delhi: Oxford University Press, 1992.

Nussbaum, Martha C., *Women and Human Development: The Capabilities Approach*, New York: Cambridge University Press, 1999.

——, *Beyond the Social Contract: Capabilities and Global Justice*, Oxford Development Studies, vol. 32, no.1, Taylor and Francis, 2004.

Panagariya, A. and V. More, 'Poverty by Social, Religious and Economic Groups in India and Its Largest States: 1993–94 to 2011–12', Columbia University Working Paper Series, Septembe 2013.

Prakash, Siddhartha, 'Political Economy of Kashmir Since 1947', *Economic and Political Weekly*, vol. 35, no. 24, 2000: 2051–60.

Punjabi, R., 'Kashmir Imbroglio: The Socio-Political Roots', *Contemporary South Asia*, vol. 4, no. 1, 1995: 39–53.

Puri, B., *Triumph and Tragedy of Indian Federation*, Delhi: Sterling, 1981.

Rai, Mridu, *Hindu Rulers, Muslim Subjects: Islam, Rights and the History of Kashmir*, Princeton: Princeton University Press, 2004.

Raina, N.N., *Kashmir Politics and Imperialist Manoeuvres (1846–1980)*, New Delhi: Patriot Publishers, 1988.

Ram, Anant and Hira Nand Raina, *The Census of India, 1931*, Volume XXIV, Jammu and Kashmir State, part 1, 1933.

Rana, Preetika and Joanna Sugden, 'India's Record since Independence', *The Wall Street Journal*, 15 August 2013.

Rao, Shiva, *The Framing of Indian Constitution: Selected Documents*, vol. 4, New Delhi: Indian Institute of Public Administration (IIPA), 1968.

Rashid, M., 'Women, Their Property and Economic Rights in Kashmir', *Greater Kashmir*, 22 June 2017.

Rather, T., 'Agrarian Transformation in Rural Kashmir: A Sociological Study of Kulgam Tehsil', PhD thesis submitted to the Centre of Central Asian Studies, University of Kashmir, 2002.

——, 'Progress in Conflict: Why poverty decreased measurably during militancy', *Kashmir Reader*, 3 January 2016, available at http://kashmirreader.com/2016/01/23/progress-in-conflict-why-poverty-decreased-measurably-during-militancy/.

'Resolution on Land Reforms', Fifth Session, Second Committee, United Nations General Assembly (UNGA), 20 November 1950.

Rostow, W.W., *The Stages of Economic Growth: A Non-Communist Manifesto*, London: Cambridge University Press, 1971.

Sadhu, A.N., 'Agricultural Transformation in Jammu and Kashmir', paper presented at the seminar on 'Economy, Society and Polity in Jammu and Kashmir', organized by Centre for Research in Rural and Industrial Development, Chandigarh, 31 October–2 November 1989, Srinagar.

Sahay, Bhagwan, ed., *Jammu and Kashmir*, Srinagar: Universal Publications, 1969.

Saxena, H.L., *The Tragedy of Kashmir*, New Delhi: Nationalist Publishers, 1975.

Schumacher, E.F., *Small is Beautiful: A Study of Economics as if People Mattered*, London: Blond & Briggs Ltd., 1973.

Sen, Abhijit, 'Economic Reforms, Employment and Poverty: Trends and Options', *Economic and Political Weekly*, vol. 31, nos. 35–37, 14 September 1996.

Sen, Amartya, *Development as Freedom*, Oxford: Oxford University Press, 1999.

Shaban, R.A., 'Testing Between Competing Models of Sharecropping', *Journal of Political Economy*, vol. 95, no. 5, October 1987: 893–920.

Shah, Khalid A., 'Students in Kashmir Attended Regular Classes for Only Two Weeks in the Last One Year', *The Print*, 8 Augus 2020, available at https://theprint.in/opinion/students-in-kashmir-attended-regular-classes-for-only-two-weeks-in-the-last-one-year/477782/, accessed 14 October 2020.

Shukla, Ajai, 'Withdrawal From Galwan Valley Puts Indian Troops Further From LAC', *Business Standard*, 9 July 2020, available at https://www.business-standard.com/article/current-affairs/withdrawal-from-galwan-valley-puts-indian-troops-further-from-lac-120070900008_1.html, accessed 17 October 2020.

Sikand, Yoginder, 'Dalits in Jammu: Demanding to be Heard', 10 November 2004, available at https://www.countercurrents.org/dalit-sikand101104.htm, accessed 22 September 2017.

Singh, G. , 'Regeneration of Forests in Jammu & Kashmir State', in S.K. Chadha, ed., *Kashmir: Ecology and Environment*, New Delhi: Mittal Publications, 1991.

Singh, Prerna, 'We-ness and Welfare: A Longitudinal Analysis of Social Development in Kerala, India', *World Development*, vol. 39, no. 2, 2010.

Singh, Vijaita, 'China Controls 1,000 sq. km of Area in Ladakh', *The Hindu*, 31 August 2020, available at https://www.thehindu.com/news/national/china-controls-1000-sq-km-of-area-in-ladakh-say-intelligence-inputs/article32490453.ece, accessed 17 October 2020.

Snedden, Christopher, *Understanding Kashmir and Kashmiris*, London: C. Hurst and Co., 2015.

Stein, M.A., trans., *Kalhana's Rajatarangini: A Chronicle of the Kings of Kasmir* [1900], vol. 5, Delhi: Motilal Banarsidass, 1989.

Taseer, Rasheed, *Tehreek-i-Hurriyat-i-Kashmir: 1931 to 1939*, vol. 1, Srinagar: Muha'afiz Publications, 1968.

Tharakan, P.K. Michael, 'Socio-economic Factors in Educational Development: Case of Nineteenth Century Travancore', *Economic and Political Weekly*, vol. 19, no. 46, 1984: 1913–67.

Thomas, M. Benson, K.S. James and S. Sujala, 'Does Living Longer Mean Living Healthier? Exploring Disability Free Life Expectancy in India', Working Paper 322, The Institute for Social and Economic Change, Bangalore, 2014.

Thomson Reuters Foundation, 'Kashmir Domicile Law Raises Fears of Losing Land, Culture', *Deccan Herald*, 28 July 2020, available at https://www.deccanherald.com/national/north-and-central/kashmir-domicile-law-raises-fears-of-losing-land-culture-866559.html, accessed 2 September 2020.

Thorner, Daniel, 'The Kashmir Land Reforms: Some Personal Impressions', *The Economic Weekly*, 12 September 1953: 999–1002.

——, *The Agrarian Prospect in India*, second edition, Delhi: Allied Publishers, 1976.

Thorp, Robert, *Kashmir Misgovernment*, Srinagar: Gulshan Publishers, 1980.

United Nations Development Programme (UNDP), *West Bengal Human Development Report*, UNDP, 2004.

——, *Jammu and Kashmir Human Development Report*, UNDP, 2010.

——, *Human Development Report 2011: India*, UNDP, 2011.

——, *Human Development Report 2014: Sustaining Human Progress: Reducing Vulnerabilities and Building Resilience*, UNDP, 2014.

Vaidyanathan, A., 'Indian Economy Since Independence, 1947–70', in Dharma Kumar, ed., *Cambridge Economic History of India*, vol. 2, New Delhi: Orient Longman Pvt. Ltd., 2005

Varshney, Ashutosh, 'Three Compromised Nationalisms', in Raju G.C. Thomas, ed., *Perspectives on Kashmir: The Roots of Conflict in South Asia*, Boulder: Westview Press, 1992.

——, 'Why Have Poor Democracies Not Eliminated Poverty? A Suggestion', *Asian Survey*, vol. 45, no. 5, 1999: 718–36.

Verma, P.S., *Jammu and Kashmir at the Political Crossroads*, New Delhi: Vikas Publishing House, 1994.

Wade, Francis, 'The Liberal Order is the Incubator for Authoritarianism: A Conversation with Pankaj Mishra', *Los Angeles Review of Books*, 15 November 2018, available at https://lareviewofbooks.org/article/the-liberal-order-is-the-incubator-for-authoritarianism-a-conversation-with-pankaj-mishra/, accessed 17 October 2020.

Wani, Gul M., 'Political Assertion of Kashmiri Identity', in N.A. Khan, ed., *The Parchment of Kashmir: History, Society, and Polity*, New York: Palgrave Macmillan, 2012.

Wani, M.A., 'Degeneration of Environment in Kashmir Valley: Need for Immediate Awakening', in S. Bhatt, ed., *Kashmir Ecology and Environment: New Concerns and Strategies*, New Delhi: APH Publishing, 2004.

Weinar, Myron, ed., *State Politics in India*, Princeton: Princeton University Press, 2016.

Whitehead, Andrew, *A Mission in Kashmir*, Srinagar: Gulshan Publishing House, 2007.

——, 'The Rise and Fall of New Kashmir', in Chitralekha Zutshi, ed., *Kashmir: History, Politics, Representation*, New York: Cambridge University Press, 2018.

Wilson, N., 'Cold, High and Dry: Traditional Agriculture in Ladakh', *Permaculture News*, 6 February 2009, available at https://permaculturenews.org/2009/02/06/cold-high-and-dry-traditional agriculture-in-ladakh/, accessed 18 October 2017.

World Bank Group, 'India's Poverty Profile', 27 May 2016, available at https://www. worldbank.org/en/news/infographic/2016/05/27/india-s-poverty-profile, accessed 19 October 2020.

Younghusband, F., *Kashmir*, London: Adam and Charles Black, 1909.

Zutshi, Chitralekha, *Languages of Belonging: Islam, Regional Identity and the Making of Kashmir*, New Delhi: Permanent Black, 2003.

Zutshi, D.P., 'Dal Lake: Environmental Issues and Conservation Strategy', in S. Bhatt, ed., *Kashmir: Ecology and Environment: New Concerns and Strategies*, New Delhi: APH Publishing, 2004.

Index